"Not only does James Merritt offer fre[...] be a person of character—and why it matters more today than ever—but he is a leader and visionary with exemplary character. The lessons you'll gain from these pages will challenge and change you in all the best ways. You can't afford not to read this book."

Margaret Feinberg, author of *Taste and See*

"One of my consistent prayers is that my gifts would never take me further than my character can sustain me. I'm so grateful for a book that not only emphasizes the importance of character, but helps cultivate it. This book will inspire you, convict you, and challenge you toward the character of Christ, our highest calling."

Mark Batterson
New York Times bestselling author of *The Circle Maker*
Lead pastor of National Community Church

"I don't know of a more important topic now than this, and I don't know anyone more qualified to speak on it than James Merritt."

Rick Warren
New York Times bestselling author, *The Purpose Driven Life*

"An important leadership book about leadership's most important topic: *character*. Merritt's insights into the human spirit, the nature of leadership, and the mores of contemporary society are always insightful, at times breathtaking. Not only does Merritt give us a clear picture of Christlike character, he shows where that character goes against the grain of society. This book glorifies Jesus and will strengthen you."

J.D. Greear, PhD
Pastor, The Summit Church, Raleigh-Durham, NC

"This is a must-read book for all aspiring leaders, parents, and educators. It gets to the heart of the most fundamentally important aspects of life—that is, the cost of poorly made decisions. Dr. Merritt talks about those decisions, how to make them, and the price one pays when you get them wrong. This book is full of real-life examples of what happens when priorities are misplaced and reputations are ruined. More importantly, it paints a crystal-clear picture of how to prevent that from happening. Read it—it could change your life."

Vice Admiral Wm. Dean Lee, USCG (ret)

"*Character Still Counts* is a necessary chalice of cool water in the desert of our anything-goes era. Honest, compassionate, biblically astute and conversational, this book paints a redemptive picture of how the kingdom of God should work its way into our hearts and practices. There is always hope."

Mary DeMuth, author of *We Too:*
How the Church Can Respond
Redemptively to the Sexual Abuse Crisis

CHARACTER
STILL
COUNTS

James Merritt

HARVEST HOUSE PUBLISHERS
EUGENE, OREGON

Published in association with the Christopher Ferebee Agency.

Cover design by Studio Gearbox

Character Still Counts
Copyright © 2019 by James Merritt
Published by Harvest House Publishers
Eugene, Oregon 97408
www.harvesthousepublishers.com

ISBN 978-0-7369-6944-4 (pbk.)
ISBN 978-0-7369-6945-1 (eBook)

Library of Congress Cataloging-in-Publication Data

Names: Merritt, James Gregory, author.
Title: Character still counts / James Merritt.
Description: Eugene : Harvest House Publishers, 2019. | Includes
    bibliographical references.
Identifiers: LCCN 2019014893 (print) | LCCN 2019019020 (ebook) | ISBN
    9780736969451 (ebook) | ISBN 9780736969444 (pbk.)
Subjects: LCSH: Character.
Classification: LCC BJ1521 (ebook) | LCC BJ1521 .M56 2019 (print) | DDC
    179/.9--dc23
LC record available at https://lccn.loc.gov/2019014893

Printed in the United States of America

21 22 23 24 25 26 27 28 / VP-CD / 10 9 8 7 6 5

It is with deep sincerity
that I dedicate this book to

BOB HAWKINS

More than my publisher, he has become a dear friend
and encourager, and this book is a mirror image
of the character I have seen in him from the first time I met him.
Every time I am around him, I am constantly reminded that
Character Still Counts

ACKNOWLEDGMENTS

Never have I worked harder on anything I have ever written (except my PhD dissertation) than this book. From the time my wonderful publishers at Harvest House suggested this book and my heart caught fire to write it, I have given it my very best effort from day one to write a work that would glorify God, edify the reader, and of course, satisfy my publisher!

I couldn't have done it without some very special people. I cannot brag enough on the great team at Harvest House, including, of course, president Bob Hawkins, editor *par excellence* Rod Morris, and the entire staff at Harvest House. Thanks for the honor of partnering with you!

I could not have done this without the help of my administrative assistant Kalli Overcash, whose tireless efforts in typing the manuscript was simply indispensable. My mind cannot conceive of a finer Christian lady, loyal servant, and faithful co-worker than Kalli. Thank you, Kalli, for staying sane and—yes—even staying with me!

My agent, my chief advisor on writing, and my guardian editor is my BFF and my beloved son, Jonathan. I wouldn't even be in the publishing game without him. I love him and his brothers more than life itself. Thanks, son, for all you have done and do for me!

I must also thank the love of my wife, Teresa. She is the "straw that stirs the drink." I couldn't pastor, preach, or publish without her help, encouragement, and support. Sweetheart, I love you forever and for always, and you will always be "still the one."

Finally, I must close by praising my Lord and Savior Jesus Christ, who, as the book closes with, is indeed the main character of all of history, whose personal character is still the only gold standard of what true perfect character looks like, lives like, walks like, and talks like. His presence in my life is a 24/7 reminder to me that *Character Still Counts*. May my character always reflect his and bring glory to him all my life.

Contents

Foreword

BY RUSSELL MOORE

A while back, I met with the elders of a church, still reeling from learning that their longtime pastor had been involved in numerous adulterous affairs and other kinds of scandalous immorality. Sadly, this wasn't the first time I've talked to people in this situation and won't be the last. I was impressed, though, by the wisdom and the maturity of the leaders of that church. Their first worry was not about the pastor's moral failing but about his evangelistic success. "Most of the people in this church first heard the gospel from this pastor," they told me. "Most of them were completely secular and disconnected from Christianity. He was the first one they ever heard preach Jesus. He was the first one they ever heard teach the Bible. He baptized all of them. He discipled all of them. We're afraid that they are going to conclude that, since everything they knew of Christianity they learned from someone they now know to have been lying to them, that Christianity must therefore be a lie."

I empathized with these people, whose names and faces were unknown to me, because I'd been before somewhat where they were now. I remembered the first time a Christian leader I'd admired had been revealed to have been living a double life of sexual infidelity and financial impropriety. The feeling was not so much that of anger

9

or disappointment as it was of vertigo. If I couldn't tell that the person teaching me so confidently didn't seem to experience, or maybe even to believe, what he was saying, then how could I have confidence in my beliefs about anything, or anyone?

Sooner or later, almost everyone will have a similar moment of vertigo. We shouldn't be surprised when we see failures of character around us, and we shouldn't be surprised when we see character constantly redefined to fit whatever purpose is deemed necessary at the moment. Jesus warned us of all this ahead of time. Moreover, Scripture gives us the revelatory tension that makes sense of both the examples of shining character we sometimes see, even in people who don't know Christ, and the debacles of twisted character we sometimes see, even in people who claim very much to belong to Christ. Humanity is created in the image of God, with a conscience that points to him (Romans 2). But humanity is also fallen, moving through a fallen world-system that seeks often to satisfy self at all costs.

The way forward, then, is also paradoxical. Those who follow Christ should be the last to adopt the sort of moral relativism that eclipses objective norms of righteousness and justice. In almost every corner of culture, people are quick to denounce the "character problems" in whomever they deem to be their "opponents," but are, at best, silent about and, at worst, justifying of those they deem to be their "allies." One can see this pattern in Hollywood, in the local workplace, and, sadly, sometimes in church congregational meetings. When we do this, we don't really believe in character or in truth or in righteousness. We believe in our "cause." In other words, we believe in ourselves.

At the same time, we could respond to the various crises of character we may see, inside and outside the church, with cynicism. We can constantly protect ourselves, assuming that there is no truth anywhere, no holiness—that everything is just marketing. This is not the way of Christ. Cynicism will seem to protect us from getting disappointed or hurt, but, in the end, all we will protect ourselves from is connection to one another. We will end up "protecting" ourselves from love.

When I think of character and integrity, one of the first faces to appear in my mind is that of the author of this book. He has exemplified, in ministry, in leadership, in family, what it means to both see himself always as a sinner in need of Christ and always as one who will follow Jesus, no matter where Jesus goes. He has given himself over neither to the conformity of the crowd nor to the isolation of cynicism. That's why so many, including me, admire his ministry and his counsel. As you read this book, you might agree with all of it, or you might, as with any book, disagree with some parts. You might even be reading this as someone who's not yet a Christian, just curious about what Christians think on this topic.

Whatever the case, I encourage you to read this prayerfully—that this book will help you not to identify those with character to emulate or those without character to mistrust, but rather to seek to identify vulnerabilities in your own character formation, and to seek to cultivate the kind of integrity that will point you, and others, to the Judgment Seat of a Christ, who is both perfectly holy and perfectly merciful. Character counts, after all, only so far as it ultimately points us to the One before whom every character falls short, and through whom any character can be reshaped.

Character—Don't Leave Home Without It

I was going to sue for defamation of character,
but then I realized I have no character.

CHARLES BARKLEY[1]

We Americans have character coursing through our veins. Or at least we used to.

At the dawn of our republic, our founders believed that individual character was critical to the formation of our fledgling nation and the communities scattered from sea to shining sea. They believed that instilling character in society carved a pathway to justice, order, and the common good. The only alternative was certain ruin.

You can hardly travel anywhere in America without being confronted by the historical importance of character. Whether you are traveling through Rocky Mountain mining towns or the sandy coastline of South Carolina, you will soon encounter a name that has always been synonymous with character. That name is Washington—as in George Washington.

Washington was surrounded by men far more brilliant, educated, and in many ways more capable than he was—a pantheon of political and philosophical rock stars such as Benjamin Franklin, Thomas Jefferson, Patrick Henry, John Adams, Alexander Hamilton, and

James Madison. At three different times in the early history of our country, the future of our nation hung in the balance. At those three critical junctures these brilliant men and their comrades unanimously chose George Washington to be the commander-in-chief of the Continental Army, president of the Constitutional Convention, and the only unanimously elected president of the United States. Why? From the numerous studies, books, and monographs written about him, the most commonly cited characteristic given for his emergence as the supreme leader is his character.[2]

No wonder a survey of the Census Bureau's geographic database found George Washington has the most "places, minor civil divisions, and counties" named after him in the United States with 127.[3] From our nation's capital to 241 townships, 26 cities, various boroughs and villages, and 15 mountains, you hear and see the name synonymous with character.

When you Google "Washington Street," the search engine returns twelve million results. This includes lots of individual addresses on Washington Street, but it still gives you an idea of how many cities and towns have named a street after George Washington.[4] Call it coincidental or providential, but in our country, we literally cannot escape the importance of character.

In a free society, authority is placed in the hands of a people rather than a sovereign monarch. Our founders knew that if citizens neglected character, the entire republic would be at risk. As Thomas Jefferson wrote in 1801, "The steady character of our countrymen is a rock to which we must safely moor." James Madison echoed Jefferson's conviction: "Is there no virtue among us? If there be not, we are in a wretched situation. No theoretical checks—no form of Government, can render us secure. To suppose that any form of Government will secure liberty or happiness without any form of virtue in the people, is a chimerical idea." When Alexis de Tocqueville traveled across America, he was struck by the centrality of moral virtue to the American spirit and its necessity for the survival of the republic: "How could society escape destruction if, when political ties are relaxed, moral ties are not tightened?"[5]

What does *character* mean? The word comes from the Greek word *charakter*, which refers to the mark or imprints on a coin or a seal.[6] *Webster's Third International Dictionary* defines it as "a composite of good moral qualities, typical of moral excellence and firmness blended with resolution, self-discipline, high ethics, force, and judgment." In other words, character is the impression your life leaves on others.

> **Character is the impression your life leaves on others.**

A lot of people confuse character with reputation, but the two are cousins rather than twins. Reputation is what other people think you are. Character is what God knows you are. Your reputation is what people perceive on the outside. Character is what you know is true on the inside. On my office desk sits a quote by nineteenth-century evangelist Dwight L. Moody: "If I take care of my character, my reputation will take care of itself."

It has been said that people are like trees. The shadow of the tree is *reputation*, the fruit of the tree is *personality*, but the root of the tree is the most important part—*character*. Abraham Lincoln said it best: "Character is like a tree and reputation like its shadow. The shadow is what we think of it; the tree is the real thing."[7] Somebody once said, "Many a man's *reputation* would not know his *character* if they met on the street."

I am reminded of a lady named Carolyn who went to a new doctor who reviewed all seventeen pages of her extensive medical history. She waited patiently until the doctor finally said, "Ma'am, you look better in person than you do on paper." Many people today, sadly, look better on paper than in person.

The Death of Character

At the beginning of the nineteenth century, most obituaries made at least some mention of the character of the person who died. By the end of the century, that practice had basically disappeared.[8] On the other hand, at the beginning of the twentieth century, obituaries seldom mentioned a person's occupation, but by 1990, occupation had become the single greatest way in which a deceased person was identified.[9] The way we viewed other people changed. What we do has become more important than who we are. We no longer value values. At least not like we once did.

New York Times columnist David Brooks reflects on this trend in his book *The Road to Character*. He makes a distinction between what he calls "résumé virtues" and "eulogy virtues." Résumé virtues are the skills you need to make a living. Eulogy virtues are the qualities you need to make a life.[10] Résumé virtues give you a temporary job. Eulogy virtues will get you eternal respect. In a reversal from the time of George Washington, American society now places more value on the former than on the latter.

As Brooks writes, "We all know that the eulogy virtues are more important than the résumé ones. But our culture and our educational systems spend more time teaching the skills and strategies you need for career success than the qualities you need to radiate that sort of inner light. Many of us are clearer on how to build an external career than on how to build inner character."[11]

If you want to measure how much America values virtues, survey the words we speak. People talk about what matters to them. They avoid topics toward which they feel apathy or antipathy. And our words tell the story of the death of character in modern America.

Google Ngram data is a collection of most of the books written in the English language stretching back hundreds of years. The database is searchable, allowing anyone to measure word usage across time. Type in a word and you can see which words occur with more frequency. In the past century, words referring to business and economics have increased while words referring to morality and virtue have decreased. Terms like *character, conscience*, and *virtue* all declined over the course of the twentieth century.[12]

In the 1950s, private morality was considered the measure of one's character. Beginning in the 1960s, however, one's stance against issues like war, racism, and sexism became far more important measures. These are important moral issues, no doubt, and people of character should oppose evil in any form. But this small shift in definition turns out to be substantial.

As author Shelby Steele notes, the result was a false dualism dividing our public and private lives. Over time, we "granted considerable license in the private realm. Sleep with whomever you wanted, explore your sexuality, expand your mind with whatever drug you liked, forego marriage, follow your instincts and impulses as inner truths, enjoy hedonism as a kind of radical authenticity. The only important thing was that you were disassociated from American evil."[13]

America is changing faster than our minds can process. Beneath these changes is a massive, often silent shift of the tectonic plates of character that were once the bedrock of our society. Most of us know this. A recent Gallup poll found that when Americans consider the trajectory of our nation, a whopping 72 percent conclude that the state of moral values in the US is "getting worse."[14]

We don't have to look far to find signs of this decline. The decrease in self-control is seen in the increase in road rage. The fall-off in honesty shows up in children cheating in school and adults cheating on tax returns. The regression of respect is apparent on most sports fields and in many workplace break rooms. And the waning of authenticity is showcased in the carefully curated photos we post on social media that bear little resemblance to our actual lives. The stench of character's corpse is all around us.

Character on Top

One of the best measures of a democratic nation's character is the leaders elected by the people. An entire bookshelf could be filled with our Founding Fathers' writings on the importance of character for those who would be elected to political office. In 1765, America's second president, John Adams, said, "Liberty cannot be preserved without general knowledge among the people who have the right to that knowledge and the desire to know. But besides this, they have a right, an indisputable, unalienable, indefeasible, divine right to that most dreaded and envied kind of knowledge—I mean of the 'character and conduct' of their rulers." Above all, Adams, perhaps conceiving in his mind a new nation to come, envisioned leaders who would place character first.[15] What a refreshing thought, particularly in today's political climate, that even our liberties depend upon the character of those who rule over us.

A unique characteristic of the office of the president of the United States is that his personal conduct relates directly to the national security of the United States. This authoritative position is unique because when he exposes himself to risk through misbehavior or criminal action, he is exposing all of us to risk. Even the way he conducts himself and maintains his character should be done in such a way that he never becomes a threat to the freedom and security of this nation.[16]

Samuel Adams, the second cousin of John Adams and one of the signers of the Declaration of Independence, gave a vigorous assertion of the connection between character and political office when he said, "He who is void of virtuous attachments in private life is, or very soon will be, void of all regard of his country. There is seldom an incidence of a man guilty of betraying his country who had not before lost the feeling of moral obligations in his private connections...The public cannot be too curious concerning the characters of public men."[17]

James Madison, the fourth president of the United States and the author of our constitution, said, "the first aim" of the constitution was to ensure wise and virtuous rulers and to prevent "their degeneracy."[18] Not only is that the reason the constitution provides for impeachment—the only true impeachable offense is when a president shows he no longer has the character to hold the office.

Our Founding Fathers' teaching about the importance of our leaders' character seemed to hold sway for many Americans—particularly people of faith—for most of our nation's history. But something shifted in 1992 when President George H.W. Bush ran for reelection against Arkansas governor Bill Clinton.

Bush was a World War II veteran who had to ditch his plane in the ocean and narrowly escaped death from Japanese captors. He had been faithful to his wife for more than forty years, and his integrity was unquestioned. Clinton had avoided the draft and admitted to illegally using marijuana. He had been credibly accused by many women of cheating on his wife and even committing sexual assault.

I had disagreements with Clinton's politics, but like many others, I was deeply disturbed by his character. Naively, I thought most Americans held character in the same regard as I did and therefore Clinton couldn't possibly beat Bush. But I was dead wrong. Clinton won handily, and the mantras of the two political movements describe why. The rallying cry of Bush supporters was "Character counts" while the phrase that energized Clinton supporters was "It's the economy, stupid." In the end, cash conquered character.

Four years later, when Clinton ran for reelection, an article asked this question: "If Americans fault the president on character, but say they prefer him over a man whom they give high marks in that area, does this mean that character doesn't matter all that much?"[19] In response, Stephen Hess, a distinguished scholar at the Brookings Institution, said, "If it is a choice between bad character and good economic news…good economic news is always going to win."[20]

The downfall of character is not a problem afflicting only one political party, as the 2016 presidential race demonstrates. In this election, character again was at the forefront of both major candidates' campaigns. Indeed, character was at such center stage that something unprecedented happened for the first time since the start of presidential campaign television advertising in 1952. In over sixty years, on average, approximately 22 percent of ads run by either opponent focused on a character-related issue while around 28 percent focused on the economy. In 2016, however, 76 percent of Democratic candidate Hillary Clinton's ads focused on the character of the Republican candidate, Donald Trump. Meanwhile, the Trump campaign's ads focused almost 50 percent of ads on Clinton's character. In more than sixty years, no other campaign from either party came close to that kind of emphasis on character.[21]

The election was summed up this way: "To judge by the daily parade of headlines and soundbites, the 2016 presidential election...boiled down to one steaming mass of invective, calumny, character assassination, and contempt: the madman verses the prevaricator, the bully versus the biddy, the devil you know vs. the devil you don't."[22]

In the end, Americans still elected a president who looked a lot like Bill Clinton—the candidate so many of them opposed just a couple of decades earlier—in terms of character. Donald Trump also dodged the draft, bragged about bedding married women, has been accused of sexual assault, and lies with impunity. According to some estimates, President Trump still tells as many as fifteen lies per day even after being elected.[23]

The same people that once shouted "Character counts" suddenly believed "It's the economy, stupid." The shift occurred with head-snapping rapidity, even among Christians. As the 2016 election approached, polls showed that both Protestants and Catholics were far more accepting of candidates who committed "immoral acts" than they had been in the past. In 2011, 30 percent of white evangelical Christians said "an elected official who commits an immoral act in their personal life can still behave ethically and fulfill their duties in their public and professional life." In 2016, that number jumped to 72 percent—more than any other religious group in the United States.[24]

Voting Republican or Democrat doesn't make you a person of more or less character. You can be a person of virtue who voted for Bill Clinton, and many people of high character voted for Donald Trump. I have friends I respect who did both. Every voter weighs a range of elements and issues when they enter the voting booth and pull the lever. However, most of us can agree that our founders' vision for the prominence of virtue in our society and among our leaders has waned in recent years. Indeed, perhaps the biggest loser in modern America is not a candidate but character itself.

Character Is Us

Low character comes at a high cost. J.P. Morgan was one of the greatest bankers and financiers in American history. He helped organize US Steel and General Electric, and his bank became the predecessor of J.P. Morgan Chase, which is the largest bank in the United States. He was asked what he considered to be the best bank collateral. Without hesitation, he replied, "Character."

One of the most successful pro-football franchises of all time is the Dallas Cowboys, otherwise known as "America's team." When they were first organized, the managers took an unusual approach. Instead of visiting successful football teams, they instead went to the boardrooms of General Motors, IBM, Xerox, and other successful corporations and asked the leading executives what they look for in their leaders. Without exception, the greatest business leaders in the world said they looked for character, for the integrity of the individual.[25]

Former Secretary of Education William Bennett describes how character, or the lack thereof, can have tremendous impact on the nation's economy. He states, "National prosperity…is largely dependent upon lots of good, private character. Lying, manipulation, sloth, lack of discipline, and personal irresponsibility become commonplace as the national economy grinds down."[26] He points out that a society filled with street predators, white-collared criminals, thugs, and divorce, and a lack of initiative and personal responsibility will mean higher bills for prison cells, drug treatment centers, government welfare, and even unemployment compensation. "Just as there are enormous financial benefits to moral health [i.e., character] there are enormous financial costs to moral collapse."[27]

When character declines, we all pay the price.

> ## Low character comes at a high cost.

So character is both a public and private matter. It is both a government issue and an economic issue. Virtue impacts our faith and touches our families. It is an individual matter and also vital for the whole. We must display character daily from our homes to our communities, to our cities, to our states, to the nation. We must instill in our children, our leaders, and our institutions the indispensable quality of character. And that brings us to, well, you.

What are you doing to stoke the spark of character within yourself? How are you training your children to grow from boys and girls to men and women of character? Do you display character from the living room to the boardroom, on social media and at the dinner table? Character must be indispensably woven into the fabric of our lives, but this does not happen by accident. We must work hard to cultivate it.

Solomon, a wise king who lived thousands of years ago, said, "A good name is more desirable than great riches; to be esteemed is better than silver or gold" (Proverbs 22:1). A good name cannot be bought, stolen, or even inherited. It can only be earned by character.

I read about a multimillionaire who asked a builder to construct a house. He showed him the blueprints and then gave him a huge amount of money. The millionaire said to the builder, "You probably won't need all this money, but I want you to have plenty to build a solid house. When you are finished, you can keep whatever money you have left over."

The builder smiled. He thought to himself, *I can build a house for a fraction of this money. Then, I can pocket most of the money for myself!* So he began to throw the house together with haste. He placed studs five feet apart; he pounded only one nail per board; he slapped on a thin coat of paint. He threw on the shingles and barely covered the roof of the house. When he was finished, he knew the house wasn't solid, but at least it looked good and he had lots of money left over. He went back to the multimillionaire and said, "Here is the key to the house." The millionaire smiled and said, "Oh, I forget to tell you…the house is yours."[28]

Each of us is constructing our lives by the choices we make. We build good character brick by brick, thought by thought, action by action, habit by habit, through daily exercising of courage and determination. The decisions we make affect others, but they also shape the place where we must live alongside each other. When we shortcut character, we shortcut ourselves. Eventually, what is on the inside of your house will show up on the outside. I hope this book will remind you of a truth that too many of our fellow citizens have forgotten: *Character still counts*. It always has, and it always will.

1

INTEGRITY:

Living Under the Microscope

> In order to be a leader a man must have followers.
> And to have followers, a man must have their
> confidence. Hence, the supreme quality for a
> leader is unquestionably integrity. Without it, no
> real success is possible…If a man's associates find
> him guilty of being phony, if they find that he
> lacks forthright integrity, he will fail. His teachings
> and actions must square with each other.
>
> **DWIGHT D. EISENHOWER**[1]

Antonie van Leeuwenhoek isn't a household name, which isn't surprising since he's been dead for almost four hundred years. And yet his life still touches the entire world. This Dutch businessman, a self-taught man in science, is commonly known as "the father of microbiology" and is credited with one of the greatest inventions in history—the microscope.

The microscope is an optical instrument that is used to see objects that are so small they would otherwise be invisible. The invention of the microscope was invaluable—children no longer have to fear the diseases of polio and smallpox, couples can now conceive children through in vitro fertilization, criminals are apprehended and convicted by DNA evidence, minimally invasive surgery is now possible because of this tool. Most of the advances of the twentieth century were made using a microscope.

The effects of a microscope can be even more devastating when an object that is so big that it is visible to the entire world is put under its viewing power. I am referring to the Catholic Church, which is facing its most serious crisis in more than five hundred years. A wave of clerical sexual abuse revelations hit the church like a tsunami. It left the world in shock and the Catholic Church reeling. Thousands of cases of child molestation by members of the clergy have been reported from Australia, to Chile, to Germany, to the United States. One US grand jury report documented one thousand children abused by three hundred priests in the state of Pennsylvania alone over seventy years.[2]

What was equally appalling was the cover-up. One cardinal, the former archbishop of Washington and a member of the College of Cardinals, had to resign when credible accusations were made that he had sexually abused a minor and harassed seminarians whom he supervised. Amazingly, he had even played a leadership role in the church's response to the last US clerical sexual abuse scandal in 2002.[3]

Protestants have their own issues. Highly visible megachurch pastors who have had to resign over sexual misconduct have become almost routine. My denomination, the largest evangelical denomination in America,[4] recently received the resignation of a former president of the convention—and the leader of the most powerful entity in the denomination—over sexual impropriety. It used to be the question was, "Is nothing sacred?" Now the question being asked is, "Is sacred nothing?"

Don't be fooled. The problem that both the largest church in the world and the largest evangelical denomination in America face is not sexual impropriety, misconduct, or abuse. The cover-up is just a symptom of the deeper problem, which is a lack of integrity. The most powerful microscope in the world can't detect one flaw in the cell of integrity.

Of course, religious institutions aren't the only ones struggling with integrity. Business leaders cook books, falsify expense reports, evade taxes, and inflate profits. In the world of sports, athletes take performance-enhancing drugs and boxers throw matches. And then there is politics, which needs no explanation. This arena might actually rank last in moral character.

The Buck Stops Here

If character were a deck of cards, integrity would be the trump card. If you were building a house of character, the foundation would be integrity. Integrity would be "the first man up."

In his book *Integrity,* Stephen Carter called this virtue the "first among virtues because…in some sense [it] is prior to everything else. The rest of what we think matters little if we lack essential integrity and the courage of our convictions, the willingness to act and speak on behalf of what is right."[5]

The fountainhead of the river of character is integrity, because all other virtues flow from this one character trait. Warren Buffet, the chairman and CEO of Berkshire Hathaway, realized the importance of integrity. He said, "We look for three things when we hire people. We look for intelligence, we look for initiative or energy, and we look for integrity. And if they don't have the latter, the first two will kill you."[6]

People are replaceable. Integrity is not. The practice of integrity may be declining, but the importance of integrity is greater than ever. In 2012, successful businesswoman and investor Amy Rees Anderson wrote:

> We live in a world where integrity isn't talked about nearly enough. We live in a world where "the end

justifies the means" has become an acceptable school of thought for far too many. Sales people over promise and under deliver, all in the name of making their quota for the month. Applicants exaggerate job interviews, because they desperately need a job. CEOs overstate projected earnings, because they don't want the Board of Directors to replace them...Customer service representatives cover up a mistake they've made because they are afraid the client will leave them. Employees call in "sick" because they don't have any more paid time off when they actually just need to get their Christmas shopping done. The list could go on and on and in each case the person committing the act of dishonesty tells themselves they had a perfectly valid reason why the end result justified their lack of integrity.[7]

Years ago, I was in Beijing, China, and I could not wait to get to the Great Wall of China. It took the ancient Chinese more than two centuries to build this wall, which stretches more than twenty-one thousand kilometers and served the purpose of holding off invasions from the barbaric armies from the north. I marveled as I walked atop that wall so thick you couldn't break through it, so long you couldn't go around it, and so tall you couldn't get over it. I could feel the security of that wall beneath my feet.

But my fascination was short-lived when my guide told me that within the first century after completion, China was successfully invaded three times by those northern barbarians. I said, "Did they go over the wall?" He said, "No." I said, "Did they go around the wall?" He said, "No." I said, "Did they go under the wall?" He said, "No." I knew they didn't go through the wall, so how did they get in? All three times they bribed the gatekeeper and walked right in.

I Know It When I See It

Integrity is a word that has such a deep and broad meaning that capturing it in a single sentence is difficult. C.S. Lewis said, "Integrity is doing what is right when no one is looking." I would tweak that to say, "Integrity is what you are when no one but God and you are looking." Someone else has said, "Integrity is doing what you say you will do unless it is wrong." As I have thought about it, I've settled on this hopefully all-encompassing definition: Integrity is always doing the right thing, at the right time, in the right place, regardless of the cost or the consequences.

> **Integrity is always doing the right thing, at the right time, in the right place, regardless of the cost or the consequences.**

Bobby Jones is considered one of the best golfers in history. He won thirteen majors before he retired at the age of twenty-eight. He was the first player to win four major tournaments in one year. I recently got to meet his grandson, Bobby Jones IV, and he recounted to me a story about his grandfather. It wasn't about a tournament that he won or a great shot that he made. It was about his integrity.

Bobby Jones took a one-shot penalty at the 1925 United States Open. He inadvertently touched his golf ball and assessed himself a one-stroke penalty even though no one else saw him touch the ball. The tournament official said he didn't see it. His playing partner said he didn't see it. No one in the gallery said that they saw it. They even tried to talk him out of assessing himself the penalty, and he would have been justified in not taking it. But Bobby Jones would not violate his conscience or compromise his integrity. He assessed himself the penalty and ultimately lost the Open by that one stroke.

When tournament officials tried to compliment him for his integrity, he said, "You might as well praise me for not breaking into banks. There is only one way to play this game." Jones could have won his fourteenth major, but he would have lost his integrity. To Bobby Jones, no win of any kind or size could ever compensate for the loss of one's integrity.

Interestingly, *Webster's Dictionary* defines integrity as "the quality or state of being complete," and uses *wholeness* as a synonym. Interestingly, in the Old Testament, the word for integrity in the Hebrew is *tom*, and it literally means "whole and complete."

The English word *integrity* derives from the Latin word *integer*, which means again, "whole and complete." In mathematics, an integer is any number that is not a fraction, decimal, or a mixed number. In other words, integrity cannot be divided. You can't have partial integrity. You can't have integrity only in certain areas. If you possess integrity it covers the whole of your life, not just certain parts. Integrity is the blanket that covers the bed of all character traits.

Many people equate integrity with honesty, but integrity is more than honesty. In a sense, you can be honest without having integrity. If you are caught stealing, and you honestly confess your crime, you still lack integrity.

As Stephen Covey asserts, "Integrity includes, but goes beyond honesty. Honesty is telling the truth—in other words, *conforming our words to reality*. Integrity is *conforming reality to our words*—in other words, keeping promises and fulfilling expectations. This requires an *integrated character*, a one-ness, primarily with self, but also with life."[8]

Live a Life of Integrity

One of the greatest pictures of integrity in history is found in the Old Testament account of Daniel. Anyone familiar with the Bible knows about Daniel and the lions' den. But what is important about this story is not Daniel being thrown into the lions' den, it is what happened before Daniel was thrown into the den and why he was thrown in. We see why integrity is so important and how to make it a part of our DNA of living.

> It pleased Darius to appoint 120 satraps to rule through-
> out the kingdom, with three administrators over them,
> one of whom was Daniel. The satraps were made
> accountable to them so that the king might not suffer
> loss (Daniel 6:1-2).

The king of the empire at this time was a pagan by the name
of Darius. Evidently, he suspected that some of the people under
him were embezzling money and being unfaithful employees. The
empire was so vast that he knew he had to surround himself with
the best people to ensure honesty and accountability. He knew that
you are no better than the people you surround yourself with, so he
sought the best people possible to help oversee the kingdom's affairs.
One choice was obvious.

> Now Daniel so distinguished himself among the admin-
> istrators and the satraps by his exceptional qualities that
> the king planned to set him over the whole kingdom
> (Daniel 6:3).

Daniel is about eighty-five years old. He has been serving the Lord
in Babylon for over seventy years and he is now under his third king.
This king is the new kid on the block, so he likely never even met
Daniel. Though not everybody knew Daniel, everybody knew about
Daniel. If you read the Book of Daniel, you will know that Daniel's
reputation preceded him. For seven decades, Daniel had proven himself to be a man of impeccable integrity. Daniel was put in charge of
everyone else and was made second in command only to the king.

Integrity trumps ability every time.

Integrity is the cream that always rises to the top. Integrity
trumps ability every time. There is no limit to how far anyone can

go if others know they can always be trusted to do the right thing. Daniel was not promoted because of his temporal seniority, but because of his moral superiority. His character was a cut above everybody else's, and his integrity got him in deep trouble.

> At this, the administrators and the satraps tried to find grounds for charges against Daniel in his conduct of government affairs, but they were unable to do so. They could find no corruption in him, because he was trustworthy and neither corrupt nor negligent (Daniel 6:4).

Evidently, a good-old-boy network had been skimming off the top, and they didn't want Daniel messing up their game. They also knew that Daniel was an outsider, a foreigner, an immigrant, and a Jew, and they couldn't stand the thought of him being over them. So, they launched a full-scale investigation into his life. They put a tail on him, hired private investigators, bugged his telephone, analyzed his tax records, and examined his bank statements. They interviewed people who went to high school and college with him. What did they find? Nothing, nada, zero, zip.

They brought in the FBI, the CIA, the IRS, and ordered them to turn over every rock, look under every bed, open every drawer and every closet, but they couldn't lay a glove on him. They thought surely after seventy years of working in the government something could cut Daniel down to size. But after putting him under the microscope, all they saw was an honest, hardworking, and holy man. How did this exhaustive investigation end?

> Finally these men said, "We will never find any basis for charges against this man Daniel unless it has something to do with the law of his God" (Daniel 6:5).

What a testimony to say about someone: that you will never find anything legally, morally, ethically wrong with them and that your only hope is to make them disobey God! When you live with integrity, your life becomes surrounded with a force field of righteousness and goodness that can withstand any investigation or accusation.

not necessarily

Count the Cost of Integrity

You are free to exercise integrity, but integrity is never free to exercise. If you know the story of Daniel, this wasn't the first challenge to his integrity, but this would prove to potentially cost the most.

> So these administrators and satraps went as a group to the king and said: "May King Darius live forever! The royal administrators, prefects, satraps, advisers and governors have all agreed that the king should issue an edict and enforce the decree that anyone who prays to any god or human being during the next thirty days, except to you, Your Majesty, shall be thrown into the lions' den. Now, Your Majesty, issue the decree and put it in writing so that it cannot be altered—in accordance with the law of the Medes and Persians, which cannot be repealed" (Daniel 6:6-8).

Give these men credit for a brilliant idea. They had just checkmated Daniel. Since they could not find anything immoral or unethical about Daniel, they decided to make his faith illegal. Daniel didn't hide that he prayed three times a day and that he prayed to the only God who exists. They passed this law with only Daniel in mind, because they knew if they made prayer to Daniel's God illegal, he would have a gold-plated printed reservation to the lions' den.

How could they be so sure it would work? How did they know what Daniel would do? Because they knew Daniel. For seven decades, when it came to integrity, Daniel's report card was nothing but straight *As*. Every test was graded *100*. They knew Daniel wouldn't fold. They knew Daniel would die first. They understood how Daniel made every decision in his life.

Theodore Hesburgh, former president of the University of Notre Dame, said, "My basic principle is you don't make decisions because they are easy; you don't make them because they are cheap; you don't make them because they are popular; you make them because they're right."[9] Though the king thought Daniel had been involved in the decision, these men had lied. Daniel knew nothing about it. So we read, "Now when Daniel learned that the decree had been published…" (Daniel 6:10).

The rubber had just hit the road in Daniel's faith. He had offered a lifetime of honesty, decency, and godly integrity in government service. He had served faithfully and loyally under every king. He had always done what was best for others. What did he get for it? A gold watch? Stock options? A lifelong pension? A severance package? No.

Now he is facing the loss of his position, his security, his income, his friends, and even his own life. I will say it again. You are free to exercise integrity, but exercising integrity is costly. You exercise integrity not so you can get what you want to have or go where you want to go, but to be who you ought to be. Daniel was going to do whatever he did next with his eyes wide open, knowing full well the cost he may incur. He came through just like his enemies thought he would.

> Now when Daniel learned that the decree had been published, he went home to his upstairs room where the windows opened toward Jerusalem. Three times a day he got down on his knees and prayed, giving thanks to his God, just as he had done before (Daniel 6:10).

Nobody ordered Daniel to pray and nobody was going to order Daniel not to pray. Now let's all ask this question: What would we have done?

You know Daniel had options. He could have played it safe and just quit praying for thirty days. He could have closed his windows and prayed in secret. He could have decided to take a month-long sabbatical and gone somewhere else. He could have lain in bed at night and prayed silently. But integrity never goes on vacation. Integrity never takes a break. Integrity never calls a time-out. Integrity never takes a pass.

Integrity doesn't go with the flow. Integrity doesn't follow the crowd. Integrity stands its ground. Integrity doesn't listen to polls. Integrity lives for principles. Integrity may even leave you all alone because you are the only one charged, as was the case with Daniel.

Whenever you are told to stand down and instead you stand up, you will stand out and you may stand alone and then become a target. Talk is cheap. Integrity never just talks the talk, it walks the walk. It never veers off course. It never takes a shortcut. It never cuts corners. It stands tall. It stands tough and it stands true to what is right.

Pay the Price of Integrity

The traitors turn tattletales, run to the king, and box him in a corner.

> Then they said to the king, "Daniel, who is one of the exiles from Judah, pays no attention to you, Your Majesty, or to the decree you put in writing. He still prays three times a day." When the king heard this, he was greatly distressed; he was determined to rescue Daniel and made every effort until sundown to save him.
>
> Then the men went as a group to King Darius and said to him, "Remember, Your Majesty, that according to the law of the Medes and Persians no decree or edict that the king issues can be changed."
>
> So the king gave the order, and they brought Daniel and threw him into the lions' den. The king said to Daniel, "May your God, whom you serve continually, rescue you!" (Daniel 6:13-16).

Pretty high price to pay for a lifetime of integrity. It is not going to be quick like lethal injection or beheading or firing squad. A lions' den death is not pretty. I was recently in Africa on a safari and I saw lions up close. They are terrifying! A lion's roar can be heard up to five miles away. It sounds like a giant bass speaker that vibrates through your whole body in order to strike a paralyzing fear into prey.[10]

They don't call him the king of the jungle for nothing. A hungry lion can eat 30 percent of his body weight in one sitting. That would be like an average person eating two hundred quarter-pound hamburgers for lunch. No man is a match for a lion because an average lion possesses the strength of fourteen men.[11]

You have to feel for Daniel. After decades of faithfulness and godliness, you'd have to assume that this eighty-five-year-old man would not be going out this way. That is the price you pay for integrity because you never outgrow integrity and you never get too old to do what is right. Daniel pays the ultimate price of being thrown into the lions' den to face a horrific death.

Some of you are thinking, *Wait a minute. Daniel was delivered from the lions' den.* But imagine that you don't know how this story ends. After all, not everybody who gets thrown into a lions' den comes out alive. The only way you will ever maintain your integrity is when you make the same decision that Daniel made regardless of how the story ends for you. You've got to make it every day before you get out of bed and go to school or work. You must realize every day God is sending you out to lead others to know Christ and get closer to Christ, which takes integrity. Otherwise, you will lead people away from Christ. You've got to make up your mind that your integrity is more important than your safety, your security, your prosperity, your position, or your popularity.

The most important question you can ask to determine whether you're living with integrity is not "Did I do things right?" but "Did I do the right thing?" After every important decision or action, take a moment to ask yourself that question, and really devote time to sit with it.

A stone was brought and placed over the mouth of the den, and the king sealed it with his own signet ring and with the rings of his nobles, so that Daniel's situation might not be changed (Daniel 6:17).

Six hundred years later, a story eerily similar to this one took place.

He was thrown into a cave. A stone was rolled across the entrance with soldiers stationed there to protect it. Sound familiar? Another man faced death like Daniel, except he wasn't thrown into a lions' den; he was nailed to a cross. Daniel didn't know whether he would live or die, but this man knew he would die. We know, of course, that Daniel was delivered from death, but this man was delivered through death. Daniel didn't die—he came out alive; this man died—but he came back alive. His name was Jesus. Both faced what they faced because of their integrity.

Technically, Daniel was guilty because of his crime, but Jesus was declared guilty because of our crimes. Daniel was guilty because he broke human laws. Jesus was declared guilty because we broke God's laws. Because Jesus lived the life, counted the cost, and paid the price of integrity, we could be forgiven and receive eternal life.

You must consider the cost and pay the price for integrity. When you do the cost-benefit analysis, the benefits far outweigh the costs, because when you are a person of integrity you never have to fear accusations or investigations. People can go through your closets because there are no skeletons in them. Your life can be an open book because you have nothing to hide. So you live a life of integrity because when those times come that you are put under the microscope, all anybody will see is the light of integrity shining in your heart and the fire of purity burning in your soul.

All-In All the Time

You may not realize it, but your integrity is most likely tested in some way every day—from filling out an expense report to filling out your income taxes, from kicking your golf ball back onto the fairway to cheating on your spouse. Whether you realize it or not, rare will be the day that someway, somehow your integrity is not tested.

So first we need to *decide to be all-in on integrity every day in every way.* It is amazing how making just one major decision—that you will always do what is right, speak what is right, and stand up for what is right—will take care of all the other decisions.

Nobody can ever take your integrity away. They may steal your money, your job, your fame, your reputation, and even your life, but they cannot take your integrity. Only you can throw that away, so when it comes to your integrity, never give in, never give out, and, never give up.

Second, we need to *determine that our integrity is not for sale.* It may cost you your job; it may cost you your inheritance; it may cost you your freedom; it may cost you a friendship. But even if the price is your life, never take the sign off your integrity that says "Not for sale."

Third, we must *dedicate ourselves to maintaining our integrity regardless of the cost.* If you do a cost-benefit analysis on integrity, the benefits far outweigh the costs. When you maintain your integrity, you don't have to spend time worrying that someone will uncover a lie about you. You don't have to worry that you will be caught doing something you will regret. You don't have to waste time trying to make up excuses or rationalize for a moral failure or ethical lapse. Integrity means you can mail your income tax return on April 15 and sleep like a baby.[12] In short, *integrity means being able to live with the most important person in your life with perfect peace and contentment—yourself.*

Jon M. Huntsman was an American businessman and philanthropist. He was the founder and executive chairman of Huntsman Corporation. He was negotiating a large business deal in 1986, and after lengthy negotiations with Emerson Kampen, chairman and CEO of Great Lakes Chemical Corporation, they agreed that Kampen would purchase 40 percent of a division of his company for $54 million. They reached across a table and shook hands settling the deal.

Huntsman did not hear from Kampen for several months, and approximately four months after their agreement, Great Lakes lawyers called to say they would like to draft some documents. Businesses often procrastinate and drag their feet, yet it took three more months for this simple purchase agreement to be put on paper. It had now been almost seven months since the handshake.

Within that period of time, the price of raw materials had decreased substantially and Huntsman's profits had tripled, but no agreement had been signed with Great Lakes and no documents had been exchanged. Kampen called Huntsman with a remarkable proposal.

"According to my bankers, 40 percent of Huntsman Chemical today is worth $250 million. You and I shook hands and agreed on a $54 million price almost seven months ago. I don't think I should have to pay the full difference, but I do think it is fair that I pay at least half." To Kampen's shock, Huntsman refused his offer. He said it would not be fair to use the appreciated value nor should they have to split the difference. He said, "You and I shook hands and made an agreement at $54 million dollars and that is exactly the price for which our attorneys will draft the documents." Kampen said, "But that is not fair to you." Huntsman replied, "Emerson, you negotiate for your company and let me negotiate for mine." For John Huntsman, integrity was the trump card of his life, but the story doesn't end there.

Emerson Kampen never forgot that handshake. He took it with him to his grave. When Kampen died he had two principal speakers at his funeral: Governor Evan Bayh (who went on to become a United States senator) and Jon Huntsman. Though Huntsman and Kampen were not close friends, Huntsman suspected why he had

a world class political hack

been asked to speak at Kampen's funeral. "Even though I could have forced Great Lakes to pay an extra $200 million for that 40 percent ownership stake in my company," Huntsman said, "I've never had to wrestle with my conscience or to look over my shoulder. My word was my bond."[13]

Kampen never forgot that, and neither will others forget that about you. Integrity is the currency that others will always gladly honor and the exchange rate will always be most favorable.

HONESTY:

Nothing but the Truth

> I think it is fair to say that honesty is on the
> ropes. Deception has become commonplace
> at all levels of contemporary life.
>
> **RALPH KEYES**[1]

They say records are made to be broken, but we should hope one record never breaks. The record was set by a man that no one ever dreamed would even try. His name is Bernie Madoff. His last name to this day makes many people incredibly *mad* and motivates them to go *off* (pun intended).

In 1960, Madoff started his own market maker firm and helped launch the Nasdaq Stock Market. He sat on the board of the National Association of Security Dealers and advised the Securities and Exchange Commission on trading securities. No one questioned the wisdom of this financial industry veteran.[2] Madoff's business was one of the top market makers on Wall Street and in 2008 was the sixth largest.

His seemingly successful financial empire collapsed like a house of cards when federal authorities arrested him on December 11, 2008. Three months to the day, Madoff pleaded guilty to eleven federal crimes and admitted to operating the largest private Ponzi scheme in history. The scale of his financial thievery and deception is unparalleled in the history of American finance.

He conned over four thousand investors out of sixty-five billion dollars and went undetected for decades.[3] It is the biggest fraud committed in the history of Wall Street. How he pulled it off and made off with twenty billion dollars is relatively simple—because lying always is.

Madoff's Ponzi scheme lured investors in by guaranteeing unusually high returns. He offered what any investor would seek— low risk and high returns, but in this case the risk was so low and the returns so high that it really should have been seen as too good to be true. For years, he was in a league of his own. No other investment firm could come close to matching the performance of his investments. In up and down years, his clients received between 12 and 13 percent returns like clockwork.[4]

Ponzi schemes are run by a controller or a central operator who takes money from new investors to pay off promised returns to older ones. No profit is actually being made, but the extra money goes to the one running the scheme, who either pockets the money or uses it to continue the deception (and the operation).

To avoid the problem of having too many investors ask for their profits, they are encouraged to "stay in the game and earn even more money." The foundation of the entire scheme is *continuous lying*.

Eventually, the scheme always falls apart after the schemer takes the remaining investment money and runs or the flow of cash dies out because new investors cannot be found or because too many current investors ask for their money. In Madoff's case, he abruptly came to the end of his financial road when his clients requested he return a total of $7 billion when he had only $200 to $300 million left to give.[5]

The results were catastrophic. Madoff was sentenced to 150 years in prison. His brother, Peter, was sentenced to 10 years in prison. His son Mark committed suicide by hanging exactly two years after his father's arrest. Madoff was also ordered to pay restitution of $170 billion. More than 2500 people lost everything they had.

The simple cause of all of this hurt and heartache can be summed up in one word, *dishonesty*. Just as the law of gravity is never broken, the road of deceit will eventually run over the cliff of defeat and lead to the rocks of destruction.

Amber Alert: Honesty Is Missing

If only the Bernie Madoff story were the entire iceberg, but unfortunately it is only the tip. Benjamin Franklin said, "Honesty is the best policy," but it is not the only policy that is followed today and it is becoming increasingly less prominent.

Little Carol Ann was trying to better understand the concept of honesty, so she asked her grandmother, "Nana, I know it is wrong to tell a lie, but is it okay to give the truth an extreme makeover?"[6] Increasingly, the truth gets an extreme makeover from lying to cheating to stealing.

A University of Massachusetts study reveals that 60 percent of adults can't have a ten-minute conversation without lying at least once.[7] We don't play favorites when it comes to lying. Americans lie the most to their parents (86 percent), their friends (75 percent), their siblings (73 percent), and their spouses (69 percent).[8] The time in which we live has been called the "post-truth era." People use euphemisms to make outright lies sound acceptable. So, for example, we no longer tell lies—we "misspeak," "exaggerate," or "exercise poor judgment." A favorite has become "mistakes were made." Recently, we were introduced to a new phenomenon called "alternative facts." Rather than calling it "dishonesty" we call it "a credibility gap" or what Winston Churchill referred to as "terminological inexactitudes."[9]

Cheating just naturally follows on the heels of lying. The evolution of technology and the devolution of morality has made cheating more acceptable than ever before. Statistics show that cheating among high school students has risen dramatically during the past fifty years. While about 20 percent of college students admitted to cheating in high school during the 1940s, today, between 75 and 80 percent of college students report having cheated in high school.[10]

Furthermore, according to the 1998 poll of Who's Who Among American High School Students, 80 percent of the country's best students cheated to get to the top of their class.[11] Some 75 percent of college students admit to cheating.[12] What is even more amazing is that 85 percent of all students think that cheating is essential and only 34 percent of college officials think cheating is a big deal.[13] Cheating has never been easier. Students can download term papers from hundreds of sites on the internet. Students can tamper electronically with grade records and transmit quiz answers via their cell phones.[14]

Contrary to what they and unfortunately much of the public increasingly thinks, honesty and its counterpart dishonesty are a big deal.

Honesty Is Free; Lying Costs

The failure to be honest is expensive and not just financially (though the cost is often tremendous). Cheating the IRS on our income taxes costs the nation $458 billion a year, which averages out to a staggering $1400 per taxpayer.[15]

Dishonesty also hits home. It drives up our grocery bills. People always complain about the cost of food, but shoplifting and "borrowing" shopping carts adds to the cost of doing business. Retailers spend about $175 million per year on replacing stolen carts and an additional $117 million on expenses to retrieve abandoned carts. The Food Marketing Institute reports that nearly two million shopping carts are stolen every year, translating into a per-store loss of $8,000 to $10,000 annually, and that's just in the food industry.[16]

Dishonesty can cost you a job, a career, a future, or a reputation.

George O'Leary, who coached several years at Georgia Tech, got his dream job when he was hired to be the head football coach at the University of Notre Dame. He was chosen out of a half dozen candidates for the most coveted job by any Catholic football coach in the country. The Fighting Irish had won eleven national titles and O'Leary dreamed of many more. But five days after he was hired he was unceremoniously and ignominiously fired.

Why? Because for two decades he had exaggerated his accomplishments as a football player at the University of New Hampshire and falsely claimed to have earned a master's degree in education from New York University.[17]

Of course, O'Leary is not alone. Nearly three-quarters of job seekers admitted to lying on their resumes in a recent survey by SelectJobs.com, a high-tech industry employment site.[18] In the world of academia, Pulitzer Prize winner Joseph Ellis was suspended from teaching at Mt. Holyoke College because he lied about serving in Vietnam. Renowned historians Doris Kearns Goodwin and Stephen Ambrose have faced charges of plagiarism.[19]

Dishonesty can also be tragically fatal. A Chinese man took out a life insurance plan worth $110,000, but he never told his wife. He was presumed dead after his vehicle was discovered in a river, although his body was not recovered. His body was not recovered because he faked his death so his wife would get the insurance. But the woman, out of grief that she was a widow, took her two children, ages three and four, and jumped into a pond after posting a suicide note where she said, "I am going to accompany my husband in the afterlife." The devastated, remorseful husband turned himself in to authorities, admitting his lie.[20]

The cost of dishonesty to business is staggering. The dishonesty of employees is widespread and damaging. Some 30 percent of people who call in because of sickness or other reasons they cannot work are lying.[21] It costs businesses up to 10 percent of their total payroll every year.[22]

A man called in to work one day and said he couldn't come in because of his grandmother's funeral. The next morning at work his boss came up and said, "Do you believe in life after death?"

"Well, yes I do," the employee said with a puzzled look.

"Boy, that makes me feel so much better!" his boss said.

"Why?"

"Yesterday, after you told me you were attending your grandmother's funeral, she stopped by to visit you."

Employers are often guilty of dishonesty too, and the resultant cost is high. According to David Horsager,

> Leaders who inspire trust [by being honest] garner better output, morale, retention, innovation, loyalty, and revenue, while mistrust [being dishonest] fosters skepticism, frustration, low productivity, lost sales, and turnover. Trust affects a leader's impact and the company's bottom line more than any other single thing.[23]

> ## Trust affects a leader's impact and the company's bottom line more than any other single thing.

Employers seeking to hire other people can't even trust recommendations from former employers anymore. Lehigh University economist Robert Thorton has come up with clever ways to recommend lousy employees to other companies. For example:

- "I am pleased to say this person is a former colleague of mine"—for a candidate with interpersonal problems.
- "In my opinion, you will be very fortunate to get this person to work for you"—for the lazy worker.

- "He is a man of many convictions and I am sorry we let him get away"—for a former felon and criminal.

- "His true ability is deceiving"—for the untrustworthy and dishonest employee.

- "I most enthusiastically recommend this person with no qualifications whatsoever"—for a totally inept worker.[24]

The bottom line is honesty is important because the lack of it erodes trust, which is the foundation of all meaningful relationships in every part of our society. Years ago, the Roper Organization surveyed the public about their perception of who is telling the truth. People said the clergy told the truth only 49 percent of the time, doctors 48 percent, their best friend 26 percent, the local newspaper 8 percent, the president of the United States 8 percent, and the leaders of Congress 3 percent. Dishonesty breeds cynicism everywhere it is planted.[25]

The Truth About Honesty

You might think *honesty* is an easy word to define, but it encompasses more than what most people think. Children are prone to believe that honesty is not lying. That is true, but in addition to telling the truth, honesty requires *doing* the truth and *living* the truth. Someone who is honest tells the truth—they do not lie. They do the truth—they do not cheat. They live the truth—they do not steal.

Honesty is sincerity's twin. *Sincere* is a Latin word that means "without wax." The word means "sun-tested." An ancient legend recounts that the ancients had fine porcelain, which was greatly valued and therefore expensive, but it often cracked during the firing process. Merchants who were dishonest would smear pearly-white wax over those cracks making it appear to be true porcelain when held up to sunlight. Honest dealers would mark their flawless wears *sinecera*—"without wax."[26] Both the words and the deeds of someone who is honest can be held up to the light of what is real and true and no cracks will ever appear. That is why you can never be honest without being sincere nor be sincere without being honest.

A cop pulled a man over and said, "Sir, I need you to breathe into this breathalyzer for me." The man said, "Sir, I can't do that. I am asthmatic and if I do I can die." The cop said, "Okay. I need you to come down to the station with me so I can take some blood." The man said, "Sir, I can't do that either. I am a hemophiliac and if I do I will bleed to death." The cop said, "Okay, then I will need a urine sample from you." He said, "Sir, I can't do that either because I am a diabetic and my blood sugar would get really low and I can go into a diabetic coma." He said, "Well, okay. Why don't you just step out of the car and walk this white line for me?" He said, "Sir, I can't do that either." He said, "Why not?" He said, "Because I'm drunk." Sincerity and honesty will always stand by and speak to the truth.

Think about your last week. Did you tell even one lie—at work, at home, on that phone call with your mother-in-law? If you said no, you probably just lied. You actually double-lied because you lied about lying. Did you know that the average person tells about ten lies per week?[27] That's nearly two per day.

Everybody Lies, a book by an Ivy League-educated former Google data scientist, analyzed new data from the internet—traces of information that billions of people give on search engines and social media and every site you could imagine. They discovered that a lot of what we think is right is dead wrong because people lie to friends, doctors, family, surveys and even themselves.[28]

A man stood on a street corner with his dog and held up a sign that said, "Talking Dog for Sale—$10." A man walked by and said, "Are you serious about that? That dog can't talk." Then the dog said, "Please sir. Please buy me. This man is mean to me. He never takes me for walks, hardly feeds me, keeps me cooped up for days, and I can't stand it anymore." The man looked at the dog's owner and said, "That dog really can talk. Why are you selling him for only ten dollars?" The owner said, "Because all he does is lie."

Unfortunately, we are living in a world where lying is common, practically expected, and seemingly just the way we do business.

An Honest Man

Many modern Christians have forgotten the name of one of the most prominent people in the Bible who was known for his honesty. Samuel is one of those unsung heroes of Scripture who deserves a higher profile than he often gets. After all, two books of the Bible are named after him, and he likely wrote both. But his literary contribution is exceeded by his sheer impact in the Jewish community of that day.

In the Old Testament, a person could hold five key positions:

- seer
- priest
- judge
- prophet
- military leader

Samuel is the only man in the Old Testament who fulfilled all five roles. A *seer* is a person who "sees." Today, we think of a seer like a psychic or a medium. But in the Old Testament, a seer was a prophet—but more than a prophet. A seer was a prophet who saw visions from God, sometimes in dreams, and then was given the ability to interpret what God was saying through those visions.

A *priest* was the religious leader of the people. He was the intercessor for the people before God and made sacrifices for their sins. For more than three hundred years after Israel entered into the Promised Land and before they selected their first king, they were ruled by *judges* or deliverers. They would ride in on a white stallion and rescue Israel whenever the people disobeyed God, fell into sin, and warred with other nations.

A *prophet* was God's spokesman. His job was to teach and preach God's word and to reveal God's truth to his people. Finally, the *military leader* was a commander who would lead the troops into battle, defend the nation, and protect the country. Samuel fulfilled all five of those roles. He was a spiritual superstar!

But that is not what set Samuel apart. That is not what made Samuel's star shine so brightly. What elevated Samuel, both in God's eyes and in his people's eyes, was his uncompromising honesty. What distinguished him was not the high positions that he held, but the honest person that he was.

In 1 Samuel 12, the nation of Israel has chosen a king for the first time in its history, and it is time for Samuel to leave the scene. Samuel is giving his farewell address, and he is going to set the record straight about who he was, how he had lived, and all that he had said. On his tombstone, you could write four words—"Nothing but the truth."

Honesty Means You Speak Truth with Your Lips

But before we get to Samuel's farewell address, we have to start when he was just a boy. At first his mother, Hannah, cannot conceive, but the Lord hears her prayer and Samuel is born. She takes Samuel to the temple and dedicates his entire life to the Lord and leaves him with a high priest named Eli. Eli became his guardian, his foster father, and his mentor.

We are told that in that day there were few visions from the Lord, but one night Samuel is on his bed about to go to sleep, and three different times a voice calls his name. All three times he gets up thinking Eli is calling him, but Eli claims he did not call him and sends him back to bed. After the third time, Eli realizes it must be the Lord calling Samuel, so he tells him, "The next time you hear this voice say, 'Speak, LORD, for your servant is listening.'" Again, the Lord calls, Samuel responds, and then the Lord reveals to Samuel in a vision what is going to happen to Eli and his family:

> The LORD said to Samuel: "See, I am about to do something in Israel that will make the ears of everyone who hears about it tingle. At that time I will carry out against Eli everything I spoke against his family—from beginning to end. For I told him that I would judge his family forever because of the sin he knew about; his sons blasphemed God, and he failed to restrain them. Therefore I swore to the house of Eli, 'The guilt of Eli's house will never be atoned for by sacrifice or offering'" (1 Samuel 3:11-14).

Samuel is saddened and shocked. Eli has shown him the ropes, taught him the tricks of the trade, and he doesn't want to tell him what the Lord said. Inevitably, this happens:

> Samuel lay down until morning and then opened the doors of the house of the LORD. He was afraid to tell Eli the vision, but Eli called him and said, "Samuel, my son."
> Samuel answered, "Here I am."
> "What was it he said to you?" Eli asked. "Do not hide it from me. May God deal with you, be it ever so severely, if you hide from me anything he told you" (1 Samuel 3:15-17).

If you were Samuel, what would you do? You are not even old enough to drive a chariot. Your mentor/hero knows more about God's word in his little finger than you know in your whole body. In situations like this, kids lie. And we can only assume that Samuel was tempted to tell a fib of his own.

Keep this in mind. This is a test for Samuel. He listened to the truth, but will he tell the truth, the whole truth, and nothing but the truth so help him God? Even though it will be tough and difficult, will he tell Eli what he wants to hear or what he needs to hear?

> So Samuel told him everything, hiding nothing from him. Then Eli said, "He is the LORD; let him do what is good in his eyes" (1 Samuel 3:18).

Samuel learned at an early age that honesty is the best policy. God is a God of truth, and when you tell the truth, God will stand with you. That is why we read the next words,

> The LORD was with Samuel as he grew up, and he let none of Samuel's words fall to the ground. And all Israel from Dan to Beersheba recognized that Samuel was attested as a prophet of the LORD (1 Samuel 3:19-20).

Samuel earned a reputation for speaking the truth no matter what. He would always relay exactly what God told him. Even as a thirteen-year-old, he is officially recognized as a prophet by the nation and would be forever known as a truth-teller.

Honesty Means You Show Truth Through Your Life

Now let's fast-forward about forty years. Samuel is in his mid-fifties, his ministry is coming to a close, Israel has decided they want a king, and he leads them to find a king. It is time for him to exit the stage, and he says his final goodbye.

> Samuel said to all Israel, "I have listened to everything you said to me and have set a king over you. Now you have a king as your leader. As for me, I am old and gray, and my sons are here with you. I have been your leader from my youth until this day" (1 Samuel 12:1-2).

Samuel has a forty-year track record. Many of these people have grown up with him, attended school with him, worshipped with him, taken their problems to him, and gone into battle for him. He then makes a bold statement about personal character:

> "Here I stand. Testify against me in the presence of the LORD and his anointed. Whose ox have I taken? Whose donkey have I taken? Whom have I cheated? Whom have I oppressed? From whose hand have I accepted a

bribe to make me shut my eyes? If I have done any of
these things, I will make it right" (1 Samuel 12:3).

He asks for a full-blown audit and instructs them to open the
books, check the records, investigate their witnesses, see what they
can find. He doesn't request a lawyer, hire a mediator, or call for an
arbitrator. He doesn't equivocate or hesitate. He boldly states, "I
have been honest every day in every way all of my life."

He defies anybody to prove that he has deceived, deluded, or
defrauded anyone. Check his tax returns or his expense reports, and
they were accurate to the penny. He had played no favorites, taken
no bribes, and never wavered on telling the truth. Wouldn't it be
great if every politician who retired from office could make that
statement before departing?

A bus full of politicians was speeding down a country road, and
the driver lost control and crashed into a tree. The farmer who
owned the field went over to investigate, and then he dug a big hole
and buried all the politicians. A few days later, the sheriff drove by
and saw this overturned bus, and he knocked on the door of the
farmer's house and asked where all the politicians had gone. The
farmer said, "I buried all of them." The sheriff said, "Were they all
dead?" The farmer said, "Well, some of them said they weren't, but
you know how politicians lie."

Not all politicians lie, of course, and this one didn't. What was
the conclusion of the people who were appointed as both judge and
jury over his life?

> "You have not cheated or oppressed us," they replied.
> "You have not taken anything from anyone's hand."
> Samuel said to them, "The LORD is witness against
> you, and also his anointed is witness this day, that you
> have not found anything in my hand" (1 Samuel 12:4-5).

Samuel is going to walk away with a divine certification of his
honesty and his integrity. Nothing is better, greater, and higher than

ending whatever calling God has given you and realizing that your lasting reputation is that you spoke the truth with your talk and you showed truth with your walk.

Honesty Means You Share Truth in Your Love

Samuel has a method to his madness. He has a reason to establish his bona fides. Samuel has forced the nation to admit that he tells nothing but the truth—that they can believe everything he says. So he is not going to stop now because the nation needs to hear a word of truth that they will not like but that they need to hear.

Do you love the people around you enough to tell them the truth? The truth of the gospel is the most important truth you can share with anyone. Jesus came to earth to tell us the truth—that we are sinners in need of a Savior—and he died for us and rose from the dead so we would tell the truth about him. Take a moment right now to jot down the name of one person in your circle of influence who needs to hear the truth about Jesus. Make a commitment today to share the truth of the gospel with that person this year.

> **Do you love the people around you enough to tell them the truth?**

Samuel loves his people enough to tell them the truth and he prepares them for what is coming:

> "Now then, stand here, because I am going to confront you with evidence before the LORD as to all the righteous acts performed by the LORD for you and your ancestors" (1 Samuel 12:7).

As the truism reminds us, the one thing we learn from history is that we don't learn from history. Samuel wanted to make sure, if possible, that the people he had loved all his life didn't make that mistake.

The words "stand here" have a judicial nuance to them. Samuel is telling them to sit still and listen carefully because court is in session. The words "confront you with evidence" mean to "decide a case of litigation." Samuel is about to present his case not only for the righteousness of God, but he is going to indict his people for their attitude toward God. He reminds them of the one thing their ancestors had done that had always gotten them in trouble: "But they forgot the LORD their God" (1 Samuel 12:9).

In 1863, President Abraham Lincoln declared a national day of prayer and fasting for the nation. He said the biggest problem that America had was "We have forgotten God." That will always be the biggest cause of our biggest problems. Many people and nations in many eras have come down with spiritual Alzheimer's during which they forget God.

Samuel pulls no punches and shares three ways we can forget God. The sin of idolatry occurs when we forget God and turn to some other god. The sin of immorality, particularly sexual immorality, is when we forget God in pursuit of pleasure. The sin of iniquity is when we pursue our own paths and place God on the shelf.

Samuel closes with these words:

> "Be sure to fear the LORD and serve him faithfully with all your heart; consider what great things he has done for you. Yet if you persist in doing evil, both you and your king will perish" (1 Samuel 12:24-25).

Samuel lets the nation know that when it comes to loving God, serving God, obeying God, remembering God, it is a matter of life and death. So this superstar Samuel began his life by being honest and telling nothing but the truth, and he ended his life in the same way.

A young lady was lying on the beach in Florida when a little boy in his swimming trunks and carrying a towel came up to her and said, "Excuse me. Do you believe in God?" She sat up surprised by the question and said, "Yes, I do." He said, "Do you go to church?" She said, "As a matter of fact, I go every Sunday." He said, "Do you believe the Bible and do you pray to God?" She said, "Absolutely!" Then the little boy looked at her with relief on his face and said, "Would you hold my two dollars while I go swimming?"

God is always looking for honest people—people who will be honest whether anyone is looking, people who will tell the truth even when it is unpopular, who will keep their promises, and whose word is their bond. When God speaks he tells us nothing but the truth, and when we speak, so should we.

Let's Get Honest

Let's get honest about being dishonest. Sometimes lying is easier. If you are determined to rededicate yourself to speaking nothing but the truth, you have to be honest in all of your life. This will take several steps.

First, be honest with *yourself.* I came across an amazing story by the legendary baseball player Ted Williams. Williams was forty years old and closing out his career with the Boston Red Sox. He developed a pinched nerve in his neck, and it so affected his hitting that for the first time in his career he batted under .300, hitting just .245 with ten home runs. At the time, he was the highest-salaried player in all of sports, making $125,000. The next year the Red Sox sent him the exact same contract.

When he looked it over, he promptly sent it back with a note telling them he would only sign a contract with the biggest pay cut allowed at that time, which was 25 percent. He went on to say, "They were offering me a contract I knew I didn't deserve and I only wanted what I deserved…" and he cut his own salary by $31,250.[29] The first step to being honest is being true to yourself and with yourself.

Be honest with *others.* That seems somewhat redundant and a matter of common sense, but when you make a rock-ribbed commitment to be honest with others, your honesty will be tested. A man came home from work after a long, arduous day, reclined in his chair, and turned on the television for an hour of rest and relaxation. His son had just gotten home from school when the phone rang. The son, being sensitive to his dad's weariness, said, "I'll get it, Daddy." He was thrilled until he overheard his son's receptionist skills. The little boy said to the caller, "Mister, I don't know if he is home or not, but if you will hold on, I'll go ask him." No one ever said that honesty would be easy!

You should be honest regardless of the actions of others or the circumstances around you. I love the story about a store owner who interviewed a young man for his first job. As a final question, the store owner asked, "If I hire you to work in my store, will you be honest and truthful?" The young man, who wanted the job badly, answered, "Sir, I will be honest and truthful whether you hire me or not."

Which leads me to say to moms and dads: Practicing honesty before your children will save you a lot of trouble in the long run. A salesman knocked on the door of a rundown and obviously poor home. The mother in the home told her little boy to tell the salesman she could not come to the door because she was in the bathtub. The little boy went to the door and said, "Mister, we don't have a bathtub, but Mom told me to tell you she is in it."[30]

We should want honesty not only for ourselves but also for our highest leaders. What do Americans want in a president? To answer this question, a random national sampling of over 1000 Americans was given a list of seventy-four leadership traits. The first question was, "What is the most important quality in deciding whether an individual has the essential leadership characteristics to be president?" The number one answer—honesty.[31] Whether you are president or not, you should want that for yourself. In the end, honesty is always the best policy.

It can even keep you out of jail or at least minimize time spent in jail. During World War II, the Dutch were forbidden from selling national art to the Nazis. But an artist named Han van Meegeren stood in court on May 29, 1945, for violating this law in "giving a national treasure to the enemy."[32] The "national treasure" he had given to the Nazis was what they thought was an authentic painting by legendary Dutch painter Johannes Vermeer. What the Nazis didn't know was that van Meegeren had become a master at emulating Vermeer and in distressing paintings to make them appear authentic when they were not. When he was faced with the possibility of life in prison, van Meegeren was forced to confess that the painting he sold was actually a forgery. The court didn't believe him.

In an ironic twist, the man who had painted himself into condemnation was also forced to paint himself out of it. He was allowed to substantiate his claim before the court by painting his last "Vermeer," earning himself a modest punishment of a year in prison.[33] In the end, his honesty about his dishonesty saved his life!

The greatest reason and motivation to be honest is that you must be honest with God. Scripture says, "It is impossible for God to lie" (Hebrews 6:18). God doesn't shade the truth or dilute the truth. He doesn't exaggerate, manipulate, or fabricate. God cannot lie.

Beginning today, do yourself a favor—tell the truth, the whole truth, and nothing but the truth. That is guaranteed to gain God's approval and will give you a clear conscience to keep your past from coming back to bite you.

HUMILITY:

It's Not About Me

Those who travel the high road of humility in
Washington, DC, are not bothered by heavy traffic.

SENATOR ALAN SIMPSON[1]

For almost a quarter of a century, the country of Iraq was synonymous with one name: Saddam Hussein. He was quirky, foolhardy, masochistic, and sadistic, but in the end, just plain foolish. He was a dictator who ruled with an iron fist. His personality and presence pervaded the entire country. Thousands of portraits, posters, statues, and murals were erected in his honor from one end of the country to the other. If you looked on the sides of office buildings, schools, airports, shops, and on Iraqi currency, you could see his face.[2]

He seemed to have nine political lives. After his crushing defeat in the first Gulf War of 1991, it took the United States, supported by Great Britain and other allies, twelve more years to finally take him out of power. But the cause of his demise was not what you think.

Foreign intelligence declared that Iraq possessed weapons of mass destruction (WMD). This intelligence was universally believed. Supporters of the war, opponents of the war, and even members of

Saddam's own regime took it to be fact. President George W. Bush, backed by Prime Minister Tony Blair of Great Britain, on March 17, 2003, gave Hussein forty-eight hours to surrender and leave Iraq. Saddam refused to do so, and after a relatively short war, he was captured on December 13, 2003, and sentenced to death by hanging on December 30, 2005.[3]

Though his death certificate will show that he died by hanging, that is not what really killed him. As it turned out, Hussein did not have WMDs and could have easily proved it to outside inspectors and probably avoided war and saved his life. Why would he gamble his regime, his power, and even his life by pretending to have something he did not? Amazingly, when he was debriefed by the FBI after his capture, he told agents that he was more worried about looking weak to Iran than being removed by the coalition of forces that invaded his country.[4] What killed Saddam Hussein was a lack of humility and an abundance of pride.

The Road Less Taken

The high road of humility is a lightly travelled path these days. We have all met people and known people who are "full of themselves"—people who could strut sitting down. The irony is we take pride in being able to spot people who have a problem with pride! We've all met people who were too full of themselves, but how many people have you met who were too empty of themselves?

In our society, we have seen a broad shift from a culture of humility to what David Brooks calls the culture of "Big Me."[5] We have morphed from a culture that once encouraged people to think humbly of themselves to a Kardashian culture where people see themselves as the center of the universe.[6]

Between 1948 and 1954, psychologists asked more than ten thousand adolescents whether they considered themselves to be an important person; 12 percent said yes. The same question was asked in 1989, and 80 percent of the boys and 77 percent of the girls said yes.[7]

Psychologists have developed what is called the Narcissism Test. Based on statements such as, "I like to be the center of attention…," "I show off if I get the chance because I am extraordinary…," "Somebody should write a biography about me…," the narcissism score has risen 30 percent in the last twenty years.[8] Not only is the road to humility unencumbered by heavy traffic, but it seems as if the traffic is getting lighter by the day.

More Humble Pie

Modern American society bombards us with encouragements to be prideful. Almost everything we hear, read, and see motivates us to look out for ourselves, elevate ourselves, get ahead, climb the ladder, and be number one. That attitude is the root cause of practically every other problem that we face in life. C.S. Lewis said it best: "The utmost evil is Pride. Unchastity, anger, grief, drunkenness, and all that are mere fleabites in comparison. It was through Pride that the devil became the devil. *Pride leads to every other vice*."[9]

Pride will keep you from doing the right thing and cause you to do the wrong thing. Pride will keep you from admitting you are wrong, even when you know you are, and will cause you to say you are right, even when you know you are not. Pride builds barriers and destroys bridges. Humility is important because it is the only antidote to pride.

Humility removes anxiety (you no longer worry about yourself because you don't think about yourself); jealousy (you not only don't compare yourself to others, you rejoice in the success of others); apathy (you realize you should care more about others than you should for yourself); and insensitivity (you desire to serve others and meet their needs).

This is why people most susceptible to pride, particularly people who have power—whether it be political power, celebrity power, or financial power—greatly need to model humility for those who follow them and look up to them.

I've had the privilege of meeting and spending time with two presidents, but my favorite president of all and one I wish I could have met was Ronald Reagan. He was a great leader, and the secret to his greatness was his humility. Peggy Noonan was the White House speechwriter for President Reagan for years and spent a lot of time with him. She tells this touching story that epitomizes what every leader should display regardless of how high they are and how much they have achieved.

> A few days after President Reagan had been shot, when he was well enough to get out of bed, he wasn't feeling well so he went to the bathroom that connected to his room. He slapped some water on his face and some of the water slopped out of the sink. He got some paper towels and got down on the floor to clean it up. An aide went in to check on him, and found the President of the United States on his hands and knees on the cold tile floor mopping up water with paper towels. The aide said, "Mr. President, what are you doing? Let the nurse clean that up!" He said, "Oh no. I made that mess and I would hate for the nurse to have to clean it up."[10]

You may be on a low-carb diet or avoid sugar, but we've all had to eat our fair share of one dessert: humble pie. It doesn't always taste good, but it is always nutritious for the soul. Former Miami Dolphins coach Don Shula learned that several years ago. He was at the height of his popularity and had difficulty with privacy.

Shula and his wife were in a small town in Maine, and they were hoping not to be recognized. They decided to go to a movie. As they entered the theater, everyone in attendance stood and applauded.

Shula was surprised at first, but then smiled and realized that just came with the territory of being a championship football coach.

As the *Orlando Sentinel* tells it, here's what happened:

> After [Don Shula] coached the '72 Dolphins to a 17-0 record, he and his late wife, Dorothy, vacationed in a small town in Maine. Entering a movie theater, they received an ovation from the few people already in the theater. Shula begged off, explaining he didn't expect special treatment just because of who he is. Said one of the moviegoers: 'We don't care who you are. They wouldn't start the movie until we had 10 people here, and you two just put us over the top.'" [11]

We could all use a piece of humble pie, because not only does it do us good, but it does all of those around us even better.

Humility: Hard to Find and Define

Before we try to define *humility*, we should undefine it. Humility is not self-deprecation. One man said, "What some people call humility I call poor posture." Humility is not seeing yourself as less than what you are—a human being with dignity created in the image of God with certain God-given gifts and abilities and talents.

Humility is not failing to appreciate and acknowledge when other people compliment you or find good in you. It is alright to let praise go to your heart as long as you don't let it go to your head. False humility is when you refuse to graciously accept a compliment that has been well-earned and deserved.

Humility is not refusing to have any ambition to be better and to do better to reach your fullest potential, both in who you are and what you can do. Someone put it this way: "Humility is not thinking less of yourself; it is thinking of yourself less."

Humility is not self-humiliation. Rather than putting yourself down, humility is putting yourself in your rightful place. That place is always second place for the good of others. As I mulled over this, I came up with this definition of humility that I hope will resonate with you as it did with me: *Humility is always volunteering to come in second in a two-man race.* A simple way to measure your humility quotient: The more pride you have, the more you desire to use others to serve you to make you successful. The humbler you are, the more you desire to serve others to make them successful.

Someone once asked Leonard Bernstein, the late New York Philharmonic conductor, what was the most difficult position in the orchestra to play. Without hesitation he said, "Second fiddle." Why? Not because second-chair violin is tougher than playing a piccolo or a flute. The point is, everyone wants to be first-chair violin. Our natural inclination is to always want the first chair, to sit in front, to be at the head of the line, to be on top of the ladder. Humility reverses that spirit. People who are genuinely humble don't think about their humility. Humble people never call attention to their character at all.

A legend is told about a man who was the humblest person in his company. He was so humble that management gave him a medal for it. The next day when the man wore the medal to work, they took it away from him.

A fine line exists between enjoying success and enjoying it too much. A fifth-grade girl came home from school so excited. She told her mother she had been voted "prettiest girl in the class." She came home the next day even more excited. The mother said, "What happened today?" She said, "I was voted the most popular girl in the class!" A week later she came dragging in the door with tears coming down her cheeks. Her mother said, "What happened?" She said, "Well, we had a third contest and I won." Her mother said, "Why are you so sad?" She said, "Because I was voted most stuck-up."

Humility is often hard to come by. The mirror never lies, and what you feel when you look into it will tell you a lot about the person staring back at you. If a person of good character is in the mirror, then you will be humble about it. Nothing will take you lower than pride, and nothing will lift you higher than humility.

> Nothing will take you lower than pride, and
> nothing will lift you higher than humility.

Wonder Woman

The most famous woman in the Bible displays humility in sparkling technicolor. Practically the whole world knows Mary by her first name. Scripture itself says that she is the most blessed and the most highly favored by God of all the women in the Bible and really, in history. Even today, she is an almost universally admired woman by billions of people around the world. There are ninety-three women in the Bible who speak, and forty-nine of them are named. Together, they say 14,056 words, 11 percent of all the words recorded in Scripture.[12] Few if any would dispute that this woman stands out above all the others, with her character and her communication, who she was and what she said. That's why both the Roman Catholic Church and the Eastern Orthodox Church place such value on her in their traditions.

When we meet Mary for the first time, God's people had not seen or heard from the God they worshipped in more than four hundred years. For four-plus centuries, there had been no new revelation from God, no new miracles, and the silence from heaven was deafening. Then, to the least likely of people, in the least likely of places, at the least likely of times, God sends an angel to make an announcement that would shake the world then and change the world forever. This angel speaks first to a teenage peasant girl who couldn't even sign her name. Then he speaks to a lowly minimum wage carpenter who had no claim to fame. Then several angels speak to shepherds who were considered to be on the lowest rung of the social ladder. (It's as if God was looking for people for whom humility would not be a problem.)

In Mary we glimpse the supreme value God places on the sublime virtue called humility. We enjoy the greatest blessings of life today because of a woman who did not go as high as she could, but got as low as she could. But because she got as low as she could, she went higher than any woman before or since.

God Looks for the Presence of Humility

> In the sixth month of Elizabeth's pregnancy, God sent the angel Gabriel to Nazareth, a town in Galilee, to a virgin pledged to be married to a man named Joseph, a descendant of David. The virgin's name was Mary (Luke 1:26-27).

Any Jewish person hearing this story would have been astounded. God hasn't spoken a word for four hundred years and he now decides to interrupt the world's programming for the most momentous broadcast in history and where does he do it? Not in Judea, which was the heart of God's work for hundreds of years, not in Rome, which was the capital of the most powerful empire in the world, not even in Jerusalem, the city that was the apple of his eye. The angel announces it in Galilee, an area where the lower class resided.

Where in Galilee did this announcement take place? Of all places, in Nazareth. The first time we ever hear about Nazareth is in Luke's Gospel. It is never mentioned in the Old Testament and you won't find it in ancient history. Nothing of importance had ever come out of Nazareth. Scholars have estimated it may have had at most two hundred people. Nazareth was the kind of town you went through, not the kind of town you went to.

Have you ever had the experience of going on a long road trip and you pull into one of those little towns to fill up your car, get a Slurpee or corndog, use the bathroom, wash the bugs off your windshield, and get away as fast as you can thanking God that is not where you live? That was Nazareth. You would thank God that is not where you were from.[13]

Nazareth housed the headquarters of a garrison of Roman soldiers. Pagan temples to Roman gods had been erected there. Many of the young girls there were known to have relations with and marry Roman soldiers to the disgrace of the Jewish people. The marketing slogan of the day could have been, "What happens in Nazareth stays in Nazareth." The town had such a bad reputation that when Nathaniel heard that Jesus was from Nazareth he wrote him off: "Can anything good come from there?" (John 1:46).

Why in the world would God make the most momentous announcement in history in a region full of hillbillies and a town full of paganism? Because God knew in that town was a teenaged girl humble enough for him to use.

God doesn't look for a diva, a beauty queen, or a movie star. God looks for a humble no-name country girl in a one-light town. God is more impressed by the dim glow of humble places than the bright lights of expansive stages.

> **God is more impressed by the dim glow of humble places than the bright lights of expansive stages.**

God Seeks People of Humility

The first time we meet Mary, an angel of God is speaking to her, a young girl living in a poverty-stricken region engaged to a lowly carpenter. If you had walked by this girl, you would not have even given her a second look.

She is an average young girl, born to the lower class, from a peasant's town, in a poor region of Israel, promised in marriage to a minimum-wage laborer. She is not a movie star, a beauty queen, or a rich socialite. Furthermore, Mary was not even a full-grown woman. She was a teenager, which wasn't unusual in the first century. Girls were often betrothed and married in their early teens. This was common practice, and most Bible scholars say that Mary was probably no older than fourteen.

Here was a nobody girl, living in a nothing town, in the middle of nowhere. But she has come face to face with an angel who spoke these words:

> The angel went to her and said, "Greetings, you who are highly favored! The Lord is with you."
> Mary was greatly troubled at his words and wondered what kind of greeting this might be (Luke 1:28-29).

Mary is confused and probably wonders whether the angel has the wrong person. She could have understood if she had been a queen or even a princess or came from a wealthy family, but she is neither royal nor rich. She has no fortune or fame.

> The angel said to her, "Do not be afraid, Mary; you have found favor with God. You will conceive and give birth to a son, and you are to call him Jesus. He will be great and will be called the Son of the Most High. The Lord God will give him the throne of his father David, and he will reign over Jacob's descendants forever; his kingdom will never end" (Luke 1:30-33).

Why did God's Son come into this world through a pregnant, unwed teenage girl in a culture that honored virginity and shamed pregnancy outside of marriage? Why would Jesus be born not in the comfortable surroundings of a royal palace, but in a feeding trough in a stable? Why would God overlook rich, famous, and powerful candidates and instead choose someone of the lowest socioeconomic class, who would suffer the apparent shame of having a child out of wedlock?

Because God values humility. God disdains the proud, but he delights in the humble. Isaiah 66:2 says, "These are the ones I look on with favor; those who are humble and contrite in spirit." Mary would have never chosen herself to mother God's Son, and she can't believe that God has. Here, we see a portrait of her humility. Humility is not just not thinking higher of yourself than you should; it is not thinking of yourself at all.

People who get God's attention are not the haughty; they are the humble. They are not the people who see how high they can stand, but how low they can stoop. It is not the people who push to the front of the line, but those who willingly go to the back. God seeks people of humility.

God Works Through the Power of Humility

Mary was Jewish, so she had heard how prophets like Isaiah, Jeremiah, and Ezekiel had foretold the coming of the king who would reclaim Israel's throne—a king like no other. He would be the Messiah. Now, she has been told she is going to give birth to the King of kings. Ordinarily, you would think that would make your head swell. The mother of God's Son! The promised Messiah! That would puff any woman up with pride, but that is not Mary's response.

She is good to go, except she did have one little question:

> "How will this be," Mary asked the angel, "since I am a
> virgin?" (Luke 1:34).

Mary may have been a young peasant girl, but she knew how babies were made and she knew she had never come within a country mile of making a baby with anybody. Luke was a doctor and he uses the word for "virgin," making it plain she had never had relations with a man. She has been told why she is going to have a baby, but she has not been told how. It is not going to be by magic but by mystery.

> The angel answered, "The Holy Spirit will come on you,
> and the power of the Most High will overshadow you.

So the holy one to be born will be called the Son of God"
(Luke 1:35).

This is a spiritual explanation, not a medical explanation. It is a
supernatural explanation, not a natural explanation. She is going
to conceive this male child in a virgin's womb. He is going to be the
heavenly child of an earthly mother and the earthly child of a heavenly Father.

Today, four out of ten babies are born out of wedlock and it is
more commonly accepted. Not so in that culture. Everyone who
knew Mary would realize she had gotten pregnant before the wed-
ding and there would be only two logical conclusions: either she
and Joseph had had sex before marriage, or worse, Mary had been
unfaithful.

If she agrees to bear this child, she knew she would be called
unsavory names, and that her children, particularly Jesus, would
be made fun of, and they would be considered second-class citizens.
Women would cross to the other side of the street when they saw her.
She wouldn't be invited to neighborhood parties. In case you aren't
convinced, on one occasion when Jesus was talking to the Pharisees
about who are truly God's children, they snidely remarked, "We are
not illegitimate children" (John 8:41).

Malicious gossip followed Mary all of her life. Common sense
suggests that she knew this was a double-edged sword. Yes, this birth
would be a blessing that she would enjoy, but it would be a burden
she would carry to her grave. Knowing the cost of this birth and the
price she would pay, she gives this response:

"I am the Lord's servant," Mary answered. "May your word
to me be fulfilled." Then the angel left her (Luke 1:38).

Now, we see the true greatness of Mary. The word "servant" refers
to the lowliest kind of servant. It refers to someone who voluntarily
sold themselves into slavery. It was the lowest act a person could

perform in that society. Do you want to know what made Mary such a great woman? It was her willingness to voluntarily conscript herself into the service of God for the sake of the world.

Humility is when obeying God's word, doing God's will, and completing God's work is more important to you than anything else, including your own life. Humility often requires stripping the word *if* out of your vocabulary. Because *if* signals a conditionality that places you and your needs first. Pride is talking when you say things like, "I will do this if it doesn't inconvenience me"; "I will go to the back of the line if there is something in it for me"; "I will give if I get what I want in return." When *if* walks into the room, humility often walks out. Humility sees a need and says yes without ifs, ands, or buts.[14]

Yes, Mary did become the mother of the Messiah. But being the mother of the greatest man who ever lived did not go to her head; it went to her heart. She never traded on her position. She never asked for a divine-mother discount. She never called attention to her role in his birth. She never asked for the spotlight or center stage. In fact, the last recorded words she spoke in Scripture are, "Do whatever he tells you" (John 2:5).

But Mary did make a prediction that came true. Speaking of her assignment from God, she said, "For he has been mindful of the humble state of his servant. From now on all generations will call me blessed" (Luke 1:48).

Mary did become the most famous woman in history. Today, billions of people do rise up and called her "blessed" because of her humility. Mary was a nobody who became greater than almost everybody because she said five words and embodied them: "It is not about me."

Humility Nobility

Of all of the building blocks of character, humility is perhaps the one hardest to cultivate. No one is ever going to write a book titled

Humility and How I Obtained It. We are not born with humility. It is not innate, inherent, or inherited. It is a seed we need to continuously plant, fertilize, and cultivate. It is a daily discipline.

The apostle Peter, who witnessed the greatest daily display of humility ever in Jesus, wrote these words: "Humble yourselves, therefore, under God's mighty hand, that he may lift you up in due time" (1 Peter 5:6). Humility is something we must do. It is not just an attitude; it is an action. Though it is said, "Practice makes perfect," you will never be perfectly humble and for sure you will never be humbly perfect! So how do we develop the discipline and hone the habit of humility? I suggest three ways.

Humility begins when you *see yourself correctly*. We are all created equal, though we may have different gifts and abilities and we may go to different places in life. No one is superior to or more important than anyone else. One of the best ways to kill pride and cultivate humility is to quit looking in the mirror and start looking out the window.

President Teddy Roosevelt was hosting a friend, William Beebe, who was a naturalist and a nature lover. They went out on the White House lawn to look at the stars, focusing on a small ray of light at the lower corner of the Pegasus Constellation. Roosevelt said, "That is the Spiral Galaxy of Andromeda. It is as large as our Milky Way. It is one of one hundred million galaxies. It is seven hundred and fifty thousand light-years away. It consists of a hundred billion suns, each larger than our own sun." After a moment of silence, the president slapped Beebe on the back and said, "Now I think we feel small enough, let's go to bed."[15]

When you keep the big picture in mind, you won't think nearly as big of yourself. There is no such thing as a self-made man. No one has ever gotten anywhere who hasn't always had the help of others. Dwight Eisenhower, soon after Germany's surrender in 1945, received the praise of the world for his great generalship. He said, "Humility must always be the portion of any man who receives a claim earned in the blood of his followers and the sacrifices of his friends."[16]

I happen to have a PhD, but every time I am referred to as "Dr. Merritt," I remember my darling wife, Teresa, who typed every word of my dissertation on an electric typewriter. While I was studying in class, she stood outside in the humidity, heat, cold, rain, or snow to catch a bus to downtown Louisville, Kentucky, and worked hours each day in a lawyer's office. I tell her all the time that she deserves at least one-half of my degree. I wouldn't be where I am today without her.

I love the story of a CEO of a Fortune 500 company who pulled into a service station to get gas. He went inside to pay and when he came out he noticed that his wife was talking with a service station attendant. It so happened that she used to date this fellow in high school before she met her husband.

After she told him about this, they drove in silence for a while, and finally the CEO said, "I bet I know what you are thinking. I bet you are thinking you are glad you married me, because I'm a Fortune 500 CEO and not a service station attendant." She said, "No. I was thinking if I had married him, *he* would be a Fortune 500 CEO and *you* would be a service station attendant."[17]

Second, *serve others consistently.* The disciple Peter wrote, "All of you, clothe yourselves with humility toward one another, because, 'God opposes the proud but shows favor to the humble'" (1 Peter 5:5). What did he mean by "clothe yourselves with humility"? The verb that he used comes from a noun that referred to a white scarf or apron typically worn by slaves. Perhaps he was thinking of the last meal he had with Jesus when Jesus served his disciples by washing their feet (John 13:1-17). Jesus went on to say that all of his followers should follow his example.

But Jesus was not referring just to the literal washing of their feet. He was referring to the attitude of servanthood that it takes to wash someone else's feet. I was invited one time to go to downtown

Atlanta and wash the feet and trim the toenails of homeless men. I must confess that my pride at first welled up within me and I thought to myself, *I'm too good to do this. This is not my calling. This is beneath me.* Then, in the mirror of my heart, I could see the reflection of the ugly face of pride and arrogance, and I realized why Jesus set such a tremendous example. You cannot look down on others when you are kneeling before them washing their feet and trimming their toenails. There are people everywhere whose feet are caked with the mud of discouragement, pain, sickness, disappointment, and failure. They need us to kneel before them and wash their feet with the tears of our compassion and the hands of our love. I remember the words of Jonathan Edwards, the great American preacher, who said, "Nothing puts a man so much out of the devil's reach as humility."

Finally, you must *surrender your ego continuously.* Every day we should run up the white flag of surrender on the poles of our ego and put our self on the shelf and be willing at every turn to voluntarily take second place in a two-man race.

Ulrich Zwingli was one of the leaders of the Protestant Reformation in Europe. He was struggling with his pride in a personal matter. To clear his mind, he decided to take a walk up a Swiss mountain. He watched two goats traversing this narrow path from opposite directions—one going up and the other coming down. At a certain point, the narrow trail prevented them from passing each other. They backed up and lowered their heads as though they were ready to lunge, but then he was astounded to see the goat going up lie down on the path. The goat going down stepped over his back. The goat then got up and continued his climb up the mountain. Zwingli never forgot that the goat went higher because he was willing to go lower.[18]

Jesus himself taught that the lower you get, the higher you will go, and greatness is found not in having others serve you, but in serving others: "The greatest among you will be your servant. For those who exalt themselves will be humbled, and those who humble themselves will be exalted" (Matthew 23:11-12).

> **When you stand beneath the cross of Christ and gaze up at God, it's impossible to look down on anyone else.**

We all face the temptation to brag on ourselves and we all love to have others brag about us, but as a Christ-follower I am reminded of the words of the apostle Paul who said in Galatians 6:14, "May I never boast except in the cross of our Lord Jesus Christ." When you stand beneath the cross of Christ and gaze up at God, it's impossible to look down on anyone else. You will find your pride crucified while humility rains down on your head. It is really not about you. The one who created you would rather die for you than live without you. We can all brag about that![19]

see p. 73

4

LOYALTY:

I'll Be There

> Loyalty is essential to the most basic things
> that make life livable. Without loyalty, there
> can be no love. Without loyalty, there can be
> no family. Without loyalty, there can be no
> friendship. Without loyalty, there can be no
> commitment to community or country. And
> without these things there can be no society.
>
> **ERIC PHELTEN**[1]

O ur children often have experiences that we as parents don't
realize at the time are deeply damaging and leave psycho-
logical and emotional scars. My middle son, Jonathan, had
such an experience when he was thirteen years old. A wonderful
family that were members of our church had a son Jonathan's age,
and he almost became one of ours because he was at our house so
much or Jonathan was at his. He wasn't just Jonathan's friend; he
was by far and away his closest friend. Jonathan has two brothers,
but Fred[2] was "a friend who sticks closer than a brother" (Proverbs
18:24). Or at least Jonathan thought he was.

They did everything together. They built tree houses. They played games and, I learned to my chagrin, would sneak into the woods to smoke cigarettes older kids had given to them. Almost every weekend they would be at Fred's house playing *The Legend of Zelda* video game, watching movies, and just hanging out. You might say Fred was not just a friend but a security blanket for my tender-hearted son.

Jonathan describes himself as an awkward, overweight teenager. He had more friends than he realized, but Fred was so close that Jonathan felt as if Fred were his only friend. He dreamed they would go through life together, college together, and be best buds forever.

I still remember the day that Jonathan staggered into our house almost hysterical. Fred had found a girlfriend, and she didn't think that Jonathan was cool enough to hang out with. She delivered an ultimatum to Fred: "It is Jonathan or me." Fred did not realize it, but God was giving him a loyalty test and he failed miserably. He abruptly told Jonathan that they could not ever hang out again, and even after Jonathan, in tears, begged him to reconsider, he threw Jonathan's friendship away like a dirty piece of paper found by the side of the road.

In Jonathan's words, "[His word 'no'] rang in my ears like the trumpet of Judgment Day and tears filled my eyes. I returned home. Loneliness followed. Depression descended. All because of a single word."[3] It wasn't just a single word that devastated Jonathan, but a deliberate act of betrayal and disloyalty.

I never had any interaction with Fred after that. He has a wonderful family, and I never let it affect my relationship with them. But as I write these words, I can only hope that Fred never experiences the heartache and the hurt caused by disloyalty. I am doubtful, however, because as someone has said, "Those who don't know the value of loyalty can never appreciate the cost of betrayal."[4]

Climate Change

Loyalty was once valued and in vogue. From the dawn of civilization, almost all the great works of literature were tales of loyalty and betrayal. To the ancient Greeks, loyalty was the defining character of a hero. The loyalty that garnered sacrifices, friends, country, faith, and great causes was celebrated and revered.[5]

There has been a climate change when it comes to loyalty. In the lore of life, loyalty is missing in action. Everywhere we look we see not loyalty but *disloyalty*. Tabloid magazines fly off the shelves when friends, boyfriends, and girlfriends share details of relationships that at one time would have been assumed to be private. Books airing someone's dirty laundry top the bestsellers lists.[6] Loyalty is now seen as old-fashioned, out of fashion, the height of naivete, and even a character flaw.[7]

The Royalty of Loyalty

Cicero, the greatest orator of ancient Rome, said this two thousand years ago: "What is the quality to look out for as a warrant for the stability and permanence of friendship? It is Loyalty. Nothing that lacks this can be stable."[8] Cicero was right, but loyalty is not just true of friendships. It is the cornerstone of stability in all relationships.[9]

The world of business is feeling the loyalty (or disloyalty) crunch. Companies lose half of their customers within five years and, on average, half of their employees within four years.[10] That sword cuts both ways. Downsizing has become the prevalent means of re-engineering corporations and companies. Employees who have been loyal for years and even decades are told that their company can no longer be loyal to them because it is not economically sensible.[11]

Customer loyalty is one of the key indicators of business success that every CEO knows has a significant impact on the bottom line. As Chip Bell put it, "Loyal customers, they don't just come back, they don't simply recommend you, they insist that their friends do business with you."[12] Researchers estimate that today it costs five times as much to acquire a new customer as it does to retain a current one. Loyalty really does matter![13]

In a significant research study titled "The Economics of Loyalty," researchers found that for all customers, "Increasing customer retention rates by 5% increases profits by 25% to 95%," and web-based customers "spend more than twice as much in months 24-30 of their relationships than they do in the first 6 months."[14]

If you are in the sales or retail business, pay attention.

- Your probability of selling to an existing customer: 60-70 percent.

- Your probability of selling to a prospect: 5-20 percent.

- 20 percent of current customers will drive 80 percent of your future profits.

- Current customers account for 65 percent of a company's business.

- If you boost your customer loyalty by just 10 percent, you boost the value of your enterprise by 30 percent.[15]

The value of loyalty is true for business, marriage, international relations, interstate commerce, and personal peace. Ultimately, only being loyal to your vows will ensure that your marriage stays together. Only being loyal to your word makes contracts viable. Only being loyal to your convictions will help you sleep well at night if you have a healthy conscience. Treaties signed between nations are only as good as the loyalty those nations give to the treaties they just signed. Every area of life that deals with interpersonal or international relationships depends a great deal on loyalty.

What do we mean by loyalty? Character is built on strong loyalty, but not *blind* loyalty. We should never incur the expense of compromising a conviction when discovering a wrongdoing or continuing a bad relationship. Loyalty does have its limits, and it always should have integrity and honesty as its bookends.

When you have your eyes open and your character leading, *loyalty is being faithful to the people you love, the principles you believe in, and priorities that are most important.* It is sticking with and standing by people who need it the most. Carroll Bryant, the author and commentator, said it well: "I don't like to give up on people when they need someone not to give up on them."[16] That sounds about right.

> **Loyalty is being faithful to the people you love, the principles you believe in, and priorities that are most important.**

A Lady of Loyalty

For technology, it is Apple. For search engines, it is Google. For social networking, it is Facebook. For airlines, it is Delta. For online retailers, it is Amazon. For quick-serve restaurants, it is Chick-fil-A. What am I talking about? I'm talking about the brands we feel most loyalty toward. These companies are just some of the recent winners of the Brand Keys Customer Loyalty Engagement Index, which means they have the highest customer retention rates in their respective industries. It is a crucial metric that business executives watch religiously, because they know nothing tops customer loyalty for retaining and building a business.[17]

Loyalty is the key driver of the best business brands in the twenty-first century. But just as it is crucial for businesses, it is central to healthy friendships, marriages, militaries, and nations. You'll be hard pressed to think of a single facet of life that does not have loyalty as a core part of its foundation.

Ruth is both a book in the Bible and the name of its main character, but we would have heard of neither if not for her incredible loyalty. Ruth is one of the greatest love stories in history. Movies, novels, and books have been written about this beautiful story, but there would have been no love story had it not been for Ruth's loyalty. What comes as an even greater shock is that the whole story begins with and is built around the loyalty of a daughter-in-law to her mother-in-law.

Understanding in-law dynamics is nearly impossible until you either have one or become one. I would be less than honest if I did not tell you in my ministry I've heard enough in-law stories that make me think sometimes that in-laws ought to be outlawed! Comedians have made fortunes off of in-law jokes.

I read about a magic show where after one particularly amazing trick, someone screamed out to the magician, "How did you do that?" The magician replied, "I would tell you, but then I would have to kill you." The same voice came back and said, "Well, then would you tell my mother-in-law?"

Many in-laws get a bad rap. I could not have asked for a better, sweeter, finer father-in-law and mother-in-law than God gave me. I will also tell you that when we read about the relationship between this daughter-in-law and her mother-in-law, it makes me think of my wife, Teresa, and the wonderful daughter-in-law she was to my mom and dad.

The book of Ruth is basically a pamphlet. The entire account is given in only eighty-five verses and it concerns ordinary people living ordinary lives who face ordinary problems. The story begins with three funerals and it ends with a marriage and the birth of a baby. But this was no ordinary baby. The story takes you from the agony of defeat to the thrill of victory, and it makes you appreciate your family, friends, future, and faith more than ever.

Two Israelites, Elimelek and his wife, Naomi, and their two sons, Mahlon and Kilion, live in Bethlehem where a great depression is occurring. Food and money have run out, so Elimelek decides to take his family to the land of Moab. Soon after, Elimelek dies and his two sons marry two Moabite women, Orpah (not Oprah) and

Ruth. After about ten years, the two sons die, and now Naomi is left without a husband or her sons. In that culture, this was an impossible situation. No way could three women, particularly widows with no children and no relatives, hope to survive for long in a time of famine. Naomi, this precious mother-in-law, proves to be as much a mother as a mother-in-law in what she tells Orpah and Ruth.

She has heard from her relatives back home that life is better in Bethlehem and she intends to go back, but it would be bad, if not perhaps dangerous, for two Moabite women to go to a country where they were not welcome. Naomi knows they will have a better chance of meeting a man, remarrying, and having children in Moab, plus they will be with the friends and family they have grown up with.

Orpah takes her up on the offer and hightails it back home, but Ruth digs in her heels. She says to her mother-in-law words that have become so famous they are used in weddings and put on necklaces and rings. They are among the greatest statements and definitions of loyalty ever written. The entire rest of the story hinges on what Ruth said.

> Ruth replied, "Don't urge me to leave you or to turn back from you. Where you go I will go, and where you stay I will stay. Your people will be my people and your God my God. Where you die I will die, and there I will be buried. May the LORD deal with me, be it ever so severely, if even death separates you and me." When Naomi realized that Ruth was determined to go with her, she stopped urging her (Ruth 1:16-18).

Do you want to know what loyalty sounds like? Play those words over again. Do you want to know what loyalty looks like? Picture Ruth in your mind. Do you want to know what loyalty smells like? Let the aroma of those words linger in the air. In that powerful statement, she tells us four ways we should manifest loyalty in our lives.

Be Loyal to Your Family

Ruth's loyalty began where the seed of loyalty is planted, fertilized, and grown—and that is in your family.

> But Ruth replied, "Don't urge me to leave you or to turn back from you. Where you go I will go, and where you stay I will stay" (Ruth 1:16).

These words are going to cost Ruth more than she could know. She is in the worst state any young woman could be in—she is both childless and unmarried. In that culture, younger women who were widowed were encouraged to find a husband as quickly as possible. Naomi is going to a country where Ruth will not only be a foreigner and an immigrant, but, because of her Moabite background, will find it all but impossible to attract any male that would want to marry her. Beyond that, he would be condemned for marrying someone out of a pagan background and from a country at enmity with Israel; she would be condemned for marrying a Jewish man and castigated for taking advantage of Naomi's hospitality.

Ruth is giving up everything—her country, her social standing, her friends, her relationships, her chances of remarrying and ever having children—all to spend it with a woman she is not physically related to who will probably struggle just to make ends meet. But when she married Naomi's son, she saw Naomi as a "mother-in-love" and not just a mother-in-law. Whether it is your mother or mother-in-law, your brother or brother-in-law, your son or son-in-law, you should be loyal to your family. My three sons know that when they need Dad, Dad will be there. I remind them often, "If the whole world walks out of your house, Dad will walk in." Be loyal to your family.

Be Loyal to Your Friends

When Ruth says, "Your people will be my people," she was talking about Naomi's family and also her friends. "Your people" means the people you grew up with, the people you went to school with, the people you knew, the people that you were friends with—they will be my people. Ruth wasn't just a daughter-in-law to Naomi— she was her forever friend.

Loyalty separates your forever friends from your fair-weather friends. So when you evaluate your friendships, don't just ask how fun they are or how nice they are or how good they make you feel or how many Instagram followers they have. Ask yourself whether they are the kind of person who will stand by your side when the bottom falls out and the electricity gets shut off and the diagnosis comes back worse than you can imagine.

When Ruth said these words to Naomi, Naomi knew that Ruth was more than just a daughter-in-law. She was a friend that would stick closer than a sister. You will never learn who your real friends are in prosperity. You will learn who your real friends are only in adversity. I promise you, none of us have as many friends as we think we have.

Facebook caps the number of friends any person can have at five thousand. Can I let you in on a not-so-secret secret? Nobody in the world has five thousand friends. If you ever exceed the limit, you get a message that says, "You have too many friends."[18] But Facebook should also send a message that says, "You have fewer friends than you think you do."

They say you can't have too many friends, but nobody has as many friends as they assume. When you find friends, be loyal to them. Always have their back.

Just three months after the scandal of Bill Clinton broke and he was catching fire everywhere, *Time* magazine celebrated its seventy-fifth anniversary dinner in New York, and a crowd of more than a thousand had gathered for the event. Billy Graham was supposed to sit at a different table than Clinton, but when former Yankee great Joe DiMaggio declined to sit with the president, Graham volunteered to take his place. Despite their disagreements, Billy Graham was President Clinton's friend. So when President Clinton's approval rating was at its lowest, Billy Graham's loyalty rating was at its highest.[19] Be loyal to your friends.

Be Loyal to Your Faithfulness

> "Where you die I will die, and there I will be buried. May the Lord deal with me, be it ever so severely, if even death separates you and me" (Ruth 1:17).

Now that is loyalty. Ruth basically is saying to her mother-in-law, "Even if it costs me my life, I am not going to leave you or forsake you. I am going to live my life with you and if necessary I am going to give my life for you. I am not going to leave you. Wherever you live I am going to live. Wherever you die I am going to die."

Naomi wouldn't have to worry when they got to Bethlehem that if things got bad, the fire got too hot, the food got too low, Ruth would abandon ship and go back to Moab. She had made a lifetime commitment that Naomi would never be alone and never be abandoned. She had made a promise on her life and she meant to keep it till death. We need to learn to be loyal to our convictions and what we believe, loyal to our promises and what we say we will do, loyal to our lenders to pay what we owe, loyal to keep our vows, and loyal to always stand for what is right and stand against what is wrong.

Two men, Jim and Philip, did everything together when they were kids. They went to high school together. They went to college together. They joined the Marines together. In World War II, they were sent to Germany where they fought side-by-side together.

During one particularly fierce battle, they were given the command to retreat. As they were doing so, Jim noticed that Philip was not with the other soldiers. He begged his commanding officer to let him go after his friend, but the officer refused, saying that it would be suicide.

Jim disobeyed his commanding officer, and with his heart

pounding and bullets whizzing by and bombs exploding around him, he kept calling out for his friend. A short time later, his platoon saw him staggering back across the field carrying a limp body in his arms. The livid commanding officer came running up to him and said, "You risked your life for nothing. Your friend was dead and there was nothing you could do." Jim replied, "No sir. You are wrong. I got there just in time. Before Philip died, he said, 'I knew you would come.'"[20]

Jim and Philip had made a promise that no matter what happened, they would always be there for each other. They would never leave each other on the battlefield, never abandon the other in a time of need. Be loyal to your faithfulness.

Be Loyal to Your Faith

The most important thing that Ruth says regards her loyalty to God:

> "Your people will be my people and your God my God"
> (Ruth 1:16).

Talk about selling all out. Ruth was a Moabite. The Moabites actually came from an incestuous relationship that a man by the name of Lot, who was a nephew of Abraham, had with one of his daughters (Genesis 19). The Moabites worshipped multiple false Gods, used temple prostitutes, and offered human sacrifices to practice their religion. The Moabite culture epitomized everything that a faithful Israelite would hate and despise. Other foreigners like Egyptians or Edomites could join God's people. The law was laid down about Moabites:

> No Ammonite or Moabite or any of their descendants
> may enter the assembly of the LORD, not even in the
> tenth generation. For they did not come to meet you
> with bread and water on your way when you came out
> of Egypt, and they hired Balaam son of Beor from Pethor

in Aram Naharaim to pronounce a curse on you. However, the LORD your God would not listen to Balaam
but turned the curse into a blessing for you, because the
LORD your God loves you. Do not seek a treaty of friendship with them as long as you live (Deuteronomy 23:3-6).

For ten generations—that is, for four hundred years—no
Moabite or a descendant of a Moabite could enter into the assem-
bly of the Lord. Here is a young woman who had everything going
against her and every reason to reject God. Her past was against
her—she was raised in a pagan family who worshipped pagan gods.
Her present was against her—all she had was a mother-in-law, no
husband, no children, no source of income. Her future was against
her—going to a land and a people where her ethnicity was a curse
word. A "not welcome" sign would be put up over all the neighbors'
homes, and yet she says, "Your God will be my God."

Her life had been radically changed by the God of Abraham,
Isaac, and Jacob. She had turned away from every other false god
she had ever known and put everything on the line to worship the
one true God. It is one of the most courageous confessions of faith
you will find in the entire Bible.

She left her blood relatives, but now she was part of a new family, not a flesh family but a spiritual family, not a physical family but
a forever family. Ruth had come to know the God of Naomi. She
had forsaken the false gods of the Moabites and given her heart to
the true God of the Israelites. Her mother-in-law of faith was more
family to her than her mother of flesh. The only family that lives
forever is the family of faith. As much as you may love your family
and as much as I love mine, the greatest family in the world that you
will ever be a part of is the family of faith.

God honors Ruth's loyalty. She does marry a wonderful man.
She has a child in a culture that places far more value on sons than
daughters. She wins the respect of the Bethlehem women, who say

to Naomi about Ruth, "For your daughter-in-law, who loves you and who is better to you than seven sons, has given him birth" (Ruth 4:15).

The greatest blessing of all was the son that she bore. His name was Obed. He became the grandfather of David, who became the ancestor of Jesus. But that is not all. When you go to the genealogy of Jesus, four women are mentioned in the family tree: Tamar (guilty of incest), Rahab (a prostitute), Bathsheba (an adulteress), and Ruth (a Moabite).

Because of her loyalty, God used her to bear a son and also change the history of the world. Our God is a loyal God. Our God will never leave us or forsake us. We owe it to him to be loyal to him and his church in worship and service. When we needed a Savior to die for us, Jesus said, "I'll be there." Now as his church needs us to serve and worship him, let's say with our presence and passion, "I'll be there."

Loyal to a Fault

You can define loyalty easier than you can find loyalty. Why? Because loyalty demands that we determine daily to be three things.

Loyalty demands that we be *candid*. Loyalty is not blind. Loyalty and honesty are joined at the hip. The military strategist John Boyd said, "A man asked me for my loyalty...I will give him my honesty. If a man asks me for my honesty, I will give him my loyalty!"[21] Your true, most loyal friends will always tell you the truth. As I recently read, "Loyalty means I am down with you whether you are wrong or right, but I will tell you when you are wrong and help you get it right."[22]

Loyalty demands that we be *consistent*. Private loyalty without public loyalty is cowardly hypocrisy. Stephen Covey wisely said, "Be loyal to those who are not present. In doing so, you build the trust of those who are present."[23]

Loyalty means that you will not broach criticism or gossip about a friend until you talk to that friend and get both sides of the story.

It is called "having their back." Loyalty means that not only will you not talk about a friend behind their back, but you won't allow others to talk about them behind their back either. I love the way the playwright Oscar Wilde put it, "A true friend stabs you in the front."[24]

Loyalty demands that we be *courageous*. Nothing takes more boldness and courage than to be willing to stand by your friends when others have abandoned them—to go against the flow, to refuse to pile on or jump on the bandwagon of criticism and condemnation just because everybody else is.

If you know anything about Watergate and Richard Nixon, then you know the name Chuck Colson. He was Richard Nixon's hatchet man, and he was convicted and served time in federal prison for obstruction of justice and defamation. During that time, he had a personal experience with Jesus Christ and, in his own words, was "born again" and wrote a book by that title. After he got out of prison, he started a ministry called Prison Fellowship that still exists to this day and is a marvelous example of how faith and government can work together to do good in the public arena.

Many people, of course, were cynical about his conversion, and bitterness was still seething toward Richard Nixon and his conduct as president. Colson, filling in for a friend, went to speak at George Washington University. Students were extremely hostile to the Nixon administration and the entire Watergate scandal. The largest speaking venue on campus was packed beyond capacity with standing room only. Colson was escorted by a uniformed policeman into the hall. Even before he spoke, several students shouted him down and condemned him in a chorus of outburst. The atmosphere in the room was raucous. Calm finally prevailed, Colson spoke, and then took questions from the audience.

The questions were pointed and they were tough, relating to everything from his income to his imprisonment to his relationship with the president. Finally, someone stood and asked the question he dreaded: "Henry Kissinger has been very critical of Richard

Nixon. Do you agree with what he said?" At that moment, Colson noticed policemen in every doorway who had been called after the initial outburst. With the anger toward Nixon in that room, Colson realized he could have easily been lighting a match of emotional dynamite that would blow the entire meeting up. It raced through his mind—*Do I duck the question? Do I jump on the bandwagon of criticism and condemnation? Or do I go with the flow?*[25]

Colson answered,

> Well, we all know Mr. Nixon's negative qualities. He has been dissected in the press like no one in history. I can tell you his good points, but I don't think I could persuade you to accept them [he then took a deep breath], but what it comes down to is, no, I don't go along with Henry Kissinger's comments. Mr. Nixon is my friend and I don't turn my back on my friends.[26]

Colson later said he thought the roof would fall due to the defiant way he had stood up for his friend, but after a moment of silence, what he received was something he never expected— a thunderous standing ovation. He reflected, "affirming loyalty to a friend, even though it was someone they despised, to my astonishment had struck a responsive chord in these people."[27] Loyalty will not always get you a standing ovation from the crowd, but it will always get you a standing ovation at least from the one to whom you are loyal.

A Tale of Two Monuments

One of the greatest victories in the Revolutionary War was won at Saratoga. At the Saratoga National Historical Park, a memorial in the shape of a boot is inscribed, "In memory of the most brilliant soldier of the Continental Army, who was desperately wounded on this spot, winning for his countrymen the decisive battle of the American Revolution and for himself the rank of Major

General." This general had his leg badly wounded in battle from which he never fully recovered. His name is curiously absent from the inscription.

A victory monument also stands at Saratoga, a stone obelisk that has four niches facing in each direction of the compass. The niches are occupied by General Horatio Gates, General Philip Schuyler, and General Daniel Morgan. The fourth niche is empty, which represents this mysterious Revolutionary War general.[28]

Just above the choir loft inside the chapel at the military academy at West Point are twelve black, marbled, shield-shaped plaques honoring the generals of the American Revolution. Each memorial has four engraved lines: name, date of birth, rank, and date of death. The last has only two lines: "Major General...Born 1740." On orders from General George Washington, this general's name does not and never will appear.

If you're an American history buff, you might have guessed these nameless icons refer to Benedict Arnold. His name, along with that of Judas in the Bible, is synonymous with "traitor." He represents the greatest act of disloyalty in United States history. Even to this day, you will be hard pressed to find anyone who will name their child Benedict Arnold or even Judas. His treachery and disloyalty is a stain that is extremely hard to erase.[29] Strangely, he may be the only person in history with monuments in his dishonor.

In Shibuya, a city of Japan, there are only two statues and both were erected in honor of a dog. Hachiko is the most famous and beloved animal in Japan, a country that adores its pets. Everyone knows who this dog is even though he has been dead for eighty years. Was it an act of heroism? No. Did the dog perform a great athletic feat? No. Was it being famous through media, movies, or a book? No. It was because of a dog's unflagging loyalty.

Hachiko's owner, Dr. Ueno, was a professor at the University of Tokyo for over twenty years and a renowned scholar in agricultural engineering. One of his students encouraged him to adopt

Hachiko, an Akita puppy. He did, and they soon became best friends and inseparable.

At two years of age, Hachiko would accompany his owner in the morning to the Shibuya train station and then would go back in the afternoon to wait for him to return home. But that year, his owner died. He had suffered a cerebral hemorrhage and he never came back.

Hachiko moved in with the Kobayashi family, but for the next nine years, he never missed a day going down to the train station at precisely when the train was due to arrive and would sit there for hours waiting for his owner to come back. He was loyal to his master until the day he died.

On the eightieth anniversary of Hachiko's passing, the University of Tokyo's agricultural department erected a bronze statue of a man meeting his dog. At both the train station and the university, you will find a statue honoring a dog of unfailing loyalty.

No one has set a greater example of loyalty than the Son of God, who was so loyal to his Father's will that he died on a cross for the sins of the world. The cross is a memorial to loyalty.

> **No one has set a greater example of loyalty than the Son of God... The cross is a memorial to loyalty.**

If we are known as someone whose heart will always say, "I'll be there" when needed, the kind of person who will walk into a house when the whole world has walked out, we can rest assured we will leave behind a monument of honor that will never be forgotten.

RESPECT:

Honor Above All

Men are respectable only as they respect.

RALPH WALDO EMERSON[1]

ob Dylan was right when he penned the song, "The Times
They Are a-Changin'." As always, some change is good and
some change is not, but indeed a battle is raging everywhere,
from the halls of Congress to the halls of schools to the halls of
our homes. You might say it is a civil war that is being fought in a
most uncivil manner. More and more in our public discourse, personal interactions, and private conversations, civility and respect are
increasingly in short supply.

Civility is in decline in America, and deep down, most of us
know it. Roughly three-fourths of Americans think that manners
have deteriorated in recent years,[2] and seven out of ten Americans
say that national politics have become less civil.[3] "Politics as usual"
has becoming staggeringly uncivil. Former Secretary of State Hillary Clinton said as much: "You cannot be civil with a political party
that wants to destroy what you stand for."[4] Pew Research says that
only 6 percent of those surveyed believe "respectful" describes the
current state of politics.[5]

CNN correspondent Jake Tapper was mourning the state of America's current political dialogue in an interview with the *Atlantic*. He noted that both sides of the political aisle were equally guilty in contributing to the climate of indecency: "There are so many lies and so much indecency…there is just a world of it exploding—and we, I fear, as a nation are becoming conditioned and accepting of it and it is horrific."[6] I couldn't agree more.

Lack of respect and civility is filtering down to our children. Only 9 percent of adults in 2002 said the children they saw in public were respectful toward adults. In 2004, more than one of three teachers considered leaving their profession or knew another teacher who had quit. The reason? "Students' intolerable behavior" according to Public Agenda, a nonprofit, nonpartisan research group.[7]

In 2005, 70 percent of people surveyed said people are ruder than they were twenty or thirty years ago. Among the worst offenders were children, according to an Associated Press poll, and the major culprit was parents. "Parents are out of control. We always want to blame the kids, but if there is something wrong with their incivility, it is the way their parents model it for them."[8]

I recently got an invitation to a conference titled "Blessed Are the Peacemakers." It began with this paragraph: "We live in a world characterized by tribalism. Forget about civility: if you are not with me you are against me. In a time when our newsfeeds are dominated by warfare and pure rhetoric, how is God calling his people to engage?"

Mean No Disrespect

Yet in spite of this culture of incivility and disrespect, the virtue of respect is not dead. Calls to respect this issue or that concern are heard almost daily. Environmentalists ask us to respect nature. Foes of abortion insist on respect for human life. Racial and ethnic minorities and those discriminated against for any number of reasons demand respect as social and moral equals. Most believe that public debates about such matters should be conducted in an atmosphere of mutual respect.

Our second president, John Adams, said, presciently, concerning our future instability as a nation: "There is one thing, my sir, that must be attempted and most sacredly observed or we are all undone. There must be *decency* and *respect*, and veneration introduced for persons of authority of every rank, or we are undone. In a popular government this is our only way."[9]

Charles Taylor in his seminal work on secularism said, "To have any kind of livable society some choices have to be restricted, some authorities have to be *respected*, and some individual responsibility has to be assumed."[10]

This is not just a philosophical or cultural issue. Respect is just a matter of common sense. Can you think of any advantage that ever comes from being disrespectful? Disrespect can get you fired from a job. Disrespect can cost you your marriage. Taylor Nelson Sofres (TNS) asked men and women what factors were most important in a successful marriage. Men by 90 percent and women by 95 percent listed mutual respect as first and foremost.[11] Disrespect can even get you killed. In certain social contexts, you may learn the price of disrespect if you violate the street law: "Diss me, and you die."

> **Respect for authority is the fabric that holds every society together.**

Respect for authority is the fabric that holds every society together. Respect for the rule of law is the only dam strong enough to hold back the waters of anarchy. Respect for others is the only foundation that will support successful, personal relationships.

R-E-S-P-E-C-T

What exactly is respect? I decided to ask my granddaughter, Presley, that question, and she looked at me quizzically. "You don't know what *respect* means, Pop? It means being nice." Being nice is a part of respect, but it is even greater than that. The word derives from the Latin *respicere,* which means "to look back at" or "to look again." Respect begins with a particular way of looking at someone or something. It means to see that person in a way that gives them the value they deserve.

Jesus himself gave the best definition of respect in the Golden Rule. Respect is treating others the way you would want to be treated, speaking to others the way you would want to be spoken to, seeing others the way you would want others to see you, and then acting towards them accordingly.

The Man Who Would Be King

That definition is on display in an incident that took place thousands of years ago between someone who was a king and someone who would be the next king. It is a great object lesson of what respect looks like especially in circumstances when disrespect might be both expected and defended.

The man who would be king was David. The man who was king was Saul. David had pulled off the greatest upset of all history when he defeated a giant named Goliath, but it brought him more headaches than honor. This would-be king had every reason not just to disrespect Saul but to destroy him and bring his kingdom to an end. But David declined, and his story serves as one of history's great portraits of character.

David's killing of Goliath was a blessing for the nation of Israel, but it turned out to be a curse for David. Just imagine. After taking on a fight no one else would and winning against all odds, parades were launched in his honor, women fell at his feet, people lined up to be his best friend, and his approval rating reached 100 percent. But all of that became a problem.

Yes, David kills Goliath and, in the process, saves King Saul's bacon. He is the MVP of the Israeli Army. He holds the Medal of Honor. He has been given the Presidential Medal of Freedom. He has won the Nobel Peace Prize. He is the heavyweight champion of the world. He is the most famous celebrity in all of Israel, and King Saul becomes insanely jealous. David's star is rising and Saul's sun is setting. Saul makes David public enemy number one and makes killing David the number one goal of his life.

After several unsuccessful attempts to kill David, from throwing a spear at him to hiring a hit squad, Saul gets his entire army together to hunt David down. He finds out that David is in the Desert of En Gedi surrounded by beautiful springs of water, lush vegetation, but also big caves. Saul thinks that he has David right where he wants him, but the reverse turns out to be true. Saul's life and his reign as king would have come to a sudden end if David had not had the thread of respect sown into the coat of his character. What happens teaches us three tremendous lessons that we need not only to learn, but we also need to pass on to the next generation who desperately need to understand the importance of respect.

Respect the Principle of Authority

Believe it or not, the story centers around some bathroom humor. Saul is looking for David when nature calls, and even a king has to answer the phone when nature is on the line.

> He came to the sheep pens along the way; a cave was there, and Saul went in to relieve himself. David and his men were far back in the cave (1 Samuel 24:3).

Now there really is no gentle way to put this. Saul needs a potty break. He has to relieve himself. What does the word "relieve" mean?

Let's just say that he took a magazine and some air-freshener with him.

Saul has taken off his armor and he is hoping that all those squatting exercises he had been doing in his workouts would pay off. While Saul is doing his business, he doesn't realize that David is in the stall right next to him. David has sized up the situation and knows this is his chance. Saul has been trying to kill him for ten years. If the situation were reversed, he knew exactly what Saul would do. David's men also know it.

> The men said, "This is the day the LORD spoke of when
> he said to you, 'I will give your enemy into your hands
> for you to deal with as you wish'" (1 Samuel 24:4).

His loyal soldiers, who love David, have a front-row seat. They can't wait for David to give Saul exactly what he deserves, but instead he does this:

> Then David crept up unnoticed and cut off a corner of
> Saul's robe (1 Samuel 24:4).

So why doesn't he kill Saul? Saul deserved it, had it coming to him. Nobody who knew the real story would have blamed David, and yet, even though David had only cut off a piece of Saul's robe, we read:

> Afterward, David was conscience-stricken for having cut
> off a corner of his robe (1 Samuel 24:5).

Why is David so bothered? Why is he feeling so guilty? What is gnawing at him? David gives us his answer and while doing so, gives us a treasure trove of truth about what respect is all about.

> He said to his men, "The LORD forbid that I should do
> such a thing to my master, the LORD's anointed, or lay
> my hand on him; for he is the anointed of the LORD"
> (1 Samuel 24:6).

David understood the principle of authority. God has built authority into the fabric of life.

I loved playing sports when I was growing up and love watching them now. Without authority, sports do not exist. You can choose the game, but you cannot choose the rules. When you play tennis, you have to serve behind the serving line and keep the ball within the sidelines. If you play basketball, you have to dribble the ball when you go up the court, you have to stay inbounds, and you can't take more than two steps after you stop your dribble. Whatever game you choose, you inherit the rules that govern the game and you play under that authority. The rules govern your behavior. Your only chance of winning the game is to follow the rules, and if you break the rules enough, you probably won't even get to finish the game.[12]

David lived in a kingdom. He was under kingdom authority. Saul, as the king, was the embodiment of that principle of authority. That is so important to grasp. You shouldn't live your life by popularity—by what everybody else thinks is right. You shouldn't live your life by practice—by what everybody else is doing. You live your life by principle—by a conviction of what is right. David respected the principle of authority. Saul was still the king. David was still under his authority. What set David apart from his men was he understood that what is right is not what we think is right or what others feel is right, but what God says is right.

One of the marks of maturity is the willingness to abide by the principle of authority even though we may not always agree with how that authority acts. It doesn't mean that we support wickedness. It doesn't mean that we approve of evil any more than David approved of what Saul was doing. It does mean that we respect all authority unless that authority asks us to do something that is immoral, unethical, or unbiblical. When we respect the principle of authority, then we respect the position of authority.

Respect the Position of Authority

David so respected the principle of authority that he felt guilty for just cutting off a piece of the king's robe, but what David does next shows how deep his respect went.

> Then David went out of the cave and called out to Saul, "My lord the king!" When Saul looked behind him, David bowed down and prostrated himself with his face to the ground (1 Samuel 24:8).

In most cultures throughout history, bowing before another person is the ultimate symbol of respect. But David is not bowing before the person that Saul is. He is bowing before the position that Saul holds. He may not be the king he should be, but Saul still sits on the throne. He may not be the kind of king that God desired, but he is still the king. He is still *David's* king.

Your parents may not always be right, but they are still the parents. Your boss may not always be right, but she is still the boss. Your teacher may not always be right, but she is still the teacher. Your coach may not always be right, but he is still the coach. The president may not always be right, and yet he is still the president. Don't confuse respecting the position that a person holds with the person that holds the position.

When John F. Kennedy was inaugurated as president, his inner circle offered him their congratulations. They were all calling him Jack until his brother Bobby, who the president had appointed attorney general, walked up to offer his congratulations. Looking at that inner circle, he said, "Congratulations, Mr. President." As a person, JFK was his brother, but in his position, he was the president. Bobby Kennedy understood the respect that was due the position regardless of who held it—even his own brother.

Notice how David continually addresses Saul: "My master, the LORD's anointed" (1 Samuel 24:6). In fact, he repeats it: "He is the anointed of the Lᴏʀᴅ." In verse 8, he calls him, "My lord the king!" In verse 14, he calls him, "The king of Israel." You can respect a person's position even if you don't respect the person who occupies it.

> You can respect a person's position even if you don't respect the person who occupies it.

The Marine Corps has a saying: "You don't salute the person; you salute the rank." In other words, you don't honor the person, you honor the position. There are good generals and bad generals, smart generals and dumb generals, nice generals and mean generals, but they are all generals. They all should be saluted. They all should be respected not in their person but in their position.

When Bill Clinton was president and the whole Monica Lewinski situation had blown up, I was preaching about it and blurted out, "Bill Clinton is an idiot!" I knew the moment I said it I was wrong. The next Sunday I said to my church, "I said something last week that was out of line, inappropriate, and wrong. I called the president an idiot. He is not an idiot. He is the president and his office deserves our highest respect."

David knew that one day he would be king and he would be in that position. If David wanted to get the respect the position deserved, then he had to give the respect the position deserved. David showed great self-respect by respecting Saul. Laurence Sterne said, "Respect for ourselves guides our morals. Respect for others guides our manners."[13]

Respect the Power Behind Authority

David uses a revealing phrase to refer to Saul six different times: "The Lᴏʀᴅ's anointed."[14] When David looked at Saul, he didn't primarily see the king on the throne, he saw the God who put him there. When David bowed down before Saul, he wasn't bowing down to the person on the throne; he was bowing down to the power behind the throne.

David didn't have a high view of Saul the man. He didn't have much respect for Saul the person, but he had a supremely, extremely high view of God and the power of God that put Saul on the throne. Did Saul personally deserve much respect? Not at all. But David's character, rather than Saul's, was on the line. He didn't focus on what Saul had tried to do to him. He focused on what God had done for Saul and would do for him.

Just because Saul was out of God's will in the way he treated David did not mean that David would get out of God's will by the way he treated Saul. God had anointed and appointed Saul. David not only respected the principle of authority and the position of authority, but above all he respected the power behind all authority, which is God.

Someone observed wisely, "If you see a turtle on a fencepost, he didn't get there by himself." Every ruler who is ruling anywhere, anytime, anyplace is allowed to rule by God's sovereign power. God is the power behind all power, and David was not going to replace what God had put in place. He was not going to dethrone what God had enthroned, and since God was the one who put Saul in, God would be the one to take Saul out. This is what enabled David to say,

> "May the Lord be our judge and decide between us. May
> he consider my cause and uphold it; may he vindicate
> me by delivering me from your hand" (1 Samuel 24:15).

David was saying, "You may be the earthly king, but there is an eternal king who made you the earthly king. I am not in your hands; I am in his hands." When you realize everything is in God's hands, you never have to take matters into your own hands.

David has taken his stand. He understands that disrespect to you does not demand disrespect from you. He also understands that if you want to get respect, you've got to give respect. Saul is forced to say,

> "You are more righteous than I," he said. "You have treated me well, but I have treated you badly. You have just now told me about the good you did to me; the LORD delivered me into your hands, but you did not kill me. When a man finds his enemy, does he let him get away unharmed? May the LORD reward you well for the way you treated me today. I know that you will surely be king and that the kingdom of Israel will be established in your hands" (1 Samuel 24:17-20).

Disrespectful people will always try to drag you down to their level. Respectful people will always try to bring you up to their level. Because someone chooses to disrespect you does not mean you have to disrespect them. If character still counts with you, you will always give respect wherever and to whomever it is due.

With All Respect

If we are going to reintroduce and recover respect and civility in our society, it has to begin with us. We cannot control how others treat us, but we can control how we treat others. Here are some practical steps to help you develop respect and, I hope, make it so contagious that others catch it.

Respect starts with an *inward attitude toward yourself.* The first step to respecting others is to respect yourself. Jesus even said, "Love your neighbor as yourself" (Matthew 22:39). Negatively, if you don't yet respect others enough to be respectful, at least respect yourself enough not to be disrespectful. At times, disrespect for others is a projection of the lack of respect we have for ourselves.

People find that being able to respect themselves is what motivates them to get off welfare and get a job, kick a disgusting habit, or defend something they believe. The ultimate loss of self-respect is when someone believes that life is no longer worth living. Respect and self-respect are deeply connected. Respecting others is almost impossible if we do not respect ourselves.

> Respect and self-respect are deeply connected.
> Respecting others is almost impossible
> if we do not respect ourselves.

Respect continues as an *outward action to others*. William Lyon Phelps said, "This is the final test of a gentleman: his respect for those who can be of no possible value to him."[15] Respect plays no favorites. The chauffeur driving the limousine is as worthy of respect as the one who owns the limousine. Too often, we are overly concerned about being respected without being as concerned with being respectful. The only way to get true respect is to "treat people the way you want to be treated. Talk to people the way you want to be talked to. Respect is earned, not given."[16]

Imagine being a bus driver in a major city. Then, imagine a woman pees in a cup in the back of the bus. As she gets off the bus, she throws it on you. That is exactly what happened to one Metrobus driver in Washington, DC.[17] That and other incidents led to a campaign in the Washington area featuring advertisements that said, "Mom. Friend. Metrobus Driver." followed by a personal plea: "I hope you will see all the things I am and respect me, like I respect you."[18]

The advertisement made an overt admission that respect and civility can only come from appealing to the human heart. Government, legislation, and slick lawyers cannot force people to respect each other. So a respected journalist said, "If we want a better society, we need to restore some of the respect that has been lost. This is a task for each one of us, in the thick of our ever busy life. Perhaps we can make a start on the bus."[19] We need to remember that we are all on the same bus in life and everybody on the bus deserves respect.

Respect flows from an *upward acknowledgment reality*. The second paragraph of the Declaration of Independence contains the most famous sentence in the document: "We hold these truths to be self-evident, that all men are created equal, that they are endowed by their Creator with certain unalienable rights." The quotation "all men are created equal" has been called an "immortal declaration" and perhaps the single phrase of the American Revolutionary period with the greatest continuing importance.[20] Sadly, we are still paying the price of our Founding Fathers not taking it that seriously by applying it to all men, including African Americans.

The foundation of respect must begin with an acknowledgment that we are all created in God's image and therefore all equally worthy of respect. Gary Chapman rightly said, "Respect begins with this attitude: I acknowledge that you are a creature of extreme worth."[21] Every creature has eternal worth. The soul of every man, woman, boy, and girl is eternal. Jesus himself even said, "What good is it for someone to gain the whole world, yet forfeit their soul?" (Mark 8:36). The whole world and this universe are temporal, but the soul of every human being is eternal, and because of that, we are all worthy of being given respect and are all obligated to give respect.

This final story says it all. Larry King spent a career spanning five decades interviewing thousands of celebrities, politicians, and world leaders. Asked to pick out the one interview that stood out, he didn't hesitate.

> I was with Martin Luther King, Jr., in 1961 when he was trying to integrate a hotel in Tallahassee, Florida. The hotel won't give him a room even though he has a reservation, and the police squad cars are coming because he's blocking the entrance. He knows he's going

to be arrested. I'm there right next to him because I was invited there by his lawyer. So King sits down on this porch in front of this small twenty-room hotel. The owner of the hotel comes out, very straightforward but not belligerently, walks up to King and asks, "What do you want?" King says nothing, so the owner asks again in the same direct tone, "What do you want?" And Martin Luther King just looked at him and said, "*My dignity.*"[22]

Dr. King was requesting something none of us should have to plead for: the respect that we all desire, deserve, and should deliver to everyone out of our respect for the God in whom we trust.

AUTHENTICITY:

The Real Deal

Be who you is, because if you is who
you ain't, you ain't who you is.

LARRY HEIN[1]

You can fantasize about being somebody that you are not, but actually pulling it off is difficult. The 2003 film *Catch Me If You Can* was based on a true story about the infamous con-man Frank Abagnale Jr. At different times, in different places, to different people, he pretended to be a doctor, an airplane pilot, a banker, an investor, an attorney, and a celebrity. Except he wasn't any of them. He was a counterfeit and a fraud who faked those professions.

Early in his life he realized he had this unusual, uncanny ability to convince people that he was something on the outside that he was not on the inside. He found he could make a lot of money doing this, and this ability became an addiction to playing a part that really was not his true self.

He conned his way into performing surgery in an operating room, cheated banks out of thousands of dollars, and even flew an airplane as a pilot with no aeronautical knowledge at all. His entire life was nothing but smoke and mirrors.

He finally realized he was in too deep and decided he wanted out of his fake life. But he had gotten caught in his own web of deceit. The FBI finally caught up to him, and he wound up spending years in a federal prison all because he pretended to be something he was not.[2]

A Zogby/Forbes ASAP poll asked respondents, "What would you like most to be known for?" Several choices were given: being intelligent, being good looking, having a great sense of humor. The number one response given by over half the people who answered the survey offered an unexpected answer: they would like a reputation for being "authentic."[3]

The postmodern generation we live in is searching continuously for what is real and authentic. They see a world that is dominated by spin and hype. They are looking for people who are the real deal.[4]

This issue of authenticity or the lack thereof is popping up everywhere. Take for example how people look. With airbrushing, Photoshop, and plastic surgery, even photographs are not trustworthy when it comes to believing whether someone's appearance is real or fake.

In the world of sports, authenticity has come under scrutiny because of steroids and human growth hormone (HGH). Is that his arm throwing the ball a hundred miles an hour or his bat hitting the ball five hundred feet or is it because he is all juiced up? Like it or not, the term "fake news" has called into question the authenticity of the media.

Get Real—Please

The rising generation in America is hungering for authenticity, and that's good news. They are not looking for perfection but rather for transparency and consistency. A sweeping survey of the next generation concluded, "Young people talk these days about the need for authenticity, for 'keeping it real'—not pretending to be something you are not. Young people are searching for this type of person, this kind of lifestyle... [authenticity] was among the characteristics young people most admired."[5]

Contrast that with the perception of many churches and Christians. When asked what someone thinks about Christianity, many young respondents say "hypocritical," "judgmental," "anti-intellectual," and "anti-gay."[6] One skeptic put it this way: "A Christian is [someone] who feels repentance on a Sunday for what he did on Saturday and is going to do on Monday."[7] Too often, perception is reality.

A study released in 2007 found that most of the lifestyle activities of born-again Christians were statistically equivalent to those of non-born-agains. When asked to identify their activities over the last thirty days, born-again believers were just as likely to gamble, look at pornography, steal something, consult a medium or psychic, physically abuse someone, get drunk, use illegal drugs, lie, and gossip.[8]

Whether the pastor of a church, a professor in a classroom, or a politician in public service, their effectiveness in their jobs, in their communication, in their ability to persuade and bring about cultural and social change rests on the level of trustworthiness people have in them. The foundation of all trustworthiness is authenticity.

When authenticity is compromised, the river of pessimism will break through the dam of optimism and the result will be a flood of negativism, cynicism, and criticism. To have real relationships, and real communication, and real interaction, which results in real productivity and real results, we must be real people.

What Is Real?

Perhaps the best way to define authenticity is to point out what it is not. As you can already see, the exact opposite of authenticity is hypocrisy. Being called a hypocrite is never a compliment. Even in the way it is used and said, disdain and disgust drip from every syllable. Preaching something different from what you practice is an intentional act.

The origin of the word *hypocrisy* is revealing. It comes from the

Greek language and originally meant "one who answers back," as an orator might do. The theater was popular in Greek culture. Actors would wear masks that would be molded or painted with different expressions to reflect the character they would play. Surprisingly, the actors were called hypocrites. A hypocrite was someone who would take on the personality of a scripted character in a story line that may or may not match their real persona. At the time, the word *hypocrite* was given to anyone who would pretend to be something they were not and "mask" who and what they really were.

Authentic people don't wear masks to hide who they are or what they believe. They are not one character in one part of their life and another character in another part. They are the same people to all people in every situation.

After going to a theater in Chicago and watching his brother play a character that bore no resemblance to him, Garry Poole said:

> Pretending to be someone we are not isn't a bad thing— if we are actors. It is part of the job description. Audience members would demand refunds if the cast refused to get into character and act out their assigned parts in the play. Actors are supposed to act.
>
> But it is a different matter in everyday life. People in the real world ought to be true to who they say they are. If someone openly claims to adhere to a set of values or beliefs, then that person had better be careful to back that up with consistent actions and behaviors— especially if he or she is a Christian. There's no room for actors on that stage.[9]

This leads to my definition of this trait: *Authenticity is when you are always true to you regardless of where you are or whom you are with.*

Authenticity is when you are always true to you regardless of where you are or whom you are with.

In the mid-twentieth century, one of the most famous comedians in the world was Groucho Marx. The secret to his humor, and his success, was his unique gift for self-deprecation. He was a master at poking fun at himself. One of his most famous quotes was, "I wouldn't join a club that would have me as a member."

I have joined a particular club more than once to my shame, and it has perhaps the lowest standards of any club. The only requirement to join is pretending to be something you are not. The chairman of this club is peer pressure and the one benefit of this club is acceptance. The club's name is hypocrisy. If you're honest, I bet most of you would say you, too, have applied for membership a time or two.

When you are authentic, you are the real deal. You aren't one person in public and another in private. You aren't one person at work and another at home. To be authentic, you are the real you in real situations. As someone has said, "Be yourself. Everyone else is already taken."

One of the greatest demonstrations of authenticity is found in a conflict between two of the greatest leaders of the early church. The conflict took place because a man who should have been authentic was not. We are going to look at a story of two spiritual and theological giants of the early church who clashed over one who sold out his authenticity for the counterfeit currency of hypocrisy. If you like drama, confrontation, and a good old-fashioned throw down, this story is for you.

The early church was led by four men who each wrote books in the New Testament: James (Jesus's half brother), John (whom Jesus called "the beloved disciple"), Peter (the leader of the original twelve disciples), and Paul (a master missionary and prolific writer). Peter and Paul are in Antioch, which was the chief city of Syria, where the Christian mission to Gentiles began and where disciples were first called "Christians." Peter was the primary gospel preacher to the Jews and Paul was the primary gospel preacher to the Gentiles. They both loved Jesus, the church, and each other.

But that doesn't mean they always got along or saw eye to eye on every theological point. In the story we're going to look at, Paul opposes Peter to his face, calls him out in public, rebukes him, and condemns him—not because of what he was saying but what he was doing. The problem was that Peter had stopped practicing what he preached. His talk differed from his walk. The person he was being was not aligned with the person God had called him to be.

Paul reminds Peter that a big part of character is authenticity, which requires you to be the same person in public as you are in private. You being you regardless of where you might be or whom you might be with. Paul shows us what authenticity looks like, how authenticity acts, and why authenticity is important.

If I Am Authentic, I Will Confront Hypocrisy

Paul is in Antioch and he has heard some rumors about Peter. So when Peter arrives in Antioch, Paul dispenses with the niceties and chitchat, gets right to the point, and cuts to the heart of the problem.

> When Cephas [another name for Peter] came to Antioch,
> I opposed him to his face, because he stood condemned
> (Galatians 2:11).

Paul did not talk about Peter behind his back. He didn't just get one side of the story. He did what we all ought to do if we hear something troubling about someone else: he went to him directly. In the Greek language, it literally says, "face to face." That is what authentic people do. Authentic people don't gossip and they don't listen to gossip. They don't talk about people; they talk to people. If they have a problem with someone, they man up and woman up and go to the person they have a problem with and talk it out. The reason Paul opposed Peter to his face was that he stood condemned.

It wasn't Paul who was condemning him. He was condemned by three things: the God he represented, the gospel he preached, and the grace that saves both Jews and Gentiles. What in the world did Peter do that left him condemned?

> Before certain men came from James, he used to eat with the Gentiles. But when they arrived, he drew back and separated himself from the Gentiles because he was afraid of those who belonged to the circumcision group. The other Jews joined him in his hypocrisy, so that by their hypocrisy even Barnabas was led astray (Galatians 2:12-13).

Evidently, when Peter first arrived in Antioch, which was a city made up primarily of Gentiles, he hung out with Gentile Christians. The tense of the verb shows that this had become a habit for him. He regularly did it. He didn't worry that they were uncircumcised and ate food that Jews normally didn't eat. They were all equal before Jesus. They had all been saved by God's grace. He would go eat at their house and they would come eat at his house.

It wasn't just who he was eating with, but it was what he was eating that was both shocking and refreshing. They were eating BBQ pork ribs, shrimp on the barbie, crab cakes, and raw oysters. They probably topped it off with a sausage biscuit from Bojangles. All of those foods had previously been forbidden by Jews to eat, but Peter had been shown by God himself that now all foods were clean. They were no longer under the ceremonial laws. He was under grace and given richly all things to enjoy. However, the little three-letter word *but* enters into the narrative.

> But when they arrived…who belonged to the circumcision group (Galatians 2:12).

Some Jewish theological policemen, spiritual busybodies who professed to be Christians, came to Antioch and preached that Gentiles still had to be circumcised and follow the Law of Moses to be accepted by God. Though they believed in Jesus and had been baptized, a circumcised Jew was not supposed to fellowship with an uncircumcised Gentile. They even claimed to come from James himself and to be speaking for him, though they probably were lying.

Regardless, Peter separated himself from the Gentiles out of fear, which delivered a crushing blow to his Gentile brothers and sisters. In the Middle East, eating with someone is the highest form of acceptance. Even though Peter knew it was wrong, he rejected the crowd he should have accepted because he wanted to be accepted by the crowd he should have rejected. He did it because he was afraid. Fear is the enemy of authenticity. Fear will cause you to bow to pressure rather than surrender to principle.

> **Fear is the enemy of authenticity.**
> **Fear will cause you to bow to pressure**
> **rather than surrender to principle.**

Peter, who had previously enjoyed unrestricted fellowship with Gentiles who were just as good as he was, just as saved as he was, just as right as he was—speaking their language, eating their food, drinking their wine, playing with their children, sitting in their homes—now treated them as if they were lepers. The word that is used twice to describe this action is *hypocrisy*.

Hypocrisy is what has kept and still keeps many churches racially segregated today. It is what has caused the church to treat certain sins as felonies and other sins as misdemeanors and caused us to slap certain sinners with the hand of judgment while turning a blind eye to other sinners that we deem acceptable. That is why we have failed to extend grace in a gracious way to everyone who needs it just as badly as we do and why many describe Christians as "hypocritical."[10] If we are going to be authentic as Christians and as a church, we must confront hypocrisy wherever we find it.

If I Am Authentic, I Will Confess Hypocrisy

The point Paul has made with Peter is let your love be authentic and your life be real. Don't be a phony. Say what you mean, mean what you say. Say the same thing with one group that you will when you are with another group, and stick by what you believe. When your life doesn't match your lips, when your behavior does not match your belief, admit it. Come out and say so.

But something even greater is at stake.

> When I saw that they were not acting in line with the truth of the gospel, I said to Cephas in front of them all, "You are a Jew, yet you live like a Gentile and not like a Jew. How is it, then, that you force Gentiles to follow Jewish customs?" (Galatians 2:14).

Paul was bothered by the hypocrisy they were displaying and the truth they were denying. The truth of the gospel was at stake. The phrase "acting in line" comes from a compound Greek word that gives us the word *orthopedic*. It means "to walk uprightly or to walk straight." They had veered off the road of gospel truth and landed in the ditch of hypocrisy.

Three things will throw you out of line with the gospel. *Racism* is when you refuse to see other people as equal just because they are not of your ethnicity or your skin color. Any racial thinking means you are not walking in line with the truth of the gospel.

Religion can also knock you offline. When we refuse to have fellowship with other people just because they may not dot the same religious *i*'s and cross the same religious *t*'s that we do, particularly those that are not essential to biblical principles, we are not walking in line with the truth of the gospel.

Righteousness will knock you offline. When we think we are superior to other people because we do things they don't or don't do things they do, we fail to realize that we are all sinners in need of the grace of God. We are not walking in line with the truth of the gospel. So Paul does Peter's confessing for him: "I said to Cephas in front of them all, 'You are a Jew, yet you live like a Gentile and not like a Jew. How is it, then, that you force Gentiles to follow Jewish customs?'" (Galatians 2:14).

In effect, Paul said to Peter, "You have been pretending to be something you are not when you are with the Gentiles. Now you want the Gentiles to pretend to be something they are not when they are with you." Peter was both denying the truth of the gospel and destroying the unity of the church.

Don't miss what a big deal this was. If Paul had not confronted Peter and at least confessed for Peter his hypocrisy, the church would have either gone back to the ways of Judaism and legalism or there would have been a permanent division between Gentile Christians and Jewish Christians. Paul did not confront Peter out of jealousy or one-upmanship. He wasn't trying to prove who the real boss of the church was. He wasn't showboating. He did it for one reason—the truth of the gospel was at stake.

Nothing will ever be more important in the life of a church or a Christian than to make sure that we preach the truth of the gospel and we practice the truth of the gospel. That may mean confessing hypocrisy in our own life.

If I Am Authentic, I Will Correct Hypocrisy

The whole problem was Peter was not being authentic in walking in line with the truth of the gospel. What does Paul do? He reminds us of what the truth of the gospel is. Paul is about to give the most succinct, simple, but stupendous definition of the gospel and what separates Christianity from every other religious faith. That is why we should walk on one street (called truth) and in one direction (toward the gospel). Paul reminds Peter (and us) that we are all in the same boat whether we are Jews or Gentiles.

> We who are Jews by birth and not sinful Gentiles know that a person is not justified by the works of the law, but by faith in Jesus Christ. So we, too, have put our faith in Christ Jesus that we may be justified by faith in Christ and not by the works of the law, because by the works of the law no one will be justified (Galatians 2:15-16).

Paul is saying that whether you are a Jew born into the covenant family of God or you are a Gentile born outside of that covenant family, neither your birth nor your behavior will make you right with God or before God. The first part of gospel truth is that everybody is born a sinner. That is the bad news. The worst news is we can do nothing to take care of our sin problem, because no one will ever be justified by the works of the law.

To press the point, Paul uses "not by works of the law" three times in verse 16. Read the Bible cover to cover and you'll discover that no one ever got right with God, no one was ever justified by God, and no one was ever accepted by God because they kept the law or because they were "good enough." The law was not given to show how good we can be but to show how bad we are. God's law is a mirror that condemns us, not a medicine that cures us. The law is like a CAT scan. It can show you what is wrong with you, but it can't cure you.

What we all need is a word that Paul uses three times here: "justified." *Justification* is a legal term borrowed from the court of law and is the opposite of *condemnation*. *Condemned* means you are declared "guilty." When you are justified you are declared "not guilty."

That word tells us that nothing is wrong with God and that something is wrong with us. If those two things are true, then something is wrong between us and God and only God can make it right. How did he do that? By justifying us. The way God does this is not the way it usually happens in a court of law.

When we stand before God, we are guilty. We know we are guilty and he knows we are guilty. We must confess we are guilty, but the moment we confess we are guilty, God declares us not guilty because Jesus has taken our sin and our punishment for us. God doesn't practice double jeopardy. We can never again be declared guilty.

Justification is not simply forgiveness, because you could be forgiven and then go out and sin again and become guilty. That is why it is different from just a pardon, because a pardoned criminal still has a record. You are justified. Your slate is clean. Your record is erased. Your file is empty.

Now you are sentenced. You are sentenced to eternal life. You are sentenced to forgiveness. You are sentenced to redemption. You are sentenced to the love, the joy, and the peace that only God can give. Since every person who comes to Jesus is justified, no Christian is more justified than any other Christian, which means if God accepts everyone on the same basis, then once God accepts us we should accept others.

The way we should accept others is the way that God accepts us—not on the basis of our skin color, our financial status, our social standing, our gifts, our abilities, or our politics. We accept others because God has accepted us. We don't have to pretend because in Jesus we are exactly who we need to be. That is what authentic Christianity is all about.

You Be You

We all know of the slippery slope from authenticity to insincerity to hypocrisy. I want to share with you three ways to make sure that you are being you anywhere, anytime, and under any circumstance. First, *stay true to who you are*. You are the best you that will ever be. You are the only you that will ever exist because God made you to be you. So, always prove to be who *you* are.

A great example is multimillionaire, world-class athlete Eliud Kipchoge. He is the world's greatest marathon runner and in 2018 set the world record for running 26.2 miles in two hours, one minute, and forty seconds. He has won nine straight world major marathons including a gold medal in the Olympics. He has not let either fame or fortune change who he is.

He still lives in his native West Kenya home, getting up every morning before 5:00 a.m. to run up to 130 miles every week. He then showers and does his chores, which range from chopping vegetables for the communal dinner, trimming the garden, and scrubbing toilets (you read that right). Why? Because he is being true to who he is.[11]

The example he sets is a great reminder that hypocrisy is when you let what others think about you go to your head while authenticity is when you allow who you know you are to stay in your heart.

The second key to being authentic is to *stand strong for what you believe*. In his acceptance speech for the 2018 MTV Awards, popular actor Chris Pratt stunned the crowd by offering his "Nine Rules for Life." It was laced with humor but punctuated with serious convictional thinking. Pratt's second rule was "You have a soul. Be careful with it." The room grew quiet. He went on to say, "God is real, God loves you, God wants the best for you. Believe that. I do." His ending was, "Grace is a gift. And like the freedom that we enjoy in this country, that grace was paid for with somebody else's blood. Do not forget that. Do not take that for granted." CNN published an article on it with this headline: "Preach, Chris Pratt." The crowd loved it. Something still attracts people to authenticity and to those who courageously stand up for what they believe.[12]

To be sure, authenticity sometimes draws boos, not cheers. Authenticity sometimes brings condemnation, not celebration. Still, Ted Koppel was right when he said, "There is harmony and inner-peace to be found in following a moral compass that points in the same direction regardless of fashion or trend."[13]

Finally, *stop living a lie.* If you are constantly using a mask to fit in where you are or with the people you are with, drop all the masks today and start being who you are. Admit when you have been living the lie.

In 2001, Nike ran an advertisement where a world-famous cyclist said, "I am on my bike, busting my [behind] six hours a day." A montage of scenes featuring weight lifting, running, and cycling was playing in the background. The ad ended with a challenging question: "What are you on?" It turns out Lance Armstrong was on erythropoietin, diuretics, and human growth hormone, plus cyclical drug doping. He was living a lie and continued to lie right up until the truth finally caught up with him. Banned from cycling for life, stripped of all of his Tour de France titles, the shame for his hypocrisy and inauthenticity will forever dwarf the fame he gained only temporarily.[14]

You have every reason to be you everywhere at all times, because you were made by God to be you. If the God who made you is proud of the you that he made, you should be as well.

Robert Redford was walking one day through a hotel lobby. A woman saw him and followed him to the elevator. "Are you the real Robert Redford?" she asked with excitement. As the doors of the elevators closed, he smiled and said, "Only when I am alone!"[15] You are never alone because God is always with you, so be authentic each day. You will sleep much better at night and people will respect you more if you learn to be the best *you* that you can be.

GENEROSITY:

Give It All You've Got

Generosity could be as contagious as
the zombie plague as long as enough
people were willing to be carriers.

JONATHAN MABERRY[1]

Generosity is one virtue that many people assume they possess but in fact do not. We Americans like to brag on ourselves as being generous, and our government does give a lot of money away to causes and needs both here and abroad. Many would call us a generous nation.

The amount of money given to charitable causes is staggering. In 2016, Americans gave over $390 billion. That sum is greater than the annual GDP of 160 countries. Most of those gifts are freely given, and the biggest charitable gifts, totaling over $280 billion, came from individuals.[2] On the surface it looks like our generosity is overflowing the banks of our wallets, but it illustrates the opposite.

A generous nation by definition is made up of generous people, and more than 85 percent of Americans give less than 2 percent of their income. Does that meet any standard of generosity?[3] Our annual giving to all charitable causes equals just over 2 percent of GDP. More to the point, our giving equals a far smaller fraction of total household wealth, which now stands at around $92 trillion. Keep in mind as well that in 2018, Americans spent over $1 trillion on Christmas gifts. We gave two-and-a-half times more to ourselves than we did to others.[4]

Now, many of us would like to believe that we would be more generous if we just had more money. Unfortunately, just the reverse is true. It is estimated that one-third of all charitable giving in the US comes from the top 1 percent of US households. In 2016, that equaled roughly $138 billion. It sounds like those in the top 1 percent are doing great except when you consider they have assets of over $30 trillion. So, as a group the wealthiest Americans gave away less than half of 1 percent of their total wealth in 2016.[5]

An inverse law of prosperity is at work here: *The more that we have, the less generous we become.* America's poor donate more in percentage terms than higher income groups do. In 2011, the wealthiest Americans—those with earnings in the top 20 percent—contributed on average 1.3 percent of their income to charity while those in the bottom 20 percent donated 3.2 percent of their income. On a percentage basis, the poorest among us give two-and-a-half times more than the richest among us.[6] Additionally, the relative generosity of lower-income Americans is extenuated by the fact that unlike middle-class and wealthy donors, most of them cannot take advantage of the charitable tax deduction and do not itemize deductions on their income-tax returns.

You Can Miss What You Never Had

Generosity, or the lack of generosity, doesn't just rob others of what they need to be given; it robs us of the need to give. The greatest disease more of us suffer from than we care to admit is affluenza. Affluenza is defined as "extreme materialism and consumerism associated with pursuit of wealth and success and resulting in a life of chronic dissatisfaction, debt, overwork, stress, and impaired relationships."[7] Indeed, David Hawkins says, "*Affluenza* is particularly rampant in the United States, where we place a high priority on financial success and material possessions."[8]

Generosity is the only remedy to selfishness, to greed, to materialism, to hoarding, and excessive spending. Too many people live in a mink-lined prison of prosperity. The only key that unlocks that door is a generous spirit. Imagine what could be accomplished in America and around the world if we were all just a little more generous. Christians in America give at 2.5 percent per capita to the church, and between 3 percent and 5 percent of Americans give regularly to the church. As little as 10 percent of any congregation gives what the Bible calls "a tithe," which is 10 percent of one's income.[9]

I was staggered to learn that if every Christian who regularly attends church were to give 10 percent of their income, churches would possess an additional $300 billion for good works.[10] To put that into perspective, that extra generosity could accomplish the following:

- $5 billion could relieve global hunger, starvation, and deaths from preventable diseases in five years.
- $12 billion could eliminate illiteracy in five years.
- $15 billion could solve the world's water and sanitation issues, specifically at places in the world where 1 billion people live on less than $1 per day.
- $1 billion could fully fund all overseas mission work.
- Even after all of that, somewhere between $150–$250 billion would be left over for additional ministry expansion.[11]

Incidentally, generosity is more than just money. The incredible exponential power of generosity can be seen in a body part like a kidney. Rick Ruzzamenti, a Californian, met a woman who had just donated her kidney to a friend she had bumped into at a Target store. Her act of generosity so inspired Rick that he decided to donate a kidney to a person in need of one. The beneficiary turned out to be an anonymous sixty-six-year-old man in Livingston, New Jersey. Here is where the story takes a remarkable turn.

The New Jersey man's niece, Teresa, had hoped to give her uncle her kidney, but their bloodwork did not match. She was so touched by Ruzzamenti's generosity in helping her uncle, she decided to donate a kidney to someone else too. That recipient turned out to be a young lady named Brooke, who lived in Michigan.

The kidney chain of donations took off! Brooke's friend then donated a kidney to a woman whose husband then donated a kidney and the chain continued. In the end, Rick Ruzzamenti's generous act moved thirty donors to share kidneys with thirty recipients and the life-giving chain spread across the entire country.

At the end of that kidney chain, four months after Rick Ruzzamenti unknowingly started it, was Donald Terry, who had been waiting for a kidney for five years and was almost dead. Because of one generous act, life and hope were given to sixty people.[12]

A Generous Definition

What does it mean to be generous? In the Roman world, generosity was regarded as a virtue that only the rich and powerful could possess. The Latin word *generosus* referred to a person's birth or nobility. The word was used to describe someone's socioeconomic status.[13]

The word evolved to mean "someone who could leverage great wealth to help other people," which unfortunately is why it became associated only with people who had great wealth. Generosity is more than an action; it is an attitude. I define generosity as coming to the place in your life when giving is more important than getting and sharing what you have with others is more important than storing it up for yourself.

Giving is not the same as being generous. You can give without being generous, but you cannot be generous without giving. Neither can generosity be measured strictly by the amount that a person gives.

I could not believe it when I read the headline "I Want the Last Check I Write to Bounce." My first thought was, *Here is someone who doesn't know how to manage their money, spends every dime they have, and doesn't realize that life is about more than just spending and getting.* But when I read about the man who said this, I realized just how wrong I was.

Charles F. Feeney is, or at least he used to be, a billionaire. He made his fortune in the duty-free shopping industry. He made a decision in 1984, which he kept a secret, to form a private foundation called Atlantic Philanthropies, and for fifteen years ran it anonymously even though it was one of the largest sources of charitable grants in the United States, Ireland, South Africa, and Vietnam. He covertly turned over the duty-free business to this foundation and continued to invest while giving money away in direct medical care, education, criminal justice advocacy, and peace-building initiatives.

Atlantic Philanthropies will close its doors sometime around 2020, having given away $8 billion, at which time it will be by far the largest such organization to have voluntarily shut itself down. Mr. Feeney isn't irresponsible after all. He just understands that personal prosperity is for the purpose of purposeful generosity.[14]

In all of my years, I have never met a selfish, greedy person of high character. I thought of someone that I know well who hoards, who is selfish and greedy, and who has more money than he can spend. In many ways, he is miserable and he makes those around him miserable. I don't believe he could even spell *generosity*.

He portrays the same traits that I see in every selfish, greedy person I've ever met. He is insecure and worries about his wealth all of the time. He is insensitive to the needs of others, and it never occurs to him how much of a blessing he could be to those who are in need.

He is inconsiderate of the feelings of others, because greed and self-ishness have a way of turning hearts ice-cold.

Generosity Commences When We Give

The most generous person ever mentioned in the Bible may come as a shock. It is remarkable that the story even made it into the Gospels, and it didn't even involve a miracle. It was just a clear example of generosity. The main character was a woman who did something that to the ordinary eye was so small, so unimport-ant, so inconsequential that nobody would have given it a second thought except Jesus. Only one person left that day talking about it, but because Jesus did, we are still talking about it two thousand years later.

Jesus is sitting on the sidelines in this story, observing people like my parents used to at the mall. I always knew when my late father and mother were bored because they would take the family down to the mall and people watch. They wouldn't buy anything. They wouldn't even window shop. They would just sit on a bench in the mall and watch people.

Which is why I think the day Jesus told this story, he must have really been bored and had nothing else to do. I mean, it has to be a slow day if you decide to go down to the temple just to watch strang-ers drop their offering in the coffer.

> Jesus sat down opposite the place where the offerings were put and watched the crowd putting their money into the temple treasury. Many rich people threw in large amounts (Mark 12:41).

Inside the temple was an area where offerings were received, and Jesus purposely got a front-row seat where he could watch what peo-ple gave. This is unique, because whenever Jesus was teaching or per-forming a miracle, normally everyone wanted a front-row seat, but this is the only time we are told that Jesus looked for a front-row seat. I could understand it if it were something exciting like a football game or a play or a concert, but this is an offering.

Today, that would be considered rude. You would be thought of as sticking your nose where it does not belong or being a busybody. News flash: Jesus still watches the offering! He still watches what we give or what we don't.

Now Jesus was not the only one watching. The treasury was a public place of deposit for the money people gave to the temple. Inside the treasury stood thirteen brass treasure chests called trumpets shaped like inverted horns. They were narrow at the top and large at the bottom. Rich people would throw their coins in such a way that they would go round and round and make a loud ringing sound so that everybody would hear and see it and everybody would know they had given a lot of money.

That is why we are told that the rich threw in large amounts. They didn't have to guess that rich people gave a lot, you could see and hear it. (It was actually called "sounding the trumpet.") Jesus was observant and often anticipated what people were giving. He knew exactly how much everybody was giving. He was well aware that rich people were donating large sums of money.

Jesus is not condemning the rich people for giving a lot of money. He loves a cheerful giver whether the giver is rich or poor. Jesus is not questioning the motive of rich people who give. There are rich people who give with a good heart and a good motive. Some of the greatest charitable work being done in the world today is done by rich people.

The point that Mark is making here is that the Lord anticipates what we give. He is marking down what we give. He knows when we give or when we don't, but that is not the point of the story.

Generosity Continues with What We Give

> But a poor widow came and put in two very small copper coins, worth only a few cents (Mark 12:42).

Talk about an unlikely hero. This lady would have been looked upon that day as a three-time loser. First of all, she was poor. Second, she was a widow (people would have known that because widows usually wore distinct clothing). Third, she was a woman (ladies, I hate to tell you, but they were considered second-class citizens compared to men).

But she makes the front page of Jesus's newspaper. Jesus is watching so closely that he sees something no one else saw. With his supernatural spiritual vision he sees her put in two small copper coins. These coins are also called "mites." These coins were the smallest and least valuable pieces of money in circulation in that day.

The average daily wage of a common laborer was fifteen cents. The two coins put together were the equivalent of about one one-hundredth of that amount or less than one-tenth of one cent. Nobody gave her offering a second thought, but Jesus gave it a second look. He is so impressed by what she gave that he calls his disciples over to see what this woman had done. He makes a statement that I promise you made the disciples question Jesus's grades in math in school.

> Calling his disciples to him, Jesus said, "Truly I tell you, this poor widow has put more into the treasury than all the others" (Mark 12:43).

Being an accounting major myself, I would say as well that maybe math wasn't Jesus's best subject in school. One-tenth of a penny is not worth more than all the money the rich gave. But generosity is not always measured by what you give. There is often a difference between giving the greatest amount and being the most generous giver. A million dollars may be a dream gift, but a tenth of a penny may make you a dream-giver.

Talk about generosity! You don't get a pass just because you are not rich or have fewer assets than your friends. This poor widow teaches us:

- You don't have to be rich to be generous.
- You don't have to have a lot to give.
- You don't have to have a lot to give a lot.

Jesus doesn't measure what people give the way we measure what people give. He doesn't look at the portion that people give; Jesus looked at the proportion of what people give. He didn't look at how much people put on the table; Jesus looked at how much people left in their pocket. We look at what is put in; Jesus looks at what is left over.

One of these days, we are going to find that some of the most generous people who ever lived were some of the poorest people we ever knew. Jesus is not impressed with the greatness of what we give but with the generosity of what we give.

Go back to that day in the temple. Everybody applauded what the rich people gave. Only one person applauded the poor widow's contribution, but it was the only person that mattered. Jesus anticipates when we give—he knows it.

Jesus calculates what we give not by how much the gift was worth, but by how much the gift really cost. By that measure, this poor widow got an A+ in generosity that day.

Giving Culminates in Why We Give

This poor widow becomes the hero of a story she didn't even know she was writing. Jesus sums up why he was so enamored with the little woman who gave such a big gift.

> "They all gave out of their wealth; but she, out of her poverty, put in everything—all she had to live on" (Mark 12:44).

Again, we are reminded just how poor she was. After being called "poor," she is now described as being a person of poverty, and two Greek words are used for "poor" and "poverty." The word translated as "poor" describes someone who is "totally destitute—a beggar." She may have been homeless. Today, she would have been dependent on public assistance. The word for "poverty" means basically "having nothing." Careful reading says that she really gave more than just money.

Jesus said she "put in everything—all she had to live on." What it literally says is she gave all of her *bios,* which gives us the word *biology* and means "life." She gave all of her life. This lady was giving her money and also giving herself. She was giving all she had and also all she was. The reason this woman could give all of her money to God was that she had already given all of her life to God.

The easy part for this woman was giving all of her money. It wasn't hard because she had given God all of her heart. What really impressed Jesus was not what she gave, but why she gave it. It wasn't the amount but the attitude that impressed Jesus.

Keep in mind she was not going to get a tax deduction. She didn't give out of show. Not only did she not know that anyone was looking, but she probably would have been embarrassed if she had known somebody was. She for sure didn't give flippantly. She carefully thought this through, and though she didn't say it out loud, she was making a clear statement to God. Actions speak louder than words, and did her actions ever speak loudly and clearly. When this woman gave everything she had, she was saying three things:

- God, I look to you to provide my needs.
- God, I love you more than I love money.
- God, I live for you and you alone.

So if you give, why do you give? The IRS doesn't care why you give. They just want your money. The mortgage company doesn't care why you give. They just want your money. The credit card company doesn't care why you give. They just want your money. God cares why you give because he doesn't want your money. He wants your heart.

Let's put something in perspective. We are talking today about a poor widow. We do not know her name, where she came from, where she lived, or how she died. Two thousand years later, we still remember her and talk about her because of her generosity. You are not going to be *remembered* by how much you made, how much you spent, or even how much you saved. You are going to be *remembered* for how much you gave.

You won't be *rewarded* by God for how much you made or how much you spent or how much you saved. You will be *rewarded* by what you gave. This woman never knew that Jesus saw what she gave. She never heard what Jesus said about what she gave, but I bet the second she arrived in heaven, the first thing Jesus said was, "I saw what you did."

The greatest reason why all of us should be generous is that we serve a generous God who is so generous that he sent his Son, Jesus Christ, to die on the cross so that we can have the most expensive gift we could ever have—eternal life. He gives it to us for free.

You have one life to live and can live it as a generous person or a greedy person. The choice is yours to make. Will you live selflessly, holding everything God has given you with an open hand, or will you live selfishly, holding everything God has given you with a closed fist?

On September 3, 1939, German troops invaded Bielsko, Poland. A fifteen-year-old girl, Gerda Weissmann, and her family survived in the Jewish ghetto until June 1942. That is when Gerda was taken from her mother, who was sent to a death camp, while Gerda would spend three years in a Nazi concentration camp. She was one of the few survivors. By the time she was liberated by American troops, she was a sixty-eight-pound skeleton. Later, she married the soldier who rescued her.

At the Holocaust Memorial in Boston, Massachusetts, are six glass towers representing the six extermination camps where six million Jews were killed. Five towers tell the story of the unbelievable cruelty these people endured, but the sixth tower stands as a testimony to generosity. Inscribed on it is a short story titled "One Raspberry," written by Gerda. This is the story.

> Ilse, a childhood friend of mine, once found a raspberry
> in the camp and carried it in her pocket all day to present to me that night on a leaf. Imagine a world in which
> your entire possession is one raspberry and you give it
> to your friend.[15]

The real measure of your heart is bound up in whether it is a heart that wants to get or a heart that wants to give. The real measure of the value of a gift is not how much it is worth on the table but how much is left in your pocket. That is true whether you possess two million dollars, two copper coins, or a single raspberry.

Financial Freedom

Generosity does not come naturally. When we were children, no matter how many toys we got for Christmas, we didn't want anybody playing with any of our toys even if we were not playing with them ourselves. Generosity is a discipline that you have to cultivate—it really is more caught than taught. It is not in our DNA, but rather must be continuously practiced.

Being a golfer, I was fascinated when I read a story about Noriaki Yamashita. He was playing the par-three fifteenth hole at the Abiko Golf Club, and he watched his tee shot fall softly toward the green, bounce twice, and then plop into the cup for a hole in one. Making a hole in one was one of the greatest thrills of my life, but not so for Yamashita. In his words, he "knew something terrible had happened."

A hole in one is a golfer's ultimate prize. The odds of the average golfer making one is 12,500-to-1, but the Japanese have a term for a hole in one—*arubatorosu,* which means "albatross." Those who score a hole in one are required by Japanese custom to buy drinks, dinner, and other presents for club members and friends, all of which can easily add up to $10,000 or more. That is why the Japanese have hole-in-one insurance. Almost four million golfers in Japan spend more than $210 million a year on policies to guard against a perfect tee shot. Why? The Japanese believe those who receive good fortune have an obligation to share it and be generous with others.[16]

There is insurance against generosity that always works, and you don't have to pay any premiums. It is called selfishness. There are only two ways you can live your life—selfishly or selflessly. I have found that the most joyful, fulfilling life is found in a life of generosity, but in order to become a generous person, we must work at it. But we can develop this discipline.

First of all, we must change the way we *look* at money. The first money I ever made was at a family reunion when my brother and I stood outside the only driveway to my grandparents' house and forced our relatives to buy crabapples we had picked and were selling for a nickel apiece. We both made about two dollars that day. When I looked at it, I thought, *This is my money* and *What am I going to buy for myself?* As we grow into adults, that childlike instinct that the money we make is ours never leaves us. Our first instinct is to *spend* money. Our second instinct is to perhaps *save* some money. Then, if we have any left over and if we happen to be feeling good (or perhaps guilty), we *share* our money with others. That is why with most people, giving always comes last.

If we are going to become a generous person, we have to reverse that order. Sharing our money must come before spending it and saving it. Giving it must come immediately after getting it. Generosity is always giving at the beginning of the meal, not giving the leftovers.

That will not happen until we change a possessive pronoun. We must go from thinking about "my money" to "God's money." Everything we have belongs to God because everything we have comes from God. The reason we get money is because God gives us money, and the reason God gives us money is not so we will get it, but so we will give it. So, unless we change the way we perceive money, we will battle becoming a generous person all of our life.

Second, we must be proactive in where we *leave* money. Everybody leaves whatever they have accumulated in this life sooner or later. We can leave it while we are living or we will leave it after we are dead. Either way, we are going to leave it. To put it another way, we can give our money away while we are alive or we will give it up when we die. We can begin even now just in little acts of generosity that train us for bigger acts of generosity.

My wife and I have what we call a Waffle House ministry. Often we will go to Waffle House and order, um, a nutritious meal. We will intentionally tip an amount larger than the bill. That may sound small, but it is motivated by this big thought: The moment we die we will never be able to give anything to anyone again.

Jesus said that if we try to hold on to our life we will lose it, but if we give up our life we will keep it (Matthew 10:39). The principle is also true about our money. All the money that we hold on to will vanish the moment we die. The money that we give to God's work—to clothe the poor, feed the hungry, educate the illiterate, provide fresh water—will bring a blessing and a benefit long after we are gone.

Finally, we must refuse to *love* money. Generosity is not what we have in hand but what we have in our heart. Let this question guide your financial management: Instead of spending money on things I don't need, why don't I give to those who are in need?

God is in the giving business, not so that we will be in the getting business, but so that we will join him in the giving business. He does not bless us just so we can live in that bigger house, drive that nicer car, or wear those nicer clothes. Nothing is wrong with those things, but God blesses us to raise our standard of giving, not our standard of living.

> ## God blesses us to raise our standard of giving, not our standard of living.

Author Stephen King has sold over 350 million copies of his novels around the world and has a net worth of over $400 million. At the commencement speech he gave to Vassar graduates in May 2001, he sounded more like a preacher than a novelist. Here is an excerpt of what he said:

> A couple of years ago I found out what "you can't take it with you" means. I found out while I was lying in a ditch at the side of a country road, covered with mud and blood and with the tibia of my right leg poking out the side of my jeans like a branch of a tree taken down in a thunderstorm. I had a MasterCard in my wallet, but when you're lying in the ditch with broken glass in your hair, no one accepts MasterCard...
>
> We all know that life is ephemeral, but on that particular day and in the months that followed, I got a painful but extremely valuable look at life's simple backstage truths. We come in naked and broke. We may be dressed when we go out, but we're just as broke. Warren Buffet? Going to go out broke. Bill Gates? Going to go out broke. Tom Hanks? Going out broke...Steve King? Broke. You guys? Broke. Not a crying dime...
>
> [A]ll the money you will earn...all the stocks you will buy, all the mutual funds and precious metals you will trade—all of that is mostly smoke and mirrors...It's still going to be a quarter-past getting late whether you tell the time on a Timex or a Rolex...
>
> I want you to consider making your life one long gift to others. And why not? All you have is on loan, anyway...All that lasts is what you pass on...

[We] have the power to help, the power to change. And why should we refuse? Because we're going to take it with us? Please...

Giving is a way of taking the focus off the money we make and putting it back where it belongs—on the lives we lead, the families we raise, the communities which nurture us...

Let it be the beginning of a life's giving, not just of money but of time and spirit. It repays. Not least of all because it helps us remember that we may be going out broke, but right now we're doing okay. Right now we have the power to do great good for others and for ourselves. So I ask you to begin the next great phase of your life by giving, and to continue as you begin. I think you'll find in the end that you got far more than you ever had, and did more good than you ever dreamed.[17]

Mr. King took quite a few paragraphs to say what Jesus said in one sentence: "It is more blessed to give than to receive" (Acts 20:35). May we all live into that truth.

COURAGE:

Go Big, Go Bold

Courage is rightly esteemed the first of
human qualities because it is the quality
which guarantees all the others.

WINSTON CHURCHILL[1]

A part of my heritage that I am not proud of is that I had two great-great-grandfathers who fought in the Civil War for the Confederate Army. One fought in the Battle of Atlanta and another is buried in a Confederate cemetery in Lynchburg, Virginia. I visited his grave many years ago and could not help but think of the cost of that war, both then and to this day, because of the immoral issue that started the conflict.

The financial cost of that war was staggering. In January of 1863, the war was costing an estimated $2.5 million every day, which is the equivalent of $47 million today. In today's dollars, the war cost about $8 trillion.

The physical devastation, almost all of it in my native South, was staggering. Possessions were burned or plundered, a countryside was pillaged, crops and farm animals were destroyed, buildings and bridges were left in ruins, college campuses were devastated, and a stretch of the nation from Virginia to Florida to most of Arkansas and parts of Texas was left in complete ruin.

Fresh estimates now say that the total number of soldiers who died from war-related causes is somewhere between 752,000 and 851,000, which is more than all the deaths we have had in all the other wars America has ever fought.[2]

The cost incurred and the price paid did not just end in 1865. It has continued up to this day where discrimination, racism, and bitter feelings still linger. A big part of the reason is the *lack of courage*.

I am speaking of the lack of courage on the part of our Founding Fathers to take the right action and do the right thing when it came to slavery. To be clear, I have great admiration for the Founding Fathers in many ways, and I do not question their courage either on the battlefield or their courage and their willingness to lay down their lives for the cause for which the Revolutionary War was fought.

But the men who waged that war did not have the moral courage to apply the principle of liberty and freedom to every person who they themselves said were all "created equal and endowed by their Creator with certain unalienable rights." As Mark Twain observed, "It is curious—curious that physical courage should be so common in the world and moral courage so rare."[3] No hero is perfect, and again in many ways we owe a debt of gratitude to the fortitude our founders displayed in so many ways. Still, we must avoid the danger that "when we venerate the saints of yesteryear as titans of faithfulness, without paying proper attention to their sins, we elevate them to a status only God possesses."[4]

Even 150 years after the Civil War was fought, we are reminded of the high cost of compromise over courage. We see the problem today repeated over and over. Our nation is drowning in a sea of debt, now over $20 trillion, because we don't have politicians with the moral courage to be fiscally responsible. The #MeToo movement has arisen because for too long we have not had the courage to face up to the problem of sexual abuse and harassment. I could continue with example after example, but as my mentor Adrian Rogers said well, "There are no problems too big to solve. Just people too little to solve them."

Secret Sauce

Courage is the fuel that powers the engine of character. Maya Angelou said, "Courage is the most important of all the virtues, because without courage you can't practice any other virtue consistently. You can practice any virtue erratically, but nothing consistently without courage."[5]

How much different would the political climate be, not to mention the political productivity or lack thereof that we see today, if courage were exercised again? How would America change if people in office quit allowing polls to become the force behind their decisions and courageously did what is best for the country? These words state it perfectly:

> Where are those who are willing to lead without regard to what is popular at the moment? Where are those who are willing to be *courageous* even if it means they will lose the next election? Where are those with the determination to stand for something, and to be consistent and unwavering in doing so? In these troubling times, we need policies that are driven by unchanging principle, and we need leaders who are willing to maintain a steady course *simply because it is right.*[6]

The problem doesn't lie just with politicians and people in office. It also lies with the people who put them in office and who refuse to exercise the courage to speak truth to power. Dietrich Bonhoeffer was perhaps the first of his German countrymen to see the need for courage to speak up and be "a voice for the voiceless." He saw the need for courage not only to speak up for the Jews but to speak against the evils of Nazism. Unfortunately, his was a lone voice crying in the wilderness. Courage was a rare commodity hardly found on the shelf of any pastor in any church, and it cost Germany and the world dearly.

Martin Niemöller, a fellow pastor and Bonhoeffer's friend, said in his famous statement:

> First they came for the socialists, and I did not speak out—
>   because I was not a socialist.
> Then they came for the trade unionists, and I did not speak out—
>   because I was not a trade unionist.
> Then they came for the Jews, and I did not speak out—
>   because I was not a Jew.
> Then they came for me—and there was no one left to speak
>   for me.[7]

Contrast that with the actions of a woman who had one seemingly small and yet hugely courageous action. She was the spark that lit the fire that burned down some of the walls of racial discrimination in the American South. It happened over six decades ago in Birmingham, Alabama. In chapter 6 and section 10 of the city code for Montgomery, Alabama, we read,

> Every person operating a bus line in the city shall provide equal, but separate accommodations for white people and Negros on his buses, by requiring the employees in charge therefore to assign passengers seats on the vehicles under their charge in such manner as to separate the white people from the Negros, where there are both white and Negroes on the same car.

Around 6:00 p.m. on Thursday, December 1, 1955, Rosa Parks sat down in the white section of a bus and refused to move. Four days later, facing charges of disorderly conduct in a trial that lasted thirty minutes, she was found guilty and fined ten dollars plus four dollars in court costs. That led to a bus boycott for over a year as the black citizens refused to ride the buses, often at great personal cost, financially and vocationally, and in the face of tremendous hostility from the white community. This led a US District Court to rule the ordinance unconstitutional, which was upheld on November 13, 1956, by the United States Supreme Court, which permanently outlawed racial segregation on buses. The courage of Rosa Parks was the beginning of the Civil Rights Movement and the rising up of Martin Luther King Jr., and the rest, as they say, is history.

Courage is important universally in all times and all places because character is important universally at all times and in all places. Real character will wither on the vine if not fertilized with the energy of courage.

You Know When You See It

What do we mean by courage? I believe courage is the refusal to allow fear to be the tail that wags the dog. You know it when you see it, and you know it when you exercise it. When you are the only one in the group willing to ask the question that everyone else wants to but is afraid to. When you are the only one to say what needs to be said when everyone else is afraid to say it. When you are the first one to apologize even if you didn't start the fight. Courage is doing what you are afraid to do and don't want to do, but you do it anyway because it is right.

On April 1, 1942, Desmond Doss joined the United States Army. Little did he realize that three-and-a-half years later, he would be standing on the White House lawn, receiving the nation's highest award for his bravery and courage under fire. Of the 16 million men in uniform during World War II, only 431 received the Congressional Medal of Honor. One of these was placed around the neck of a soldier who, during combat, had not killed a single enemy soldier and refused to carry a gun. His only weapons were his Bible and his faith in God.[8]

In May of 1945, Japanese troops were fiercely defending, to

their last man, the only remaining barrier (Okinawa and the Maeda Escarpment) to an Allied invasion of their homeland. The men in Desmond's division were repeatedly trying to capture an imposing rock face the soldiers called Hacksaw Ridge. After the company had secured the top of the cliff, the Americans were stunned when suddenly enemy forces rushed them in a vicious counterattack. Officers ordered an immediate retreat. Soldiers rushed to climb back down the steep cliff—that is, all except one.

Less than one-third of the men made it back down. The rest lay wounded, scattered across enemy soil—abandoned and left for dead, if they weren't already. One lone soldier disobeyed orders and charged back into the firefight to rescue as many of his men as he could before he either collapsed or died trying. His iron determination and unflagging courage resulted in at least seventy-five lives saved that day, May 5, 1945, as he lowered them down one by one. Some of these men had berated him, bullied him, and even beat him when he first enlisted because he refused to carry a weapon. They had witnessed firsthand the moral courage that steeled his heart to risk his life for them. In October 1945, he became the only conscientious objector in military history to be awarded the Medal of Honor.[9]

When I speak of courage, physical courage probably comes to mind. The kind of courage that Hollywood loves to celebrate: the power of superheroes, the athlete who pushes through pain to win contests, or the soldier who races into a hail of bullets to save a comrade (as in the movie *Hacksaw Ridge*). We see and hear about those acts of courage often.

But the type of courage that most of us need to learn—and the one that has almost become an endangered species—is moral courage. It may expose you to ridicule, criticism, ostracism, and the judgmental wrath of others. This kind of courage was described by W. Clement Stone: "Have the courage to say 'no' and have the courage to face the truth. Do the right thing, because it is right. These are the magic keys to living your life with integrity."[10]

Lady Lionheart

It is the kind of courage described in the story that has been preserved for more than twenty-five hundred years. The Book of Esther is unique because the name "God" is never mentioned in its pages. Not one time. And yet it is included in the Bible because God's fingerprints are all over the story. If this story were not in the Bible, you would swear that some Hollywood screenwriter had penned it. It has intrigue, mystery, deceit, treachery, romance, murder, and a you-are-not-going-to-believe-how-this-ends conclusion.

The story takes place in the ancient kingdom of Persia. Israel had been taken into captivity by the Babylonians, who were then conquered by the Persians. They were under the authority of the Persian king Xerxes. He ruled over what is now known as the Medo-Persian Empire that stretched from modern-day Libya in Africa to Pakistan in Asia. It was the largest empire up to this point in history with about fifty million people. Persia ruled the Middle-Eastern world for two centuries.

Esther enters this historical thriller and transforms it into a Cinderella story. She is just an unknown Hebrew girl who, in a miraculous turn of events, is selected from among twenty-five thousand women to marry the most powerful man on earth and become the queen of Persia. But as we'll soon find out, this transformation doesn't just make her queen for a day; it ends up saving the Jewish people.

She has a cousin named Mordecai who had adopted and raised her because she was an orphan. As she becomes queen, he tells her to keep her Jewish identity a secret because no Jewish woman would ever be allowed to become a Persian queen. Jews were considered to be captured immigrants.

Then a villain named Haman enters the scene. Haman is the prime minister of the empire, second in command only to the king. Haman has a big ego. He wants everyone to bow down to him whenever he walks by, but Mordecai refuses to do so for religious reasons. That infuriates Haman, and when he finds out that

Mordecai is a Jew, his hate shoots through the roof. Haman was an Amalekite, a tribe that had a blood feud with Israel stretching more than a thousand years. The two groups were the Hatfields and the McCoys, they were Alexander Hamilton and Aaron Burr, they were Taylor Swift and Kanye West. So Haman decides to take Mordecai out, and also to exterminate the entire Jewish race. He doesn't just hate the person of Mordecai; he hates the people of Mordecai.

> When Haman saw that Mordecai would not kneel down or pay him honor, he was enraged. Yet having learned who Mordecai's people were, he scorned the idea of killing only Mordecai. Instead Haman looked for a way to destroy all Mordecai's people, the Jews, throughout the whole kingdom of Xerxes (Esther 3:5-6).

Haman persuades the king to go along with this plan, and so every Jew, including those who had moved back to Israel, is going to be annihilated. Haman is going to end the Jewish race once and for all. (Hitler tried the same thing about twenty-four hundred years later.) Haman has now manipulated the signing of the death warrant of an entire nation. We are talking genocide on an unprecedented scale.

All that stands between the Jewish nation and complete annihilation is a Jewish peasant-turned-queen named Esther. She is the only person in the world who can change the mind of the king and turn the tide from tragedy to triumph. To do this, she will have to go big and go bold. We learn from this great woman what courage is all about.

Courage Shows Up

When news gets back to Mordecai about the edict that has been issued, he collapses in a heap of sackcloth and ashes and sits outside the city gate wailing and mourning. Esther hears about it and gets some of her attendants to find out what the problem is, because she obviously knew nothing about this plan. Mordecai realizes that

Esther is his ace in the hole. He sends word back to her about what has happened, and then says to her that she must go into the king's presence and beg for mercy for him to spare not just Mordecai's people, but her people. The problem is, that isn't as easy as it sounds.

> Hathak went back and reported to Esther what Mordecai had said. Then she instructed him to say to Mordecai, "All the king's officials and the people of the royal provinces know that for any man or woman who approaches the king in the inner court without being summoned the king has but one law: that they be put to death unless the king extends the gold scepter to them and spares their lives. But thirty days have passed since I was called to go to the king" (Esther 4:9-11).

Feminism and gender equality are still a long way off at this point in history. So the queen couldn't just stroll into the king's office anytime she wanted to chat. Back in the day, nobody had an open door to the king—not the queen, not the prime minister, not the secretary of state—nobody. Leaders feared assassination, so the king surrounded himself with his own version of the Secret Service.

If you wanted to see the king, you had to send a formal request in writing, and he had to respond with a formal invitation. Then, when you went into his presence, he had to hold out his golden scepter to show his approval. If he held out the golden scepter, you were welcome to speak. But if you walked in unannounced and uninvited, you probably weren't going to walk out.

Esther now faces a choice. If she stays in the comfort of her lovely estate, she can keep the Mercedes, the Rolex, the servants, the crown, the jewelry and nobody would know she is Jewish and at least she could live happily ever after. The only other option is to rise to the occasion, go for broke, and risk her life to do the right thing, say the right words, and be the right person.

When Mordecai hears her response, he realizes the spot she is in and the decision she faces. If this were a movie, you would be on the edge of your seat with eyes riveted, wanting to know what she will do. Then Mordecai makes one of the most life-changing statements in the Bible:

> He sent back this answer: "Do not think that because you are in the king's house you alone of all the Jews will escape. For if you remain silent at this time, relief and deliverance for the Jews will arise from another place, but you and your father's family will perish. And who knows but that you have come to your royal position for such a time as this?" (Esther 4:13-14).

Being courageous is expensive and courage never goes on sale. We are going to face times in life where risk and fear are staring us in the face. That is why the Bible says "fear not" 365 times, because God knows every day offers a chance for fear to show up and make us crawl under the bed, hide in the closet, retreat from the battle.

That is why the first step of courage is just showing up. Bestselling author Brené Brown says, "Sometimes the bravest and most important thing you can do is just show up...Vulnerability is not winning or losing; it's having the courage to show up and be seen when we have no control over the outcome."[11]

Each of us will face a time when we have to decide if we are going to do the right thing or the wrong thing, our thing or God's thing. Are we going to be courageous or a coward? Are we going to show up or wimp out?

I heard this recently: "A ship in harbor is safe, but that is not what ships are built for."[12] The ship of your life should sail the seas it was meant to travel. You can't stay in the harbor. You have to courageously ship out and show up.

Courage Stands Up

One of the reasons why courage is difficult is that often we don't have time to think about doing the courageous thing, saying the courageous word, taking the courageous action. It is thrust upon us like a lightning bolt out of the blue, and then we discover whether we have it or we don't. There will be no doubt whether we bleed red or you bleed yellow. In this case, Esther didn't take long to decide.

> Then Esther sent this reply to Mordecai: "Go, gather together all the Jews who are in Susa, and fast for me. Do not eat or drink for three days, night or day. I and my attendants will fast as you do. When this is done, I will go to the king, even though it is against the law. And if I perish, I perish" (Esther 4:15-16).

We all have those "such a time as this" moments when we have to on-the-spot decide if we are going to keep our seat or stand up. Are we going to go with the crowd, go with the flow, do as the Romans do, or do the right thing even if we have to do it alone? Stand up even if we have to stand alone, and take the right path even if we have to take it alone?

In that moment, courage will always be asking us not what is the easiest or most popular, but what is right. Fear will be screaming in our ear, "Say no!" Courage will quietly speak to our heart, "Say yes." Esther realizes the cost of her decision with these unbelievably courageous words, "And if I perish, I perish."

Someone has said that courage is not the absence of fear; it is the mastery of it. The Bible adds an important element to courage: trust in God. Courage is being willing to do what we know God wants us to do even when the consequences are unseen and unknown.

> **Courage is being willing to do what we know God wants us to do even when the consequences are unseen and unknown.**

The cowardly way is often easy and comfortable, but the queen has made her decision. In between Esther chapters 4 and 5, a three-day pause in the action occurs during which the people are praying and fasting. Then we read these words:

> On the third day Esther put on her royal robes and stood in the inner court of the palace, in front of the king's hall. The king was sitting on his royal throne in the hall, facing the entrance (Esther 5:1).

She is standing in the inner court and doesn't know whether she will live or die. Will the king hold out his scepter or not? Esther teaches us that courage is being willing to pay the price for doing the right thing. Courage is going where we need to go and taking our stand.

Courage Speaks Up

We fast-forward to where Esther has carried out a brilliant plan to expose Haman and his evil plan. There before everyone, she makes this breathtaking announcement:

> So the king and Haman went to Queen Esther's banquet, and as they were drinking wine on the second day, the king again asked, "Queen Esther, what is your petition? It will be given you. What is your request? Even up to half the kingdom, it will be granted."
>
> Then Queen Esther answered, "If I have found favor with you, Your Majesty, and if it pleases you, grant me my life—this is my petition. And spare my people—this is my request. For I and my people have been sold to be destroyed, killed and annihilated. If we had merely been sold as male and female slaves, I would have kept quiet, because no such distress would justify disturbing the king" (Esther 7:1-4).

You could have heard the proverbial pin drop from one end of the empire to the other. Queen Esther is Jewish! Her family is Jewish. Her blood is Jewish. Her people are Jewish. The only one that could speak up spoke up. And the rest, as they say, is history. Since the decree that had been ordered could not be revoked, Xerxes issues another decree. He gives the Jews the right to gather together, arm themselves, and defend their lives. The fight ensues, and the Jews kill over seventy-five thousand Persians and the process saves an entire nation, all because of a woman who was willing to go big and go bold.

Winston Churchill said, "There comes a special moment in everyone's life; a moment for which that person was born. That special opportunity that when he seizes it will fulfill his mission—a mission for which he is uniquely qualified. In that moment, he finds greatness. It is his finest hour."[13] This was Esther's finest hour, and it has never been forgotten.

The Jewish calendar is built around three major holidays. On Passover, Jews celebrate their deliverance from Egypt and the exodus. On Hanukkah, they remember the victory of a leader named Judas Maccabeus over the Syrians and the restoration of the temple. On the Feast of Purim, they commemorate how this incredible wonder woman placed God first, others second, and herself last to display rare courage. On that day, Jews assemble in synagogues where her story is read aloud from beginning to end.

Nothing will measure you or mature you like those times when life puts you on the spot—you've got to make the call, choose the path, and make the decision. You know there is a right way and a wrong way, a right door and a wrong door, a right call and a wrong call. The choice that you make will make you. Will we have the courage to love those most unlike us? The courage to stand up against discrimination, racism, sex trafficking, sexual abuse, abortion, education inequality and proclaim we follow a just God who demands justice?

Will each one of us who claim to know Christ have the courage to choose just one person that we are going to pray for, go to, and share the love of Christ with? We are here to make disciples. A disciple should be like his or her master. Your master had the courage to leave the comfort of heaven and come to a planet he created that would ridicule him, reject him, scorn him, and crucify him so that we might have eternal life and forgiveness. Oh, by the way, Jesus did that because God raised up an Esther to preserve the people that would bring the Messiah into the world.

In the early 1970s, the Iraqi government arrested a group of American students on some trumped-up espionage charges. Saddam Hussein wanted confessions and admissions of guilt, and they tortured the students. They were told that if they would confess, they could go free. One by one, as the pressure and the pain mounted, the prisoners confessed to crimes they had not committed. Every prisoner except one.

Recounting his friend's story in *The Wall Street Journal*, Mark Helprin wrote,

> They announced they were finished with his case—that
> he could simply confess or die. A confession lay before
> him as they raised a pistol to his head and cocked the
> hammer and started the countdown. He had heard exe-
> cutions from his cell. "Sign your name, and you will live,"
> he was told, but he refused. He closed his eyes, grimaced
> and prepared to die. They pulled the trigger. When he
> heard the click, he thought he was dead. The gun how-
> ever had not been loaded.[14]

Helprin's friend was eventually released. He discovered later that all the other prisoners who had confessed were hanged in the public square.

The cost of courage is great, but the cost of cowardliness and compromise is even greater. So, teach your kids and model for them a life that shows up when the rest of the world is hiding, stands up when the rest of the world is sitting, and speaks up when the rest of the world is listening. Go big and go bold.

Take Courage

When all is said and done, how do we develop this crucial character trait? Well, one person who has spent ten years studying this subject and talking to people about it said she came to realize that courage is not something we have or don't have. It is something we practice.[15] Courage is not a trait we possess; it is a trait we do. It can indeed be taught and modeled for a younger generation.

The first thing we must do to practice courage is to be willing to *face fear*. Recently, while on a safari in Kenya, I learned how lions stalk their prey. The females do the killing rather than the males. They stalk their prey from behind while the king of the jungle comes from the front and lets loose a bloodcurdling roar heard up to five miles away. The prey do not know that the one roaring is more bark than bite. Instead of running away from danger, they run to danger—the waiting lioness. To survive, they should have run *toward the roar*.[16]

The one way to get rid of fear is to face it, because if you fail to face your fear, it will follow you wherever you go. So you must decide before you even leave your house that when you hear the roar of fear, if at all possible you will run to it, not away from it.

Second, we need to be willing to *stand strong*. We develop courage by deciding ahead of time that truth is worth standing up for, and then when necessary, being willing to stand up for the truth. John Stewart Mill said in 1867, "Bad men need nothing more to accomplish their ends than that good men should look on and do nothing." Sometimes courage means, "Don't just stand there. Do something!" When Abraham Lincoln led a nation into war to free slaves and issued the Emancipation Proclamation, he was advised not to do so.

Courage also means, at times, "Don't do something. Just stand there." "Tank Man" did just that, a solitary man who stood before a column of Chinese tanks in Tiananmen Square, silently but courageously defying the brutal crackdown against peaceful protests.

Third, *respond righteously.* There are times when it takes courage to speak up, because it has been well said, "To sin by silence when they should protest makes cowards of men."[17] But sometimes we must also practice the courage of staying silent. This means refusing to respond to personal attacks, harsh words, and vitriolic language in like kind.

Finally, be willing to *act alone.* All of this must be done realizing that to exercise courage is actually countercultural. Mark Batterson put it so well when he said,

> One of my prayers for my children is that they will have soft hearts and strong spines…but I also want them to stand straight and stand strong for what is right. We live in a culture where it is wrong to say something is wrong. Not only is that wrong, but it makes it even tougher to do what is right. That is why moral courage is the rarest kind of courage.[18]

When a judge ordered New Orleans to open its public schools in 1960 to African-American children, the white parents decided that if they had to let black children in, they would keep their children out. They let it be known that any black children who came to school would be in for big trouble, so all the black children stayed home too—except six-year-old Ruby Bridges. Her parents sent her to school all by herself.

In the morning, she would walk alone, having to face a crowd of people lining the street yelling and screaming epithets at her, threatening her, ridiculing her. White people lined up on both sides of the entrance, shaking their fists at her. They threatened to do terrible things to her and her family if she kept coming to school. But every morning at ten minutes to eight, Ruby Bridges walked head up, eyes ahead, straight through that screaming mob into that school building. Led by US marshals she would spend the day alone with her teachers inside that big silent school building.

Harvard professor Robert Coles was curious about what would cause such a child to be so courageous. He talked to Ruby's mother, and she said, "There's a lot of people who talk about doing good, and a lot of people who argue about what's good and what's not good," but there are other folks who "just put their lives on the line for what's right."[19]

Six-year-old Ruby Bridges went big and she went bold. "And a little child will lead them" (Isaiah 11:6). Let's follow a little child's lead and go big and go bold!

9

PERSEVERANCE:

Run the Stop Sign

If I falter, push me on. If I stumble, pick
me up. If I retreat, shoot me.

MOTTO OF THE FRENCH FOREIGN LEGION[1]

Over four decades ago, on April 1, 1976, three cofounders
signed Apple's partnership agreement: Steve Jobs, Steve
Wozniak, and Ronald Wayne. Practically everyone has
heard of Steve Jobs, many have heard of Steve Wozniak, but you
have probably never heard of Ronald Wayne.

The three men met while working at Atari. By his own account,
Ronald Wayne joined Apple to keep an eye on the two other guys
who were somewhat "crazy." He wrote the partners' agreement piece
where they agreed he would receive 10 percent of the company. He
wrote the manual for Apple I and drew Apple's first logo. But for a
number of reasons, after twelve days at Apple, he quit. He sold his
10 percent of the company for eight hundred dollars.

Well, you can guess the rest of the story. Apple became the biggest company in the world. Ronald Wayne's 10 percent share that
he sold for eight hundred dollars is now worth over sixty billion

dollars. He probably will have the all-time record for the highest cost of quitting too soon.[2]

Perseverance is perhaps the biggest key ingredient to being successful by any definition. As pastor and author Mark Batterson said,

> I am absolutely convinced that the greatest predictor of success in any endeavor is persistence. It is not only how hard you try, it is also how long you try. We tend to overestimate how much we can accomplish in the short-term, but we underestimate how much we can accomplish over the long haul. Why? Because energy is exponential. The harder you work and the longer you work the more it pays off. Energy turns into synergy. And that persistence pays off.[3]

Sadly, perseverance and the things that go with it—like loyalty, responsibility, keeping your word, honoring contracts, staying until you are finished, and making sure the job is done right—are in shorter and shorter supply today. Being a Baby Boomer, I agree with this perspective:

> We Baby Boomers have been raised to view success as ease, most of us are not very good at enduring. When the boss is unreasonable, we quit. When the subjects are too difficult, we drop out. When marriage gets unbearable, we get a divorce.
>
> Our great mobility has allowed us to get to places faster than ever before. It has also allowed us to leave faster. It has become easy to "*quit*." No-fault divorce is the natural result of a society that likes to leave itself an easy out in almost everything.[4]

Disney World, Lightbulbs, and Dr. Seuss

Perseverance touches every part of the world that we live in, and the perseverance of people we will never meet or know affects our lives every day. Because of the power of perseverance, we can light up the night, send a text message around the world, take our children and grandchildren to the greatest children's entertainment center on the planet, and teach our children some of life's greatest lessons found in the most popular children's books of all time. All of our lives have been impacted by people who refused to quit.

Think about the importance of perseverance the next time you flip a switch and turn on a light in a dark room. When you do, be thankful for the perseverance of Thomas Edison. *Life* magazine named Edison the number one man of the millennium. He is credited with 1093 different inventions, including the lightbulb, phonograph, motion-picture camera, printing telegraph apparatus, and typewriting machines.[5] He owned more patents than any other person in the world and was granted at least one every year for sixty-five consecutive years. He developed the modern research laboratory.[6] By his own reckoning, the secret to his success was not that he was a genius but that he persevered. Take for example the lights we turn on every day.

Edison had to try *600* different materials before he found the right one to serve as the filament to work in his lightbulb. He had more than 10,000 failed experiments until he finally created the lightbulb. What if he had quit on material 599? What if he had quit after experiment 9999? We would still be sitting in the dark. So, he definitely has street cred when he says, "Our greatest weakness lies in giving up. Many of life's failures are people who did not realize how close they were to success when they gave up. The most certain way to succeed is always to try just one more time."[7]

Have you ever heard of Mickey Mouse? I know—stupid question. His face is one of the most recognized logos in the world. Mickey Mouse and all that he has spawned is with us today because of the power of perseverance. Has anyone in the world ever had a more vivid imagination than Walt Disney? He was fired as a newspaper editor because, according to his boss, "He lacked imagination

and his ideas were no good." His first cartoon company went bankrupt. His concept of a theme park was trashed more than three hundred times by banks and investors, but Walt Disney refused to quit.
Because of his perseverance, his grandson watches Mickey Mouse
every day. Fifty-two million people visit Walt Disney World every
year (two-and-half-times the population of Florida). Disney himself won thirty-two Academy Awards and holds the record by an
individual for most Oscars ever won. Today, Walt Disney Enter-
prises has assets worth ninety-eight billion dollars.[8] So Walt Disney
knew whereof he spoke when he said, "Everybody falls down. Getting back up is how you learn to walk."[9]

You may not know the name Theodor Geisel, but you would
surely recognize his pen name: Dr. Seuss. He is the author of the
most popular children's books ever written, sixty books in all, translated in twenty different languages with over 600 million copies
sold. His first children's book was rejected by twenty-three publishers. Had he not submitted it to the twenty-fourth publisher, it
would have never sold six million copies, and his other books would
never have been heard of, nor would he.[10]

So, maybe Dr. Seuss was on to something when he said, "Think
left and think right and think low and think high. Oh, the things
you can think up if only you try!"[11] And I would add—keep trying!

And when something "absolutely, positively has to be there overnight," you call Federal Express. Fred Smith was turned down a
hundred times before someone finally gave him the money to start
a delivery company.[12] He's glad he didn't quit as Federal Express
delivers 3.5 million packages every single day. His business attitude
is summed up best in this personal quote: "If you keep working at it,
in the last analysis, you win. They've got to kill us a hundred times.
All we have to do is kill them once."[13]

I could go on and on, but imagine what our world would be like
today if leaders, scientists, businessmen, and inventors had quit. We
wouldn't have electricity, running water, cars, televisions, computers,

and all the other things that make our life so comfortable and easy.[14] We are all born with the knowledge that "quitters never win and winners never quit." I was amazed to find that since *Billboard* magazine first published its "Hot 100" chart in 1958, sixteen different songs titled "Hold On" have made the list. In that sense, "Hold On" is the most popular song in American music history.[15]

The Will to Win

Holding on is really what perseverance is all about. I define perseverance this way: Perseverance is the determination that as long as you are in control, you will hold on until things beyond your control force you to let go. Defeat is not disgrace. There is disgrace only if you quit fighting despite the possibility of victory.

The defeatist attitude is a major part of why the United States exists. The defeat at Yorktown on October 19, 1791, basically ended the Revolutionary War. General Cornwallis was surrounded by American and French forces, supplies were depleted, and he decided to surrender his troops. To their shock, American soldiers found in the British Camp 144 cannon and mortars, thousands of big-gun cartridges, 120 barrels of powder, 800 muskets, 266,000 musket cartridges, 53,000 pounds of flour, 60,000 pounds of bread, 75,000 pounds of pork, 30,000 bushels of peas, and 1250 gallons of liquor—enough materials and foodstuffs to hold on for many more weeks. The British did not surrender at Yorktown because they lacked the resources to fight but because they lost the will to win.[16]

Job Did His Job

Perhaps the oldest book in the Bible tells the story of a man who is one of the most famous examples of perseverance in history. Job had every reason to quit on life, on himself, and even on God, but he persevered, and even 3500 years after this man lived, his story is still worth reading and hearing. He was coasting down the highway of life with nothing but blue sky and bright sunshine in front of him until he rounded a curve and ran head on into the destruction of his wealth, the death of his children, and the disease that would wrack his body. Not only was he tempted to quit, but even his closest friends and his own wife told him to quit.

Life is like that for all of us sooner or later. You round a curve in your life and all of a sudden you see a sign. But it won't say "stop"; it will say "QUIT!" You will be broadsided by events you never anticipated and you will be tempted to quit, or you will be discouraged because of something somebody said and you will be tempted to quit, or you will fail where you thought you were going to succeed and you will be tempted to quit, or you just get tired of trying and you will be tempted to quit. You may be thinking of doing that right now.

Well, consider…you will never read biographies of great quitters. You will never see a long line of followers behind great quitters. You will never see trophies and awards given to great quitters. Former president Calvin Coolidge said, "Nothing in the world can take the place of persistence. Talent will not; nothing is more common than unsuccessful individuals with talent. Genius will not; unrewarded genius is almost a proverb. Education will not; the world is full of educated derelicts. Persistence and determination alone are omnipotent."[17]

No man in the Bible, outside of Jesus Christ himself, suffered more than Job. It would even be fair to say that outside of Jesus, no man suffered more unjustly and more unfairly than Job. Job did not bring any of his troubles on himself.

> In the land of Uz there lived a man whose name was Job. This man was blameless and upright; he feared God and shunned evil. He had seven sons and three daughters, and he owned seven thousand sheep, three thousand camels, five hundred yoke of oxen and five hundred

donkeys, and had a large number of servants. He was the greatest man among all the people of the East (Job 1:1-3).

Talk about a man that had it all. Job had hit the trifecta lottery of life! He was healthy, happy, and holy. He had a beautiful wife and ten precious children. He was filthy rich. He was the most respected, revered man in the entire land. He was the Wizard of Uz!

What is even more remarkable is what God said about him:

> Then the LORD said to Satan, "Have you considered my servant Job? There is no one on earth like him; he is blameless and upright, a man who fears God and shuns evil" (Job 1:8).

God knew everybody everywhere and said, "There is nobody like this guy. There is nobody that loves me, looks to me, and lives for me like Job."

Yet, Satan questions Job's sincerity and his motives, saying that the only reason Job loves God and serves God is because of God's goodness to him. He asks God to allow him to test Job's faith, and God permits it. That is when the fun begins. Before you can blink an eye, Job loses his fortune. Thieves come and steal his oxen, his donkeys, and his camels. Then they kill all of his servants. Lightning strikes and kills all his sheep and their shepherds.

Then, before he can even call his insurance company, he loses his family. A tornado sweeps in and kills all of his children. Then, the coup de grace—he loses his health. He is afflicted with pus-filled sores and boils that cover his entire body with not a doctor in sight.

Job went to sleep with everything and woke up with nothing, except the most important thing—God. If Job were a country songwriter, he would have penned a song titled, "I Can't Eat by Day, I Can't Sleep by Night, and the Woman I Love Don't Treat Me Right." If Job had responded the way most people do, this book would have never been written and Job's name would have never been known. We learn about a great character trait called perseverance from this man who teaches us that tough times never last, but tough people do.

We Will Face Problems That Will Make Us Want to Quit

The next time you think you're overwhelmed by problems, go read the book of Job. It may not make you feel better at first, but it will put your problems in perspective. They call the day the stock market crashed—that caused the Great Depression—"Black Monday." Job had the blackest of all Mondays. He didn't just lose his retirement; he lost everything. One of the greatest estates anyone has ever had was wiped out in less time than it takes for Earth to rotate once on its axis. A few enemies had slaughtered all of Job's cattle, lightning had destroyed all his sheep, thieves and murderers had killed all of his servants, and a tornado had left all of his children dead and buried under the rubble of their own homes. That was just the first day.

Now round two begins. A day or so later, Satan raises the stakes even higher. He now asks God for permission to attack Job physically, and God allows it again. Satan drops a disease bomb on Job and utterly obliterates his health. Here are some of the physical problems he had:

- inflamed ulcerous sores (Job 2:7)
- persistent itching (Job 2:8)
- degenerative changes in facial skin and disfiguration (Job 2:12)
- total loss of appetite (Job 3:24)
- fears and depression (Job 3:25)
- insomnia (Job 7:4)
- purulent sores that burst open, scab over, crack, and ooze with pus (Job 7:5)

- worms that form in the sores (Job 7:5)
- foul breath (Job 19:17)
- breathing difficulties (Job 9:18)
- weight loss (Job 19:20)
- chronic, excruciating, continuous pain (Job 30:27)
- high fever and chills (Job 30:30)

Nobody really wants to be around Job and he doesn't want to be around anybody else. So he is now rejected, isolated, and he relocates to the city dump, which is what we would call it today: "Then Job took a piece of broken pottery and scraped himself with it as he sat among the ashes" (Job. 2:8). This was a place where they burned garbage, rubbish, and excrement.

I remember visiting the World Trade Center in December after 9/11. I went to Ground Zero, the place where the World Trade Center had collapsed. All that was left was rubble, and smoke was still coming up from the ground. Job had now become a "human ground zero."[18] Job asked the most natural questions: "Why?" and "Why me?" and "How do I get out of this mess?"

But the question we should be asking in the midst of our trials is, "What should I get out of this?" Life's difficulties are not meant to defeat you, depress you, or even discourage you; they are meant to develop you. Problems are not tools to tear you down; they are tests to build you up.

But Job's troubles are not finished yet.

> **Life's difficulties are not meant to defeat you, depress you, or even discourage you; they are meant to develop you.**

We Will Hear People Tell Us to Quit

Job had been bathed in an ocean of defeat, devastation, death, disease, and depression. Then came a wave of discouragement, which Job didn't see coming. It is one thing to be tempted to quit, to give in, give out, and give up. It is another thing to be told to do it by the people closest to you.

Job is drowning in a sea of sorrow, his head barely above water. He needs a helping hand to pull him up and out, but instead those he loves and trusts the most put their foot on his head. It begins with his wife. Job is sitting on a pile of garbage, scraping the sores on his skin, despair surrounding him like flies at a picnic, and his wife comes up to him with these warm, encouraging, uplifting words,

> His wife said to him, "Are you still maintaining your integrity? Curse God and die!" (Job 2:9).

That word "integrity" reminds us that even though Job appears to have lost everything, he still possesses the one thing he can't afford to lose. Job's wife is asking him to throw away his character and end his life. Just imagine your husband or your wife, the best friend you have in the world, telling you to commit suicide, to end your own life—and do it while you are cursing God and shaking a fist in his face. Two temptations accompany tough times: quitting God and quitting our faith in God.

Job continued to do the right thing by not responding in the wrong way. Later, he will confront God, but he will never curse God. He will reason with God, but he will never reject God. He will stand up to God, but he will never walk away from God.

The good news is Job still has some great close friends. The bad news is Job still has some great close friends. They are the original Dumb and Dumber. Lloyd and Harry in *Dumb and Dumber* were always trying to do the right thing, but they wound up doing the wrong thing, the wrong way, and making things worse. Job has three friends who do the same thing.

Even though Job knew that he had done nothing to deserve what had happened to him, that he had not brought any of this on himself, these three stooges made it their job to be prosecuting attorneys. They tried to convince Job that he should quit on himself. They tried to convince Job that he didn't have integrity and that he was a hypocrite.

Here was their argument:

1. God is holy and must punish sin.

2. God is punishing Job.

3. Therefore, Job has done something wrong and is getting exactly what he deserves.

Job's wife said, "Why don't you throw away your integrity?" Job's friends asked, "Why don't you admit you never had any integrity to begin with?" Now, not only does everything seem to be against Job; everybody seems to be against Job.

Everything and everybody has joined to become one choir singing a one-word song, over and over and over: "Quit!" We have all either been there or one day will be. We have been knocked down, flat on our back, lying on the mat; the referee has reached the count of nine, and we've got one of two choices: lie there and quit or get up and fight. Both his wife and his friends thought they had solved Job's problem, but if Job had taken their advice, we wouldn't be telling this story and we would never have heard of a man named Job.

So, what is Job going to do? When those times come in your life, what are you going to do? That leads to the third lesson.

We Must Have the Perspective that Ensures We Don't Quit

Job looks like he is on his last leg, as if he has no fight left. You couldn't really blame him if he decided to throw in the towel. Most people would have and a lot of people do.

Let's go back to that first devastating day when Job lost almost everything, including his tremendous fortune and his beautiful family. We read one of the greatest passages in the entire Bible. Job 1:20 has nine words in the Hebrew text and they describe what Job did before they tell us what Job said. When Job's world collapsed, he collapsed. But Job peels himself off the ground, gets up, and goes back into the boxing match called life to fight one more round.[19]

Gentleman Jim Corbett, the former heavyweight boxing champion of the world, said,

> Fight one more round. When your arms are so tired that you can hardly lift your hands to come on guard, fight one more round. When your nose is bleeding and your eyes are black and you are so tired that you wish your opponent would crack you one on the jaw and put you to sleep, fight one more round, remembering that the man who fights one more round is never whipped.[20]

Even more amazing is that after Job got up, he voluntarily went back down for a different reason.

> At this, Job got up and tore his robe and shaved his head. Then he fell to the ground in worship and said:
>   "Naked I came from my mother's womb,
>   and naked I will depart.
>   The LORD gave and the LORD has taken away;
>   may the name of the LORD be praised."
>   (Job 1:20-21)

Job didn't wallow in self-pity. He didn't walk away from God, but went to God in worship. No blame, no bitterness, no whining, no cursing, no "How dare you do this to me knowing what an upright man I've been." He gave God what God always deserves in good times and bad: worship. Job's entire world had walked out on him, but he would not walk out on God.

What does he say to his wife?

> He replied, "You are talking like a foolish woman. Shall we accept good from God, and not trouble?" (Job 2:10).

This is one of the most incredible statements in the Bible. Job is saying, "We may not always like what life gives us, but we can always trust the God who loves us and gives us life."

No, Job didn't quit on God or his faith in God. Because of God and his faith in God, Job did not quit on himself, and that is why we read this fantastic testimony about him:

> In all this, Job did not sin by charging God with wrong-doing (Job 1:22).

> In all this, Job did not sin in what he said (Job 2:10).

Perseverance is the reason we have this book in the Bible and why we know about this man. Eighteen hundred years later, the brother of Jesus, a man named James, pointed to Job as an example: "As you know, we count as blessed those who have persevered. You have heard of Job's perseverance and have seen what the Lord finally brought about. The Lord is full of compassion and mercy" (James 5:11). The story of Job is about his suffering, but also about his standing. He refused to quit.

A history professor once said, "If Columbus had turned back no one would have blamed him, but nobody would have remembered him either."[21] When life goes sideways and a wave of trouble smacks you in the face and knocks you flat on your back, you will either lower your view of God or you will raise your faith in God. As you make your decision, remember God is still in charge. Even if you lose everything you own and tragedy wipes out everyone you love, God is still in charge. If your business goes bankrupt, God is still in charge. If the doctor calls with bad news, God is still in charge.

You may question God but don't ever quit on God, because God never quits on you. When God starts a work in you, he finishes it. God promises he will never quit on you: "Being confident of this… he who began a good work in you will carry it on to completion until the day of Christ Jesus" (Philippians 1:6). What if Jesus had quit before he got to the cross? What if Jesus had quit on the cross—but he didn't, so we wouldn't, and we shouldn't.

> **You may question God, but don't ever quit on God because God never quits on you.**

God has a process for how he wants your life to flow, he has a plan for how he wants your life to go, and he has a purpose for how he wants your life to grow. Don't quit on God, because he will move his process, work his plan, and accomplish his purpose so that in the end everything works out for your good and for his glory.

Keep Moving Forward

In a day when quitting, throwing in the towel, walking off the job, cutting and running when the going gets tough seem to be more and more accepted, how do you put the steel in your spine, the fire in your heart, and the will in your soul to persevere? Perhaps, the greatest example of perseverance in the twentieth century was Martin Luther King Jr., who said, "If you can't fly then run, if you can't run then walk, if you can't walk then crawl, but whatever you do you have to keep moving forward."[22] I suggest this moment that you make three irrevocable, set-in-concrete resolutions:

Resolution 1: Don't give out in difficulty. I've accomplished a lot in my life, but every significant success required me to break walls, climb barriers, and battle difficulties. Though at the time the experience of persevering was not pleasant, I've learned that the things that have counted the most to me cost me the most. It also strengthened me the best.

If you talk to any mountain climber, they will tell you that the joy is not so much in standing on top of the mountain; the joy is in climbing to the top of the mountain. I did not know that the word *mediocre* was first used to describe rock (or mountain) climbers. *Mediocre* literally means "middle of the rock," and it was used to describe climbers who didn't finish the climb but stopped halfway.[23]

We all find ourselves "halfway up the mountain" at times when we have to dig in and keep climbing. We all, like marathon runners, sometimes "hit the wall" when we are trying to reach a goal, and that is when we have to keep moving forward.

Resolution 2: Don't give in to discouragement. My greatest inner battle in my profession is discouragement, and the biggest cause of discouragement is failure. Though it may sound counterintuitive, the secret to success is not avoiding failure; it is handling failure correctly. Michael Jordan is the greatest basketball player who has ever lived. He once wrote, "I've missed more than 9000 shots in my career. I've lost almost 300 games. Twenty-six times, I've been trusted to take the game-winning shot and missed. I've failed over and over and over again in my life. And that is why I succeed."[24]

John C. Norcross is a distinguished professor of psychology at the University of Scranton. He has done extensive research in the area of success and failure with goals. There is a difference between those who reach their goals and those who don't. During the first month of pursuing a goal, the people who ultimately succeed will fail as often as those who eventually give up on their goal. The key difference is perspective. The victors see their failures as "a reason to recommit, a reminder to refocus on their goals with more and more determination…Those who are unsuccessful say a relapse is evidence that they can't do it." In other words, Dr. Norcross says that the success of a goal is determined not by how many times you fail, but by how you view your failures.[25]

Failure neither has to be final nor fatal. The fear of failure has kept far more people from succeeding than failure itself. When you sow the seed of hard work, the soil will only produce the crop of success if it is fertilized with failure. Herbert V. Prochnow said, "The fellow who never makes a mistake takes his orders from one who does."[26]

Resolution 3: Don't give up on your dream. William Wilberforce, a member of the British Parliament, had a dream to abolish the slave trade in his country. In 1789, he regularly introduced bills in Parliament to ban the slave trade. He was fiercely opposed by everyone making money from the trade. He kept bringing the bill up only to face defeat after defeat. Finally, on March 25, 1807, after eighteen years, the Abolition of the Slave Trade Act was established in the British colonies. The House rose to its feet and cheered, but Wilberforce's dream had not yet come to full fruition. This was not a vote to abolish slavery as a whole throughout the empire, it just dealt with the trade of enslaved people. He continued to work for the abolition of all slavery within all the British colonies.

He continued to fight for another seventeen years, until he was so seriously ill he had to resign from Parliament in 1825. But he continued writing and speaking another nine years, even in the last days from his bedside. He wrote one last petition to Parliament. The parliamentary debate lasted three months, but on July 26, 1833, thirty-four years after Wilberforce first took up the fight, the Abolition of Slavery bill passed, and a messenger rushed to his house to tell him that slavery was finally going to be abolished throughout the entire British Empire. Wilberforce died three days later.[27]

Some 130 years later, another man brimming with the spirit of William Wilberforce, Martin Luther King Jr., gave a speech to 250,000 people at the Lincoln Memorial titled "I Have a Dream," which became the final spark to light the fire of the greatest civil rights movement in history. Both men refused to give up on their dream.

An old naval expression captures the spirit of perseverance. When a captain was headed into battle where surrender was not to be contemplated, he would order that "the colors be nailed to the mast." Having the flag nailed up high meant the captain refused to lower it in the heat of battle and replace it with the flag of surrender. A ship might go under, but it would go under moving forward.

No victory in any endeavor has ever been won by going backward. In World War II, the people of England were being bombarded nightly by the Nazis, and they were scared speechless. In view of a cry for the British to surrender, Winston Churchill famously said in his thundering speech to the British nation, "Victory is not won by evacuation."[28] No, it is not. It is won only by determination. Run fast, and don't slow down.

SELF-CONTROL:

Caging the Lion

In reading the lives of great men, I found
that the first victory won was over themselves.
Self-discipline with all of them came first.

HARRY S. TRUMAN[1]

Raynald III was a fourteenth-century duke in what is now Belgium, and he was morbidly obese. His Latin nickname, *Crassus*, means "fat." Raynald's younger brother, Edward, revolted against Raynald's rule. Edward captured Raynald, but he did not kill him. Instead, he built a room around Raynald in the Nijenbeek castle and promised him he would be restored to his throne and regain his title and all that he owned only when he left the room.

For most people, this would have been easy since the room had several windows and a door of near-normal size, and neither the windows nor the doors were locked or barred. But Raynald had one problem—his size. He was extremely overweight and to regain his freedom he needed to lose it.

Edward knew his older brother, and every day he would send a variety of delicious foods into the room. Instead of dieting his way out of prison, Raynald grew fatter. When Duke Edward was accused of being cruel to his brother, he said, "My brother is not a prisoner. He may leave whenever he so wills." Raynald stayed in his room for ten years and wasn't released until Edward died in battle, but by then, Raynald's health was so ruined that he died within a year—a prisoner of his own appetite.[2]

In the 1988 Olympics, Ben Johnson won the one-hundred-meter dash, trimming four one-hundredths of a second off the world record. Many thought the record would last for decades. It didn't last three days. At the Olympic Doping Control Center, less than half a mile from where Johnson had received his gold medal, doctors discovered his urine sample contained stanozolol, a dangerous anabolic steroid. Johnson was both disqualified and disgraced. He was banned from racing for life in 1993 after he tested positive again.[3]

Pete Rose is the all-time Major League Baseball leader in hits (4256), games played (3562), career at-bats (14,053), and singles (3215). He owns three World Series rings, three batting titles, one Most Valuable Player award, two Gold Gloves, and the Rookie of the Year award, and he made seventeen All-Star appearances at an unequaled five positions (second baseman, left fielder, right fielder, third baseman, and first baseman).[4]

But he is not eligible for the Hall of Fame because he admitted to breaking the cardinal rule against betting on baseball. Amazingly, he has applied for reinstatement four times, all of which have been either ignored or denied in large part due to his acknowledgment that he *continues* to legally bet on baseball.[5]

Bill Clinton had remarkable achievements during his administration. He reduced the national debt by $363 billion—the largest three-year debt pay-down in American history. He converted the largest budget deficit in history ($290 billion) to the largest surplus ($237 billion). He was president over one of the longest economic expansions in American history—one that lasted 115 months and created more than 22 million new jobs.[6] Whenever Bill Clinton is mentioned, three words will always come to mind and stand at the fore: *Impeachment* and *Monica Lewinsky*.

Why are the stories of a king, two world-class athletes, and the most powerful man in the world—a president of the United States—all afflicted with a sad commentary? Why are they in the shadow of the valley of defeat instead of enjoying the sunshine on the mountaintop of victory? In every case it was due to *a lack of self-control*. We've seen it in the past and it continues in the present. Reputations can be impugned. Athletes can be impaired. Presidents can be impeached. CEOs can be imprisoned because of a lack of self-control.

I candidly admit that, at times, I am desperately in need of exercising this emotional muscle. Perhaps you are like me. There are times I have kept eating when I should have quit eating. I have said something when I should have said nothing. I have put my nose where it didn't belong and made the mistake of not just losing my temper, but also finding it. We all at times suffer from the same sickness, which is the lack of self-control. Someone has described life in Western culture this way, as "living in a giant all-you-can-eat buffet, one that offers more calories, credit, sex, intoxicants, and just about anything else we can take to excess…with more possibilities for pleasure and fewer rules and constraints than ever before. *The happy few will be those able to exercise self-control.*"[7]

Discipline Dividends

The lack of self-control is evident everywhere and affects almost all of us daily, from road rage to the vitriol we see on social media to the problems of alcoholism, drug abuse, the opioid epidemic, obesity, family discord, and marital breakups. Often the problems either began or continue because of a lack of self-control. This is in no way meant to discount the problem of addiction many people face that is beyond their self-control and in need of professional help and counseling. The flip side of this is there are tremendous benefits that accrue to someone who learns self-discipline. A brighter future awaits those who decide to be in control of themselves. Science backs this up.

Stanford University psychologist Walter Mischel conducted a series of studies on deferred gratification in 1972 now known as "the marshmallow test." It was performed on children ages four to six. A single marshmallow was offered to each child, but the child was promised two marshmallows instead of one if they could resist eating the first marshmallow right away. Researchers wanted to know how long children could resist the temptation. Some kids grabbed the marshmallow the moment the researchers walked out of the room. But others, doing their best to resist, employed a variety of tactics to bolster their resistance. They sang songs, played games, covered their eyes, looked away, or talked to themselves. Some put their heads on a desk and tried to go to sleep.

The objective was to see if the ability to maintain self-control and to defer instant gratification would correlate to long-term academic achievement. Sixteen children participated, and their academic record was tracked all the way through their high school graduation. Amazingly, researchers found a tremendous difference between the "one marshmallow now" and "two marshmallows later" kids. Kids who exercised the greatest self-control were more academically accomplished. They scored on average 210 points higher on the SAT and, equally incredibly, the "marshmallow test" proved to be twice as powerful as the child's IQ as an indicator of academic success.

The more self-controlled kids were also more socially competent. They took more initiative, were better at problem solving, and handled pressure more effectively. A follow-up study conducted when these children were in their early forties discovered that the "two marshmallows later" children had higher incomes, stronger marriages, and happier careers.[8]

Sociologist Bradley Wright and psychiatrist David Carreon shared research that found: "People with more self-control live longer, are happier, get better grades, are less depressed, are more physically active, have lower resting heart rates, have less alcohol abuse, have more stable emotions, are more helpful to others, get better jobs, earn more money, have better marriages, are more faithful in marriage, and sleep better at night."[9]

Lest you doubt the vital importance and exponential power of self-control, think about the following words: *civil rights* and *racial equality*. Who comes to your mind? None other than one of the greatest proponents and practitioners of self-control the world has ever known, Dr. Martin Luther King Jr. The iconic civil rights leader was given plenty of reasons and opportunities to uncage the lion. He was provoked relentlessly, was physically threatened and attacked by bigoted people, and was repeatedly jailed by state authorities (thirty times in twelve years). King was harassed by the FBI and even vilified by fellow black leaders who urged him to be more aggressive, more violent, and more confrontational. But he lived by his own statement: "No matter how emotional your opponents are, you must be calm."[10] He was.

Only by taming his anger and maintaining self-control did King earn the right to become a messenger of peaceful struggle to his nation. In 1964, the preacher was awarded the Nobel Peace Prize for his work during the civil rights movement. He summed up his legacy when he remarked, "The time is always right to do what is right."[11]

Self-control is an indispensable quality for those who would be leaders, for leaders must first lead themselves before they can properly lead others. In Ronald Reagan's first inaugural address as governor of California, he said, "If no one among us is capable of governing himself, then who among us has the capacity to govern someone else?"[12]

Deny Thyself

What exactly is self-control? Twenty-four hundred years ago, Greek historian Xenophon put it this way: "Temperance [self-control] may be defined as: moderation in all things healthful; total abstinence from all things harmful."[13] Someone else has said that "self-discipline is choosing to do what is right when you feel like doing what is wrong," but that definition is not always accurate. Sometimes self-control is a matter of choosing between two things that are right, but choosing the one that is more right or better. Self-discipline or self-control could also be described as knowing you can do something, but you won't do it if it is wrong or harmful. On the other hand, self-control may mean to do the costly action that you'd rather avoid. My definition of self-control is, "Lining up your 'want to' with your 'should do' and then doing it."

A Man Under Control

Two of the three greatest home-run hitters of all time, Hank Aaron and Babe Ruth, couldn't do it. The winningest pitcher of all time, Cy Young, couldn't do it. The hitter with the all-time best batting average, Ty Cobb, couldn't do it. The all-time strikeout king and the one with the most no hitters, Nolan Ryan, couldn't do it. But a part-time player who couldn't hit—a pitcher who won only eighty games over a nineteen-year career—became the only person in history to do it. New York Yankees relief pitcher Mariano Rivera became the first player unanimously elected into the National Baseball Hall of Fame.

If a Christian Hall of Fame existed, perhaps only one person would be elected unanimously. The apostle Paul wrote thirteen of the twenty-seven books in the New Testament, the most of any author. Because of that, he is Christianity's greatest and most influential theologian, and the greatest missionary in the history of the church. On three mission trips that lasted over ten years, Paul traveled ten thousand miles, taking nine months of actual travel time. He visited more than fifty cities in those travels and preached the gospel to the emperor of the Roman Empire.

Beyond that, Paul was responsible—more than any other person— for shifting the focus of the Christian religion from the proclamation of Jesus to the proclamation about Jesus.[14] Because of his influence, Christianity spread to the point that after several centuries the Roman Empire officially adopted Christianity as its singular religion. Paul shifted Christianity from a Jewish emphasis to a Gentile emphasis, so Christianity would not be just a sect within Judaism. It would become a worldwide faith, and the Christian church became the dominant religious, cultural, social, political, and economic institution of the Western world.[15]

Paul was a paragon of self-control. He traced the tremendous success he had in his life directly to this virtue. He reminds us why self-control is important and instructs us on how to achieve it.

A lion named "self" lives within each of us. This animal is wild and destructive but tamable. The biggest enemy you will have to your success, to going where you can and should go and being who you can and should be, will always be you. If you want to win the battle of life, you have to tame that lion within.

You Must Have a Real Desire to Win

I love Paul because, like me, he loved sports. He talked about living the Christian life, which is a life lived for God's glory and under the power of the gospel, in terms of running a race. And he tells us that if we are going to win this race and live what we call the cross-shaped life, it begins and ends with self-control:

> Do you not know that in a race all the runners run, but only one gets the prize? Run in such a way as to get the prize (1 Corinthians 9:24).

Since the time of Alexander the Great, athletics had dominated Greek society. They were a sports-crazy culture. The most important athletic events were the Olympic Games, which were held every fourth year in Athens, and the Isthmian Games, which were held every other year in Corinth. These events had something for everybody: running, jumping, spear throwing, boxing, wrestling, and chariot racing. Everyone that competed was required to take an oath that said, "I trained for at least ten months and I will not resort to unfair tricks." This was back before the days of HGH, steroids, and stimulants.

Everyone was eligible. Everyone could enter and anybody who wanted to compete could compete, but only one could win. There would be only one who would win the race, who would win the wrestling match, the boxing match, the long jump, and the spear throw. So, Paul says rightly, "If you are going to be in it, be in it to win it." There was great motivation to win. Your name and your hometown would be announced to the crowds as you were awarded first place. You would be given a triumphant parade in your hometown. You would receive a financial gift of five hundred drachmas. You would be given the right to sit at a place of honor for all succeeding games for the rest of your life. Your children would receive a free education for life. You would be exempt from military duty for the rest of your life, and you would never have to pay taxes again.

Everybody wanted to win. In the race of life, we are all born running. If you have to run anyway, why not run to win? Why not make every day of your life count for God? The first step to doing that is to have a real desire to win—a real desire to live a life that pleases God and blesses others.

The first step to winning is wanting. Almost without exception, when two individuals or teams are competing for a championship, it is the one that wants it the most that wins. Their fire burned a little bit hotter. Their desire was just a little bit higher.

> ### The first step to winning is wanting.

The bottom line is we all do what we really want to do and what we really have a desire to do with our life. If you really want to come to church, you will. If you really want to read your Bible, you will. If you really want to spend time with God, you will. If you really want to be faithful in your finances, you will. If you really want to worship, and serve, and be sent and grow as a disciple, you will.

You Must Exercise Rigorous Discipline to Win

Winning doesn't come automatically; it is more than just showing up. As Paul states,

> Every athlete exercises self-control in all things. They do it to receive a perishable wreath, but we an imperishable (1 Corinthians 9:25 ESV).

You have to pay a price to be a winner and the currency is called discipline. The Greek word used for exercising self-control gives us the word *agonize*. Athletes in Paul's day trained hard just to be able to compete. In order to enter the games, you had to give proof that you had been training ten months full-time. Then, for thirty days before the event, you trained together daily in public view. Saying you wanted to compete was not the same as proving it.

This is where most people fail in going as high as they could go and as far as they could go and doing what they really could do. Discipline is kind of like eating vegetables. You don't want to do it, but you know you really need to. Parentally, we don't like to discipline our kids and we don't like to discipline ourselves.

Discipline is what we need most in our life but want the least. It is the difference between ability and achievement, between potential and the prize. I've never met anyone who was successful in life that always did only what they wanted to do. Zig Ziglar, my dear friend, said, "When you do what you need to do, when you need to do it, then you can do what you want to do when you want to do it."

It takes discipline to do that extra rep when you are lifting weights. At 211 degrees, water is just hot; at 212 degrees, it boils. With boiling water comes steam and with steam you can power a locomotive. It takes discipline to exercise that one-degree difference.[16] You may not love discipline, but you are going to have to live it if you are going to win your race and live the life that glorifies God and blesses others.

Michael Phelps is not only the greatest swimmer who has ever lived, but he is the most successful and decorated Olympian of all time with a total of twenty-eight medals. He holds the all-time record for Olympic gold medals with twenty-three, Olympic gold medals in individual events with thirteen, and Olympic medals in individual events with sixteen. He won eight gold medals in 2008, an all-time record. He won the most medals of any athlete in four Olympics in a row. The key? Discipline and self-control.

Phelps would swim eighty thousand meters every week, which is nearly fifty miles. He practiced twice a day. He trained five to six hours a day, six days a week doing both vertical kicking and underwater kicking. He used gear from kickboards, pull buoys, training paddles, and snorkels to make his swimming even more difficult. To have the energy to do that, he had to eat twelve thousand calories a day.[17]

He paid a price to go for the gold. Do you want to know something amazing? That gold medal that he worked so hard for? The highest value of all time was the London gold medal, which was worth only $708. It is not even really gold. It is made up of 95.5 percent silver and 1.34 percent gold, with the remainder copper.[18] In time, it will tarnish and fade.

In the ancient Olympic and Isthmian Games, you would either get a winner's crown made out of olive branches or a wreath made out of pine branches. But as soon as you received it, it would have already started to wither. Crowns are fleeting and titles are temporary.

Paul says we are running a race for a crown that will last forever. Would you rather have a gold medal or God's approval? The fame and fortune of this world or the favor of God? To win the only prize that matters, it takes rigorous discipline.

You Must Go in the Right Direction to Win

If you are running in the wrong direction, it doesn't matter how hard you run, how fast you run, or how far you run. Paul says,

> I do not run like someone running aimlessly; I do not
> fight like a boxer beating the air (1 Corinthians 9:26).

You don't win a race by just running around in circles or running where you think you ought to run. You have to run toward the finish line. You don't win a boxing match by just throwing punches in the air, swinging wildly and hoping something connects. In both cases, you've got to be focused on the finish and focused on the fight. If your aim is not right, you will hit the wrong target every time.

You've got to decide, "Who am I? Why am I here? Where am I going?" Too many people are just shadowboxing. Most people are not serious about life because a person is not serious about life until they are serious about God. If you are not headed toward God—the will of God, the work of God, the worship of God—you are headed in the wrong direction. You are just running around in circles.

The finish line is not temporal but eternal. The finish line is not making the most money, having the most stuff, climbing the highest corporate ladder, being the most popular or famous. The finish line is God's glory and the spread of the gospel. This may sound narrow-minded and arrogant, but if Jesus Christ is the real deal, a life lived apart from Jesus Christ as Lord is a wasted life. A life lived for the gold of this world and not the glory of God is a wasted life. A life that is lived for the fame and fortune of this world and not for the favor of God is a wasted life.

> A life lived for the gold of this world and
> not the glory of God is a wasted life.

I don't want to run the race of life only to realize that I was running in the wrong direction. If you are living life the way it was meant to be lived, every day draws you closer to Jesus. Every day positions you on the inside of God's will, looking out, not on the outside of God's will, looking in.

I read a sign one time that said, "If most people drove their cars the way they plan their lives, they would never get out of the driveway." You need to focus on the finish, and the finish is not a place; the finish is a person named Jesus. To win the race, you've got to go in the right direction.

You Must Maintain a Relentless Determination to Win

In order to run the best race that you can, to fight the best fight that you can, you have to be in the best shape that you can be in. Paul concludes with this striking picture:

> No, I strike a blow to my body and make it my slave so that after I have preached to others, I myself will not be disqualified for the prize (1 Corinthians 9:27).

Either self will control you or you will control self. The one that wins is the one that has the greatest determination. Many people want to be in shape but aren't determined enough to exercise. Lots of people wish to be financially stable but aren't determined enough to stick to a budget. Many people want to lose weight but aren't determined enough to watch what they eat. We want the prize of success, but we are not determined enough to pay the price of success. Every day you must determine how you run your race.

You can never let your guard down. You can never take your eye off the finish line. You can never slack off or take shortcuts. The only runner that wins is the one who crosses the finish line. You need to remember your race is not over, and your fight is not finished, until you draw your last breath. It is how you finish, not how you start, that counts. My biggest goal in life today, and until the day I die, is to finish well. I don't want to run my race only to be disqualified at the end.

In Greek culture, nothing was more shameful for a community or a town than the disqualification of one of its athletes. What Paul was talking about here was being disqualified from being the representative of Jesus and the messenger of the gospel that we are all called to be.

Paul was not talking about losing your salvation, but rather losing the tremendous privilege of being a positive example for Jesus, of being a credible messenger of the gospel and being used of God as greatly as he wants to use you. That is why every day what you may assume are little things are actually big. It is the little things that will keep you in the race, will keep you going in the right direction and making the right decisions. It takes discipline and determination. It takes discipline and determination to get into God's word. It takes discipline and determination to be discipled in a small group. It takes discipline and determination to make worship with God's people a regular habit. It takes discipline and determination to be sent to share the gospel both here and around the world.

If you are an unbeliever, if you are not a follower of Jesus, you aren't even in the race. In order to run in the Olympics or the Isthmian Games you had to be a Greek citizen. You have to be a part of the family of God to be in the real race of life. If you are not a follower of Jesus, you can't possibly win because you are not running in the race. The good news is that the moment you give your life to Jesus Christ, you are in the race; you are qualified to run. This is one race where everybody can win. We are not competing with each other; we are competing against ourselves.

Haile Gebrselassie, who won two Olympic gold medals in the 10,000-meter run, said, "When you run the marathon, you run against the distance, not against the other runners and not against the time." You run your own race. It will be up to your desire, your discipline, your direction, and your determination whether you win or are disqualified.

The good news is we can win. That is why the Bible is filled with examples of ordinary people just like you and me who won their race—Joseph, Moses, Paul, Peter, James, John, Daniel. They were all people just like us, but they ran and they won. By God's grace and power, so can we.

Cotton Fitzsimmons used to be the coach of the Atlanta Hawks. He was quite a character and also a great motivator. One year the Hawks weren't very good and they were getting ready to play the Boston Celtics. The Hawks were in a long losing streak and the Celtics—well, they were the Boston Celtics. So, Fitzsimmons got his players together right before the game and gave a pep talk centered around the word *pretend*. He said, "Men, when you go out there tonight, forget that you are in last place. Pretend you are in first place. Forget you have been in a long losing streak. Pretend you are on a long winning streak. Forget this is a regular game. Pretend this is a game for the championship."

The Hawks went out on that court fired up, and the Celtics blew them out. They came into the locker room, and Fitzsimmons was upset and about to read them the riot act. But then one of his players came up with a big grin on his face, slapped Fitzsimmons on the back, and said, "Cheer up, coach. Pretend we won!"

Life is too short and too valuable to pretend. We must quit pretending we can do what we want, buy what we want, go where we want, say what we want, and take what we want without respecting other people and certain principles and practices. That's what the lion inside all of us wants to do, and it must be tamed or we will never win the race of life we are all running and become all we can be and do all we can do.

Getting Hold of You

As with most character traits, talking about self-control is easier than practicing it. Self-control is more like a muscle than a power switch you turn on and off. It weakens immediately after use, but it strengthens with frequent use.[19] That is why maintaining self-control is so hard for us, because it is a muscle that will either strengthen with constant practice or atrophy from inactivity. Every part of a productive life is joined at the hip to self-control, whether it is playing a musical instrument, learning a new language, a new skill, or just learning to work a computer. Self-control is essential, which may be why Aristotle called self-control "the hardest victory."

So how do we constantly win that victory? How do we triumph over the greatest enemy we all face—ourselves? I suggest three steps. First of all, *we must expect our self-control to be tested.* If temptation didn't exist, we wouldn't need self-control. A civil war rages inside every human being. Describing his own inward battle, the apostle Paul spoke for all of us when he said, "I do not do the good I want to do, but the evil I do not want to do—this I keep on doing" (Romans 7:19). The battle for self-control is a real battle and one that never takes a break, never calls a truce, and never ceases fire. Never. The time to be alarmed is when the battle is no longer raging.

David Brooks stated the issue perfectly: "We have a side to our nature that is sinful—selfish, deceiving, and self-deceiving—but we have another side to our nature that is in God's image, that seeks transcendence and virtue. The essential drama of life is the drama to *construct character,* which is an engraved set of *disciplined habits*, a settled disposition to do good."[20]

What Brooks said leads to the second step we must take: *we must expose our weaknesses.* The most important part of any battle is making sure that we know our enemy better than our enemy knows us. That is why counterintelligence is so important in any war. We must honestly face up to those areas that test our self-control the most so we can be prepared when that temptation comes. For example, if you know you have a sweet tooth or if you know you have a problem with overeating, be honest enough to admit that is a point of weakness for you and use that weakness to help you develop your strength by practicing self-denial. Also, realize when you are trying to lose weight that food is an opportunity for you to learn to say no to your feelings and your impulses—skip dessert after a meal, drink a glass of water instead of a soda, or drive by the donut shop and just keep going.

There are two keys to self-control: learning to say yes to what is right and learning to say no to what is wrong. Many times the latter step must precede the former. About ten years ago, I finally had to realize and own that I was a Coke-a-holic. Atlanta is the home of Coca-Cola, and since Atlanta is basically my home, I assumed drinking Coke was my civic duty. One evening at dinner with my wife, however, I looked at the Coke can in my hand and thought, *It cannot be good for me to drink this—at least not as much as I am drinking.* I made a decision that night to say no to sodas for the rest of my life. I have kept that now for almost eleven years and the thrill of knowing that Coca-Cola no longer controls me has been worth the price I paid to give it up. I had to admit first that I was addicted to it before I could say no.

> There are two keys to self-control:
> learning to say yes to what is right and
> learning to say no to what is wrong.

Finally, *we must exercise the discipline muscle.* The best way to start is to take the advice of the author of "the marshmallow test": "The core strategy for self-control is to cool the *now* and heat the *later*—push the temptation in front of you far away in space and time, and bring the distant consequences closer in your mind."[21]

There are three major areas that we all deal with daily. We need to hit the discipline gym and exercise our self-control muscle in these three areas.

Think about the *tongue* where we need to exercise verbal self-control. Did you know that you have the right to remain silent even when you are not being arrested? All my life I've never had to apologize for anything I didn't say. Begin today to make a habit of expanding your listening capacity and decreasing your speaking capacity. It is better to be quiet and let people think you are a fool than to open your mouth and remove all doubt. Today when words are flying through the air like supersonic jets, crashing into feelings everywhere and leaving broken relationships behind, let's dial it back. You always learn more by listening than you do by talking.

Think about our *temper* where we need to learn to exercise emotional self-control. Honestly, at times this can be my weakest area. The wisest man who ever lived, a king named Solomon, said, "Whoever is slow to anger is better than the mighty, and he who rules his spirit than he who takes a city" (Proverbs 16:32 ESV). Whatever you have to do—count to five, walk away, bite your lip—become the master of your temper and not its slave.

The way we use our *time* is another critical area in which we must exercise self-control. The father of modern management, Peter Drucker, said, "Nothing else, perhaps, distinguishes effective executives as much as their tender loving care of time…unless he manages himself effectively, no amount of ability, skill, experience or knowledge will make an executive effective."[22] People talk about killing time. You don't kill time; time kills you. So plan your day, prioritize your time, don't let the urgent take the place of the important. If today were to be your last day, make sure it would be your best day.

Here's how Admiral William H. McRaven describes the job of the Navy SEALs:

> One of our jobs as Navy SEALs is to conduct underwater attacks against enemy shipping. We practiced this

technique extensively during basic training. The ship-attack mission is where a pair of SEAL divers is dropped off outside an enemy harbor and then they swim well over two miles underwater using nothing but a depth gauge and a compass to get to their target. During the entire swim, even well below the surface there is some light that comes through. It is comforting to know there is open water above you, but as you approach the ship, which is tied to a pier, the light begins to fade. The steel structure of the ship blocks the moonlight; it blocks the surrounding streetlamps. It blocks all ambient light. To be successful in your mission, you have to swim under the ship and find the keel, the center line and the deepest part of the ship. This is your objective, but the keel is also the darkest part of the ship where you cannot see your hand in front of your face, where the noise from the ship's machinery is deafening, and where it is easy to get disoriented and fail.

Every SEAL knows that under the keel, at the darkest moment of the mission, is the time when you must be calm—composed—when all your tactical skills, your physical power, and all your inner strength must be brought to bear. If you want to change the world, you must be your very best in the darkest moment.[23]

McRaven was saying if you don't cage the lion of fear at that crucial moment, you will fail to complete your mission. Upon examination, no one has ever changed the world for the better unless they were self-controlled. The good news is you can change the part of the world you live in. You can be your brightest at your darkest moment. It is just a matter of caging the lion.

FORGIVENESS:

When the Doctor Heals Himself

Everyone says forgiveness is a lovely idea,
until they have something to forgive.

C.S. LEWIS[1]

No virtue will test your character like forgiveness. That is true regardless of whether you are the one who needs to forgive or the one who needs forgiveness. Forgiving someone who has wounded us is difficult. But asking forgiveness from those we have wounded may be harder. We think forgiveness is a great idea if we are the ones who need it, but not so great if we are the ones that have to give it.

We consistently tell ourselves that we have a right to carry a grudge. A study in the *Journal of Adult Development* found that 75 percent of those surveyed believe they have been forgiven by God for past mistakes and wrongdoing, but only 52 percent say they have forgiven others. What is even more amazing is that fewer than 43 percent say they have actively sought forgiveness for harms they have done.[2]

People everywhere carry invisible backpacks every day filled with bitterness. I sometimes refer to bitterness, the refusal to forgive, as "the secret killer." Refusing to forgive, carrying grudges, and swimming in a sea of bitterness affects people physically, emotionally, mentally, relationally, and spiritually. Neither the human mind nor the human soul was designed to carry a grudge. Bitterness is a weight that is too heavy to carry and a poison too deadly to swallow, and it greatly affects everyday life.

How often do you read the story of a disgruntled employee who goes in and kills his or her boss and other innocent victims because he or she lost their job or didn't get the promotion? Or how about domestic violence ending in the death of a spouse, a boyfriend, or a girlfriend due to the bitterness of a divorce or a breakup? I've never read a more heartbreaking story than the one titled "A Cold Dose of Vengeance." It still leaves me saddened and dumbfounded every time I read it.

Amy and Ron Shanabarger seemingly had a storybook marriage. They met at the supermarket where they both worked, and he brought her roses nearly every week. He gave her a beautiful diamond ring when he proposed, and her parents loved him. They had a baby boy named Tyler, who was just seven months old and the picture of health until Amy found him facedown in his crib on Father's Day. Instead of waking their son as they often did, Ron had jumped into the shower and told her to go wake Tyler. When she went to turn him over, she discovered his stiff body. Ron told her to dial 9-1-1, but it was too late. The doctor said it was SIDS (sudden infant death syndrome), and they buried Tyler two days later.

But that is not how Tyler died.

Amy sat sobbing in her living room, wondering if she could have saved her baby, if she should have checked on him during the night. And then Ron told her what really happened. As Tyler was cooing and playing with his feet in the crib, Ron wrapped the baby's head in plastic wrap, sat down for dinner, and brushed his teeth, before turning to see his son's last breath. He removed the wrap and turned the baby onto his stomach, switched off the light, and went to bed.

He deliberately wanted Amy to be the one to discover the body. Then he looked at her and said, "Now we're even."

For what? Amazingly, Ron said he had never forgiven Amy for refusing to cut short an ocean cruise with her parents to come home and comfort him when his father died. So, he said he decided to marry her, have a child with her, and kill it.[3]

There may not be a more destructive force on earth than bitterness. I hope I don't offend cat lovers, but I am not one of them. I don't like cats and I never have. I have discovered why. Amazingly, cats never forgive. Primates, like mountain gorillas and chimps, often follow confrontations with friendly behavior like embracing or kissing. Similar behavior has been observed in nonprimates like goats and hyenas. The only species that has so far failed to show outward signs of reconciliation is the domestic cat.[4]

You may be like the woman who was bitten by a dog that was later discovered to be rabid. Hospital tests confirmed it. The woman had rabies. This was at a time before a cure had been fully developed. The doctor had to tell the woman that nothing could be done for her. He said, "My only and best advice to you would be to put your affairs in order as soon as possible."

The dying woman sat back in shock, but finally rallied the strength to request a pen and paper. She wrote furiously. The doctor, wanting to give her time to herself, left and came back after a half hour, and the woman was still writing. The doctor said, "Well, you are a brave woman to be writing out your will." She said, "This is not my will. This is a list of people I plan to bite before I die."

Too many people, I fear, carry a list like that around in their pocket. We live in a culture full of walking volcanos where people appear calm on the outside, but just beneath the surface is a boiling, seething cauldron of bitterness.

The Healing Feeling

I was fascinated recently to read how carrying a grudge weighs you down. Researchers at Erasmus University in the Netherlands asked people to write about a time when they either gave forgiveness or withheld it. These human guinea pigs were then asked to jump as high as they could five times without bending their knees. Incredibly, the forgivers jumped the highest, about 11.8 inches on average, while the grudge holders jumped 8.5 inches—a 40 percent difference! It was a startling illustration of how forgiveness can actually unburden you.[5]

Drs. Frank Minirth and Paul Meier researched ten thousand patients and diagnosed the top three reasons for burnout. Most would have guessed that stressful overextension and overwork would be the number one reason people burn out, but "burning the candle at both ends" came in third. The second cause of burnout was workaholism that causes someone to be compulsive and perfectionistic. And the most dominant cause of burnout? Bitterness. Our unwillingness to forgive, either others or ourselves, is the number one reason for burnout.[6]

The famed Mayo Clinic has documented that forgiveness is good for the mind and also the body. It gives both mental and physical health. It can lead to:

- healthier relationships
- improved mental health
- less anxiety, stress, and hostility
- lower blood pressure
- fewer symptoms of depression
- a stronger immune system
- improved heart health
- improved self-esteem[7]

I majored in accounting in college. I was taught early on the value of the bottom line. Just thinking logically from a cost-benefit analysis, the bottom line of choosing to exercise forgiveness rather than holding on to bitterness makes it a no-brainer. The benefit of forgiveness far outweighs the cost of forgiving, but the benefit of bitterness is far outweighed by the price of remaining bitter.

Dale Carnegie tells about a visit to Yellowstone Park where he saw a grizzly bear. This huge bear was in the center of a clearing, feeding on some food that campers had left behind. He was eating alone. No other creatures were around or dared to draw near, but after a few moments a skunk walked through the clearing right toward the food and took his place next to the grizzly. He began helping himself to the meal. The bear didn't object, growl, or even move, and Carnegie knew why. He said, "The grizzly knew the high cost of getting even."[8]

You can never really get even with anyone. No matter what you do to them, it will not remove the effects of what they have done to you. When all you try to do to someone is get even, you actually shortchange yourself. Famed football coach Lou Holtz said, "You will never get ahead of anyone as long as you try to get even with him."[9] Bitterness will always keep you under the power of the person who harmed you. Forgiveness sets you free.

What do we mean by forgiveness? I struggled to define this word, and I am not sure why. Perhaps because the word is so emotionally charged. It is one of the hardest character traits to produce under certain circumstances. Indeed, the thought of it brings almost as much pain as the hurt calls for forgiveness. The best definition for this word I've come across is Archibald Hart's: "Giving up my right to hurt you for hurting me."[10]

Jesus Christ told a parable in the Gospel of Matthew in which he describes a man deeply in debt who is about to be thrown into debtors' prison, but instead the holder of the debt forgives the man and cancels the debt (Matthew 18:21-35). Jesus actually uses two Greek words to describe what this forgiveness entailed. One word meant "release" or "to let go of." The other word was a financial term that meant "to cancel a debt." That really is a perfect picture of forgiveness.

Forgiveness is making a conscious decision to drop the backpack of grudges you have been carrying around, to let them go and leave them behind, and in the process, tear up the debt of repayment for someone's wrongdoing.

From the time you are born you immediately interact with other people. You grow up in a family, go to school, play on a team, join a club, get into business, and your life is filled with personal interactions. You will discover there are two situations no one can avoid regardless of how good a person may be, how hard a person tries, how nice someone is. You will be in both of these two situations: You will need to be forgiving and you will need to be forgiven.

Forgiveness demands more character than we even realize. Have you ever been hurt, mistreated, disappointed? Right now, think about the person or the persons who have hurt you the most, mistreated you the worst, disappointed you the greatest. Either you have forgiven that person or you haven't. If you have and you are honest, it may be the hardest thing you have ever done. If you haven't, you may assume it is too difficult for you. But before you convince yourself, consider one man's story.

Good Old Joe

One of the reasons why the Bible is so valuable is that it gives us real life examples of real people who faced real hurt and heartache just like we do. Rather than becoming victims, they became victors. Rather than sinking into the quicksand of bitterness, they were able to get to the oasis of forgiveness. One such man dominates much of the first book of the Bible, and his *Survivor* story climaxes with one of the greatest displays of forgiveness found anywhere.

To say Joseph grew up in a dysfunctional family would be a gross understatement. If his family were alive today, we would have never heard of the Kardashians! His dad fathered thirteen children by four different mothers (two were his wives and two were his mistresses). He had eleven brothers and one sister, and ten out of eleven brothers hated his guts because they were actually just his half-brothers. If you have ever experienced sibling rivalry, then you know what Thanksgiving was like at Joseph's house.

His mother is his father's favorite woman. He is the favorite son of both the favorite woman and the dad. His brothers grow to hate him so much that they hatch a scheme to kill him. They put him into a pit to leave him for dead only to be persuaded by another brother not to kill him. So, instead, they sell him to human traffickers for twenty pieces of silver. Joseph is taken away from his family at seventeen years of age, never (he thought) to see his father again.

Murphy's Law kicks in for Joseph and everything worsens. He becomes a slave on a plantation for eleven years. When he refuses to sleep with his master's wife, she falsely accuses him of rape, and he is thrown into prison. Because of his brothers, Joseph has gone from the pit to the plantation to prison, and he hasn't done anything wrong.

But the story has a great ending because he eventually becomes the prime minister of Egypt. Through a series of events, the narrative comes full circle, and now his brothers are at his mercy. He can do whatever he wants to them, and he would be justified in the eyes of most people and the law. Even our own president has admitted that his two guiding principles in business are: "Always get even," and "Hit back harder than you were hit."[11] Joseph doesn't do what many consider to be normal or even expected. Instead, he forgives his brothers, and he shows us not just how but why we should forgive. He did it by taking a wide-angle view.

Anyone who knows photography can tell you that one of a photographer's staples is a wide-angle lens because it has a short focal length and a wide field of view. It allows the camera to capture much more of the scene than a normal lens can. When Joseph took a wide-angle view of his life, a view of what had really happened, forgiveness was the best option.

How did Joseph keep from being burned by the fire of bitterness, avoid drowning in the sea of bitterness, become immune to the poison of bitterness? He refused to do four things that we should all avoid if we believe character still counts.

Never Take God's Place

> When Joseph's brothers saw that their father was dead, they said, "What if Joseph holds a grudge against us and pays us back for all the wrongs we did to him?" (Genesis 50:15).

Joseph has been reunited with his brothers and his father, and they live together for seventeen years. Joseph has forgiven his brothers and has treated them with kindness. Now their dad has died, and although Joseph had already forgiven them, told them he had forgiven them, and showed them he had forgiven them, they doubted it. They had convinced themselves that the only thing holding Joseph back from getting even was dear old Dad; but now he is gone. They were still feeling guilty over what they had done to Joseph even though they had been forgiven.

As this text reveals, there are two kinds of guilt. Legitimate guilt is when you have not asked for forgiveness. Illegitimate guilt is when you have not accepted forgiveness. One of the reasons why they had never accepted forgiveness is that they had never asked for forgiveness. For the first time, they do what they should have done seventeen years ago and confess.

> So they sent word to Joseph, saying, "Your father left these instructions before he died: 'This is what you are to say to Joseph: I ask you to forgive your brothers the sins and the wrongs they committed in treating you so badly.' Now please forgive the sins of the servants of the

God of your father." When their message came to him,
Joseph wept (Genesis 50:16-17).

They are so fearful and so desperate they even make up a story
about their dad leaving word for Joseph to forgive them. His brothers are still lying and conniving, trying to save their own skin. Joseph
breaks down weeping because he realizes that his brothers didn't
believe him. Even though he had affirmed forgiveness, they had not
accepted forgiveness.

The Old Testament uses four different words for sin, and the
guilty brothers use three of them: *transgression*, *sin*, and *evil*. They
have finally given a full, faithful confession and total, truthful admission of what they have done. They have been in a prison of guilt and
living under the shadow of guilt and fear for seventeen years. The
brothers want to be forgiven, and they realize that confession is the
key that unlocks the door to the prison of guilt.

Now we are introduced to Joseph's amazing response. Churchill
would have called this "Joseph's finest hour."

> His brothers then came and threw themselves down
> before him. "We are your slaves," they said.
> But Joseph said to them, "Don't be afraid. Am I in
> the place of God?" (Genesis 50:18-19).

Joseph understood that God is like us in that he needs to forgive
others who do wrong to him. He is continuously in the position
of the forgiver. But he is unlike us in that he never needs to be forgiven. The simple reason why we always need to forgive others and
we must forgive others is that we are not God. Joseph has no desire
to play God and he is not going to take God's place. You never have
to fear being wronged by a person who is right with God. And when
a person has wronged you, if he gets right with God, he will right
the wrong. If you are right with God, and you keep God in his place,
you will keep you in your place.

Joseph was saying, "I may be the prime minister of Egypt, but God is the Preeminent Master of the universe. Since I sometimes need to receive forgiveness, then I must always be willing to give forgiveness." C.S. Lewis said, "To be a Christian means to forgive the inexcusable because God has forgiven the inexcusable in you."[12] You can forgive, you must forgive, and you will forgive when you remember that just as God has forgiven you, you are to forgive others.

Never Forget God's Providence

Joseph is just getting warmed up. With a wide-angle-lens view, he is about to give us a theological truth that once you believe it, will permanently change your behavior forever. The reason Joseph was able to behave the right way in this situation is that he believed the right thing. Belief always determines behavior. What Joseph is about to say about his life is true about your life:

> "You intended to harm me, but God intended it for good" (Genesis 5:20).

Joseph acknowledges that his brothers had done him wrong. He didn't sugarcoat what they did and he didn't overlook it. When people hurt you, mistreat you, disappoint you, throw you under the bus, the first step to forgiving them is to acknowledge what they've done. At the same time, you have to remember that when it seems as if everything is out of control, God is in control. Behind everything that happens to you—even the bad, the evil, the horrible—God intends to use it ultimately for your good.

Belief always determines behavior.

God could have prevented Joseph's brothers from throwing him into the pit. God could have prevented Joseph from being sold into slavery. God could have prevented Joseph from being falsely accused. God could have prevented Joseph from being thrown into prison. But what his brothers and a scorned woman and a gullible master intended for evil, God intended for good. The sentence structure gives us a wide-angle view of all the bad things that will ever happen to you:

> "As for you, you meant evil against me, but God meant
> it for good" (Genesis 50:20 ESV).

Do you see it? Those three words—"evil," "God," "good"—sum up the providence of God. Providence is God working in your life and in the entire universe where everything is for your good and his glory. Have you heard the saying, "The devil is in the details?" Well, that isn't right. God is in the details!

God never has to say, "Well, that wasn't in the script." With God, everything is in the script. In the movie of your life, there are going to be valleys and deserts, bad times and good times, good and evil, but when the movie ends it will all work out for your good. Joseph was not sold into slavery, put on a plantation, or thrown into prison because he was in the wrong place at the wrong time. Because of God's providence, he was in the right place at the right time.

I hate the word *lucky*. We call someone a lucky dog, thank our lucky stars, and talk about lady luck, tough luck, good luck, bad luck, rotten luck. We even have a cereal called Lucky Charms. If you think every or any event in life is random, then you are out of luck. Nothing is up to chance—everything is up to God.

Joseph had not gotten to be prime minister of Egypt because of luck, because of his resume, because of people he knew, or because of his politics. It was due to God's providence. Remember, all the bad events that happen to you and all the bad people that orchestrate them will be providentially used by God for your good and his glory.

204 CHARACTER STILL COUNTS

Never Doubt God's Plan

The next part of this story has the power to shift our perspective on this entire topic:

> "You intended to harm me, but God intended it for good
> to accomplish what is now being done" (Genesis 50:20).

Just exactly what was being accomplished? God's plan. God has a plan for everything and everyone, and his plan will always accomplish what is for your good and for his glory.

My wife makes some of the best cakes you will put in your mouth. But those spongey masterpieces do not just appear out of thin air; they are the result of a plan. When I look at all the ingredients that she lays out—the butter, the sugar, the flour, the eggs—she doesn't ask me to eat each of those individually. By themselves they would taste terrible, but when she mixes those ingredients together, according to her plan, my soul is it good! There are two words Joseph says to his brothers that you need to write over everything that happens to you, especially the bad, and those are "but God."

This all started when Joseph's brothers sold him into slavery. The situation looked bad, but God had a plan. Joseph says to his brothers, "You sold me, but God sent me." Those two words, "but God," changed everything.

- Their plan was to eliminate Joseph, but God's plan was to elevate Joseph.

- Their plan was to lower Joseph into a pit, but God's plan was to lift Joseph onto a throne.

- Their plan was to desert Joseph, but God's plan was to deliver Joseph.

- Their plan was to sell Joseph out, but God's plan was to pick Joseph up.

That is why Joseph could say with 100 percent confidence, "You intended to harm me, but God intended it for good" (Genesis 50:20).

I don't know what you have gone through in your life or what you are going through right now. I don't know how unfairly you have been treated or are being treated, how unjust your circumstances have been or are now, what kind of bad hand you have been dealt or are being dealt now, but I will tell you what I do know. Whatever else you think or you are hearing, God is saying to you right now, "Everything is going according to plan."

This does not mean that all the events of Joseph's life were good, and not everything that is happening to you is good either. His kidnapping wasn't good, his enslavement wasn't good, and neither was his imprisonment. What you are going through right now may not be good, but God will take all of the bad and turn it into good because that is God's plan for every one of his children. So, when somebody throws you under the bus, leaves you holding the bag, gives you the short end of the stick, or leaves you high and dry, God will use it to accomplish his plan.

God's plan for you is bigger than you and bigger than your plan for you. Events do not happen by coincidence; they happen by providence. Providence guarantees that everything is progressing according to God's plan.

Never Question God's Purpose

God doesn't play games with your life. God has a purpose for your life. He has a purpose for every life. He has a purpose for everything—even for Joseph in the midst of his darkest hour.

> "You intended to harm me, but God intended it for good
> to accomplish what is now being done, the saving of
> many lives" (Genesis 50:20).

Joseph didn't know it, but the purpose of everything that happened to Joseph was so that God could put Joseph in a place to be a savior for his people—and not just to be a savior for his people, but so that his people could bring the Savior into the world.

Every plan has a purpose. Almost twenty years ago Teresa and I built our house according to the plan that she picked out over many months. The purpose of that plan was not just to build *a* house but *the* house she wanted. That was the purpose of our house plan, and every doorknob and paint color was meticulously chosen according to our plan.

Behind every plan is a purpose, and the same is true for God's plan for your life. It wasn't drawn up last night. God didn't make it up on the fly, and he doesn't have to improvise or adjust it as time progresses. God's plan for all of us is wrapped around God's purpose for the entire world.

God doesn't react when things go awry in your life because God never reacts. God acts before anything happens, and he providentially funnels everything into the container of his plans and purposes. It took Joseph twenty-three years to understand that God's purpose was "the saving of many lives."

> God doesn't react when things go awry
> in your life because God never reacts...
> he providentially funnels everything into the
> container of his plans and purposes.

What lives was he referring to? Who needed to be saved? Earlier, he had said to his brothers, "But God sent me ahead of you to preserve for you a remnant on earth and to save your lives by a great deliverance" (Genesis 45:7).

He wasn't just trying to save his family. He was trying to save his family who would become a nation that would send a Savior into the world. If his brothers don't sell Joseph into slavery, he doesn't go to Egypt. If he doesn't go to Egypt, Israel wouldn't exist. If Israel didn't exist, neither does Jesus. If Jesus doesn't exist, salvation never comes to the world.

Joseph didn't know that one day a famine would come that could destroy his family, but God did. Joseph didn't know that being in prison would lead him to the palace and put him in a position of such power he could save an entire nation, but God did. Joseph didn't know that God had to send him to Egypt so ultimately his family would give birth to the nation of Israel from which Jesus Christ, the Savior of the world was born, but God did.

God had a purpose for the pit and for the prison. It was all so that Joseph could be placed into a palace where he would have the power and the position to save a family, a nation, and a world. Every time Joseph was put where he didn't want to be, he was right where God wanted him to be, because God had a bigger purpose in mind. That is why Joseph lovingly and honestly says to his brothers,

> "Don't be afraid. I will provide for you and your children." And he reassured them and spoke kindly to them (Genesis 50:21).

And that is when you know you have really forgiven someone. Forgiveness is comprised of words spoken and also action taken. Forgiveness is both said and shown.

Only the water of forgiveness can quench the fire of bitterness. When Joseph's first son was born, he named him Manasseh, which literally means "one who causes to forget." That is exactly what Joseph did. He didn't hold a grudge and he didn't look back. This was a doctor that healed himself, because he didn't take God's place, forget God's providence, doubt God's plan, or question God's purpose.

The God controlling every event in his life is still sitting on the throne of the universe, and he is still over all the circumstances of your life. Yes, he will allow evil to be done to you, but in the end, he promises he will make it good for you. The God in you is bigger than the evil that others do to you. Our job is to forgive what others do to us. God's job is to providentially fit what others do to us into his plan and purpose for our good and his glory. By the way, he has a 100 percent success rate!

If you doubt this can happen, consider that God took the greatest evil ever done to anyone—the crucifixion of his own Son—and transformed it into the greatest good of all, which is the salvation of all who accept him.

All Is Forgiven

I want to be careful that I don't make forgiveness sound easy. If it were, everybody would practice it. It takes every ounce of your best character to exercise forgiveness, but you can do it. I have learned that there are necessary steps to bring forgiveness to completion.

First of all, *face it*. You cannot cancel a debt that you have not acknowledged. You cannot forgive a wrongdoing by sweeping it under the rug. Acknowledging the hurt that someone has done to you is healthy. It helps you lance the boil and deal with the impacts of the emotional pain to your mental health. Admitting your pain is actually the easy part, but next comes the hard part.

Forgive it. Write this on your mirror because you'll do well not to forget it: Forgiveness is a choice. No one has ever been forced into the prison of bitterness and no one can be forced to stay in the prison of bitterness. Everyone holds the key of forgiveness in their pocket, and they can choose to unlock that prison door and get out of jail any time they want to.

Don Colbert pulls no punches when he rightly says, "Those who forgive are those who choose to forgive. Forgiveness is not automatic, unintentional, or happenstance. It is a choice and an act of the will...Saying 'I forgive' is like taking an emotional shower—forgiveness cleanses and frees the entrapped soul." [13] The shower of forgiveness is never turned off. It never runs out of water. You can step into it anytime you choose and allow its cleansing waters to wash away the dirt of bitterness that has covered you.

No offense is unforgiveable. Robert Enright, a psychologist who pioneered the study of forgiveness, said, "I have never found a particular injustice in the world that I don't know of at least one person who has forgiven those who have perpetrated it." [14]

Finally, *forsake it.* It is not enough just to cancel the debt that someone owes you for doing you wrong. You've got to tear up the document, bury it, and refuse to ever dig it up again. In our justice system, we are immune from what is known as double jeopardy. That is, once you are acquitted of a crime, regardless of what other evidence comes up, you can never be tried for that crime again. The case is permanently dismissed.

When you forgive someone, you must dismiss the case. You must resolve to never expose the person who wronged you to double jeopardy. You must "distinctly remember forgetting what that person has done to you."

You will never erase the memory of great hurt and heartache that someone caused you. It may be unrealistic to expect you will. But you can choose to refuse to let it ever control you, have power over you, and never bring it up again, including to the person who hurt you.

Joe Reynolds, a prominent attorney in Houston, Texas, at the time of his death had tried more cases in the state of Texas than any attorney in modern history. He was a dear friend of mine and a wonderful man of God. One day he told me one of the most fascinating stories I have ever heard.

He had cosigned a note with one of his most trusted friends for a piece of property for one million dollars and thought nothing further about it. But one day he got a call from a bank outside of Houston.

"Are you Joe Reynolds?"

"Yes."

"Are you partners with this man and have you cosigned a note with him?"

"Yes."

"Mr. Reynolds, your partner has defaulted on his loan, and you owe this bank one million dollars. We want our money in two days or we are going to foreclose on the property and sue you for damages."

Joe was flabbergasted. To make matters worse, he had cosigned the note without even telling his wife. He told the banker he could not come up with that amount of money, but the banker reiterated that he expected to hear back in two days.

Joe went home and told his wife, who was panic stricken. She said, "What are we going to do?" He said, "Well, we're going to have to sell our home." They lived in a beautiful home on eleven acres of prime property in midtown Houston. They had worked all their lives to save up enough to have this dream home, but now they were going to lose it.

He said not two hours after he told his wife the bad news, as he was sitting in his chair depressed and discouraged, a real estate agent he had never met phoned him.

"Are you Joe Reynolds?"

"Yes."

"Mr. Reynolds, I have a client who would like to buy two acres of your property."

"Well, lady, I am not interested in selling two acres. I need to sell my whole place, so thanks but no thanks."

"Mr. Reynolds, before you say no would you at least let me come to your house and give you this proposal?"

"No, it would be a complete waste of time. But do keep me in mind if you have someone that would like to buy the entire property."

"Mr. Reynolds, please let me just run this proposal by. It won't take you two minutes to look at it, and I will be out of your hair."

"It's a waste of time, but come on out."

This lady drove out to his home, sat down, and said, "Mr. Reynolds, my client would like to buy two acres that are just on the fringe of your property."

"And what is he offering?"

"A million dollars."

At this point, I would have given a million dollars to have seen the look on his face! My friend could hardly believe it. In the span of two hours, God had answered his prayer in a way he never imagined.

Joe called the banker the next day and said, "I will have your money in the office to you tomorrow."

"I knew it," the banker said. "I just knew it!"

"You knew what?" Joe said.

"When I met with our board yesterday, talking about your situation, one of the men said not only would you try not to pay us, but that you would take us to court and sue us. I said, 'I have heard of this Joe Reynolds. He is a man of his word, a godly man, and he will pay us the money.' The board told me if I was right and you did agree to pay, that I could negotiate with you any sum I wanted to, and Joe, the board agreed to cut the debt in half to $500,000."

So, not only did Joe Reynolds come out $500,000 to the good, but he also wound up with a piece of property and kept his home.

That is not the end of the story. Joe never heard again from his so-called friend until about seven years later. They happened to run into each other, and his friend was talking as if nothing had happened.

"I understand from reading the paper that you just cut a deal that netted you over $5 million," Joe said.

"As a matter of fact, I did," the man said.

"When are you going to pay me the $500,000 you owe me?" Joe said.

212 CHARACTER STILL COUNTS

"Joe, I'm not going to pay you. The statute of limitations has run out and there is not a thing you can do about it."

Joe looked at him and said, "Yes, there is one thing I can do about it."

"What is that?"

"I can forgive you and I do. You have to live with it; I don't. God has taken care of me and God will take care of you."

What was true of Joe in the Bible, and what was true of Joe in Houston, Texas, is true of me, you, and every Joe everywhere at any time. When you choose to forgive the way God (and sometimes others) has forgiven you, you will become the doctor that heals yourself.

FAITHFULNESS:

You Can Count on Me

We are not here to be successful,
we are here to be faithful.

MOTHER TERESA[1]

My wife, Teresa, and I love the mountains. Every year we take a week and get away to the beautiful Smoky Mountains. We hang out in one of our favorite places, Pigeon Forge, Tennessee, but on the way, we always pass through Cherokee, North Carolina, an Indian reservation that I have visited many times since I was a little boy. I thrilled then, as my grandchildren thrill now, at the heritage and the customs of Native Americans.

But I am also painfully reminded of the plight of these people who inhabited America before the first immigrants ever came. About 400,000 American Indians living on reservations have the highest rates of poverty, unemployment, and disease of any ethnic group in America. They are faced with a suicide rate that is double that of all other nonwhites and higher levels of school dropouts, alcoholism, and unemployment (45 percent average). One half of all American Indian families currently live below the poverty line.[2] Today, Indians are the poorest of all American ethnic groups.[3]

But the plight of these Indians and the sight of them living on reservations are a reminder of something even greater and that is, candidly, the lack of faithfulness on the part of the American government. History tells us that the spiritual aspect of making treaties escaped the United States government. The US federal government entered into more than 500 treaties with Indian nations from 1778 to 1871, and every one of them was "broken, changed, or nullified when it served the government's interest."[4]

But we see a lack of faithfulness everywhere in our society today. We see it in sports, where the moment an athlete finds that someone is making more money, they want to renegotiate their contract. We see it in an epidemic of divorce, when people no longer want to be faithful to the sacred marital vows they made. We see it in the rash of bankruptcies, when people decide for whatever reason they are no longer going to pay a debt they legally incurred. We see it in the broken promises of politicians, who are faithful in making promises to get elected but unfaithful in keeping them after they are. Have you ever considered just how potent and poisonous faithlessness is? One act of unfaithfulness can cost you:

- your job
- your marriage
- your reputation
- your happiness
- your legacy
- your peace of mind

Sticky Factor

If you want to know just how important being faithful is, just think about the nation we live in and the foundation of its law, which is the Constitution. Had it not been for faithfulness, our nation might look different today and we might not even have a constitution. When the Constitutional Convention met, the delegates adopted certain parliamentary rules for them to live by. But the most significant rules did not come from the parliamentary committee; they actually came from the floor. The most important rule suggested and adopted was that the Convention keep its proceedings secret. The Convention rules provided that "no copy be taken of any entry on the journal and nothing spoken in the house be printed, or otherwise published or communicated without leave."[5] Every delegate was asked to faithfully keep the deliberations and conversations secret for life.

How important was their faithfulness? James Madison later said, "No Constitution ever would have been adopted by the Convention if the debates had been made public."[6] The document that provides for the rule of law in our nation was built on the foundation of faithfulness.

Even though our world struggles to value character, people still take notice of faithfulness. If you want to advance in the corporate world, try displaying good old-fashioned faithfulness. Show up every day on time ready to work, give a full day's work for a full day's wage, and do not quit until the job is done. You will rise above the rest in no time.

One of the most popular tourist attractions in America is Yellowstone National Park. It welcomes up to four million people a year. One site everyone wants to see when they visit is a hole in the ground that spits out hot water. It was discovered in 1870 and given its name because, at the time, it erupted every nine minutes. Since Yellowstone became the world's first national park in 1872, it has erupted more than a million times.

This famous geyser currently erupts on average around twenty times a day or every seventy-four minutes and can be predicted with a 90 percent confidence rate within a ten-minute variation.[7] Amazingly, this geyser is not the tallest or the largest geyser in the park.[8]

Old Faithful is so popular not because it spews water the longest or the highest but because it is faithful.

We sometimes fall into the trap of evaluating people on the basis of their *competency*, when an even more important test is their *consistency*. Successful people don't do things right just occasionally or when they feel like it; they do it consistently. The word *faithfulness* assumes the factor of a reoccurring, repeated action.

Certain batters in baseball are called clutch hitters. These are the hitters who win the game with a crucial hit when the score is close in the last few innings. The assumption is that certain great ballplayers can turn the switch on in a clutch situation when others can't. Studies have proven that the phenomenon of clutch hitters is a myth and "what a hitter does in most clutch situations is pretty much what he does all the rest of the time."[9]

The study goes on to say, "What occurs on a baseball diamond is no different than what happens in every aspect of life. When things are tough the person who comes through is generally the same person who consistently comes through day in and day out when things aren't so tough." The concluding sentence is, "By practicing consistent excellence every day we will not only get the job done when life is mundane, but we'll have a far greater likelihood of coming through in the clutch."[10]

You've Got Mail

What do we mean by faithfulness? I define it this way: *Faithfulness is to be where you are needed to be, do what is needed to be done, and stay until the job is complete.* Every time you go by or into a post office or receive mail you are being reminded of the definition of faithfulness. Inscribed on the James Farley post office that faces Penn Station in New York City is a motto that reads, "Neither snow, nor rain, nor heat, nor gloom of night stays these couriers from the swift completion of their appointed rounds." Even though this is not an official creed or motto of the United States Postal Service, it has long been associated with the American postman, and the postal service officially acknowledges it as its informal motto.[11] Postal service is suspended in severe weather, but their goal is to always faithfully deliver the mail.

I have heard it said that the greatest ability is availability. But in my experience, the greatest ability is reliability. If you are available without being reliable, it would be better off if you were unavailable. The wisest man who ever lived asked this question thousands of years ago: "Many claim to have unfailing love, but a faithful person who can find?" (Proverbs 20:6). Answering Solomon's question is more difficult now than when he wrote it.

> I have heard it said that the greatest ability is availability. But in my experience, the greatest ability is reliability.

The First Marine

We are going to look at a man who was inducted into God's Hall of Fame because of his faithfulness. A Savior ultimately came into this world because of this man's faithfulness. A nation that at one time history had given up for dead is in miraculous existence today because of his faithfulness. He has been called "the father of the faithful" and "the brightest star in the Hebrew heaven" because of his faithfulness. His name is Abraham, and one incident took place in his life that gave him an opportunity to demonstrate and define true faithfulness. He proved himself to be faithful in one of the most difficult circumstances any person has ever faced.

The story actually begins twenty-five years earlier. God called Abraham (at the time his name was Abram) from his home country to begin his plan to redeem the world. His faithfulness kicks in the first day of the story. God told Abraham to leave his country, his people, and his family. He was asking for a tremendous sacrifice. In that day, your identity was wrapped up in the clan you belonged to and the land you lived on. Your security depended upon your clan, because police didn't exist. Your family protected you from robbery or assault or any crime. Your future prosperity was at stake because in your old age, the only people that would care for you would either be your children or your extended family.

Abraham obeys God and leaves with the assurance of God's promise that he would make from Abraham a great nation and he would bless him for eternity.

> Now Sarai was childless because she was not able to conceive (Genesis 11:30).

At the time, Abraham and his wife, Sarai (her name was later changed to Sarah), had been married for at least fifty years. So, even though at the time Abraham had no idea how God would make him into a great nation, seeing that he had no children, he trusted God. Now, twenty-five years later, we come to this story, an inspiring lesson on faithfulness.

Go Where You Need to Go

Spoiler alert—the beginning of the story will leave you dazed, confused, and maybe even angry.

> Some time later God tested Abraham. He said to him, "Abraham!"
>
> "Here I am," he replied.
>
> Then God said, "Take your son, your only son, whom you love—Isaac—and go to the region of Moriah. Sacrifice him there as a burnt offering on a mountain I will show you" (Genesis 22:1-2).

Never before had God ever asked for a human sacrifice. Now, here is God telling Abraham to take the son that he had promised him, the son that carried his every hope, and sacrifice him. But the first sentence of this story is the key to the entire story. God is testing Abraham. The Hebrew word translated "tested" (*nāsāh*) has the idea of proving the quality of something or putting it through some kind of trial. The writer of this story is teaching us an important lesson: We are in the trusting business. God is in the testing business. And testing can be a good thing.

You wouldn't want to fly on an airplane that has never been tested. You wouldn't want a doctor to perform surgery on you if he'd never taken a test in medical school. You wouldn't want an accountant filing your taxes who had never taken a course in finance.

That opening line is to help cushion us from the shock of the story that follows. Keep in mind that the entire story is a test. Why does God test us? God tests us for two primary reasons:

- Testing is an opportunity for God to prove his faithfulness to us.
- Testing is an opportunity for us to prove our faith in God.

We are in the trusting business and God is in the testing business. Faith is shown in faithfulness and faith is grown through faithfulness. God not only gives us faith, but he grows our faith by testing our faith.

> **We are in the trusting business,**
> **and God is in the testing business.**

Probably no one has ever been tested like Abraham. The test

comes in the form of three commands—"take, go, and sacrifice [as a burnt offering]." Now the words hide how graphic this is. When you offered a burnt sacrifice, you first had to kill the animal by cutting its throat. Then you had to dismember the animal and offer the body parts as a sacrifice by fire. This is what God is asking Abraham to do.

How strange that God would ask Abraham to sacrifice the son he had promised him and given him, the son that would become the forerunner of the Jewish nation. It is the son that Abraham loved and this is the first time the word *love* (*'āhab*) is found in the Bible. (Incidentally, the first time *love* is found in the New Testament is in Matthew 3:17 where the heavenly Father affirms his love for his Son.)

How does Abraham respond? Before I tell you, how do you think you would respond? It all depends on how faithful you are.

> Early the next morning Abraham got up and loaded his donkey. He took with him two of his servants and his son Isaac. When he had cut enough wood for the burnt offering, he set out for the place God had told him about (Genesis 22:3).

Amazing—no hesitation, no deliberation, no argumentation, just a simple "I go where I need to go." The ultimate test of faithfulness is whenever we are willing to lay whatever we hold most dear in God's hands.

Ask yourself this test question: "Which do you love more: the _____ God has given to you or the God who has given you the _____?" You can fill in the blank with any word you want to. You could insert *children*, *money*, *life*, *success*, or anything else. Then ask, "Am I willing to go where I need to go no matter what I have to sacrifice or give up?"

Give What You Need to Give

This next sentence paints a picture we need to see and ponder:

> Abraham took the wood for the burnt offering and
> placed it on his son Isaac, and he himself carried the fire
> and the knife (Genesis 22:6).

Abraham and Isaac are going up Mount Moriah. At only twenty-seven hundred feet above sea level, Mount Moriah is not a particularly high mountain. But no one has ever climbed higher than Abraham and Isaac did that day. Today we think of success as becoming wealthy or having a lot of power and influence. In Abraham's day, success was tied to family. The greatest hope a person could have to live a meaningful life and leave a valuable legacy would be to become the father or mother of many descendants who would become people of wealth and influence. Now, God is asking Abraham to sacrifice the only chance he has.

God even reminded Abraham, "This is your only son. This is the son you love." So Abraham has a dilemma. Does he love the son that God gave him more than he loves the God that gave him the son? Is God really his one and only God? Because anything we love more, desire more, want more, crave more, or serve more than God is an idol. This is a checkpoint of Abraham's faith in God and faithfulness to God. God asks him, "Abraham, is your love for me greater than your love for your son? Is your faith in me greater than your feelings for your son?" We have to answer this question almost daily. Will I be faithful now to the God that is always faithful to me?

The way our faith and God's faithfulness operate is this: God will not reveal his faithfulness to us until we reveal our faith in him. Faith means going all in. You can't be half faithful to God. You can't be faithful part of the time to God. You can't be faithful to God only when you feel like it, when it's convenient, when it doesn't cost you anything.

Imagine I said to my wife, Teresa, "I haven't always been faithful to you. But I only messed up one day in the last month." Or how about this? "Honey, I met a woman the other day and you will be so proud of me. I was almost faithful to you." No, she wants me to be faithful on every day that ends in *y*, and God demands, desires, and deserves no less. Abraham comes through with flying colors.

> Abraham took the wood for the burnt offering and placed it on his son Isaac, and he himself carried the fire and the knife. As the two of them went on together, Isaac spoke up and said to his father Abraham, "Father?"
>
> "Yes, my son?" Abraham replied.
>
> "The fire and wood are here," Isaac said, "but where is the lamb for the burnt offering?"
>
> Abraham answered, "God himself will provide the lamb for the burnt offering, my son." And the two of them went on together (Genesis 22:6-8).

Isaac had seen many sacrifices before and he realizes that Dad forgot to bring the lamb. He asks, "Where is the sacrifice?" You have to love Abraham's answer: "God will provide." Abraham was teaching Isaac a valuable lesson. God's business is to keep his promises. Our business is to believe he will keep them and live accordingly.

Abraham was declaring his faith, expressing his faithfulness, and even though he didn't know it, prophesying about the future. This story is a perfect type and picture of what happened nearly two thousand years later. God would provide a sacrificial lamb, but in this case it would be his own Son so our sins could be forgiven. As you go through life, God will test you and stretch your faith, and in the end, he will provide. God always has provided and always will.

Get What You Need to Get

The story is coming to a breathtakingly climatic and surprising conclusion.

> When they reached the place God had told him about, Abraham built an altar there and arranged the wood on it. He bound his son Isaac and laid him on the altar, on top of the wood. Then he reached out his hand and took

the knife to slay his son. But the angel of the LORD called out to him from heaven, "Abraham! Abraham!"

"Here I am," he replied.

"Do not lay a hand on the boy," he said. "Do not do anything to him. Now I know that you fear God, because you have not withheld from me your son, your only son."

Abraham looked up and there in a thicket he saw a ram caught by its horns. He went over and took the ram and sacrificed it as a burnt offering instead of his son. So Abraham called that place The LORD Will Provide. And to this day it is said, "On the mountain of the LORD it will be provided."

The angel of the LORD called to Abraham from heaven a second time and said, "I swear by myself, declares the LORD, that because you have done this and have not withheld your son, your only son, I will surely bless you and make your descendants as numerous as the stars in the sky and as the sand on the seashore. Your descendants will take possession of the cities of their enemies, and through your offspring all nations on earth will be blessed, because you have obeyed me" (Genesis 22:9-18).

Abraham is about to do the unthinkable, the unbelievable when the angel of God stops him. What is the whole point of this story? This is a test. Now Abraham understands that God did not want Isaac; he wanted Abraham! He did not want Abraham's son, but Abraham's surrender. He did not want Abraham's family; he wanted Abraham's faith demonstrated in faithfulness. God knew what was in Abraham's heart, but God wanted Abraham to know what was in his heart.

God tested Abraham, Abraham passed the test, and this is how Abraham got a *test*imony! Every test is an opportunity to gain a testimony. And Abraham's testimony is even more amazing because there is a secret to Abraham's faith and faithfulness:

> On the third day Abraham looked up and saw the place in the distance. He said to his servants, "Stay here with the donkey while I and the boy go over there. We will worship and then we will come back to you" (Genesis 22:4-5).

Abraham said "we" will return because he is convinced they are going to come back together. He didn't understand what he was being asked to do, but he trusted the one who was asking him to do it. Why? The answer is found in a Bible passage that looks back over two thousand years to what happened:

> By faith Abraham, when God tested him, offered Isaac as a sacrifice. He who had embraced the promises was about to sacrifice his one and only son, even though God had said to him, "It is through Isaac that your offspring will be reckoned." Abraham reasoned that God could even raise the dead, and so in a manner of speaking he did receive Isaac back from death (Hebrews 11:17-19).

God had made Abraham a promise that Isaac would be a part of a great line of people who would bless the world. Although God was asking him to sacrifice Isaac, Abraham knew that God would never break a promise, so he concluded that God would rescue Isaac, even raise him from the dead if necessary. He was unwittingly prophesying an event that would occur two thousand years later. God would provide a sacrifice with God's own Son. He would die for our sins, but God would raise him from the dead. The proof of your faith in God is your faithfulness to God. If God never fails to do what he says he will do, we never have to hesitate to be faithful to do what he tells us to do.

When you put this story in context, it reads like a preview of coming attractions. It is a picture of a God who makes the ultimate sacrifice, who put his one and only beloved Son on the altar of sacrifice for our sin so that we would never have to be sacrificed for our sin. By the way, do you know where Mount Moriah is? It is the mountaintop where Jerusalem and the temple stood. It is the place where Jesus Christ did die for the sins of the world, the place where the Lord did provide a Savior for the world.

Note God's final words to Abraham: "'I swear by myself, declares the LORD...I will surely bless you...and through your offspring all nations on earth will be blessed, because you have obeyed me'" (Genesis 22:15,17,18).

God swears an oath by himself. No higher oath could be given. No surer promise could be made because God always keeps his word and never breaks a promise. God will never give you a reason to distrust him even though your reason may say you can't trust him. Because Abraham remained faithful he became not only the father of all the Jews but of all the faithful who come to believe in the one who was sacrificed—Jesus Christ. Because of his faithfulness, he became the father of a family that will number more than the sands of the sea.

> **God will never give you a reason to distrust him even though your reason may say you can't trust him.**

Your faithfulness will never exceed God's favor. If you honor God with your faithfulness, God will honor you more. If you bless God with your faithfulness, God will bless you more.

Join the Marines

Though I never served in the military, I respect those who have. I show affection for Marines because my brother-in-law served in the Marine Corps, as did one of my best friends. More than two hundred years ago when the United States Marine Corps was being formed, a lot of time and thought was given to an appropriate motto. They finally chose the Latin phrase *semper fidelis*, which means "always faithful." Those are two powerful words and the most important is the word *always*. Always means—well, always, because of the cost you may have to pay, the climb you may have to endure, or the conflict you may have to face. You go where you need to go, you do what needs to be done, and you stay until the job is complete. Fortunately, faithfulness is a discipline that can be developed.

First of all, *begin with being faithful in the little things*. One of the best practices parents can instill in their children at an early age is to teach them to be faithful in seemingly small ways. Teach them to be faithful to do what they say they will do, to finish any job they are given, and to do the best they can. Teach them to make their bed, pick up their clothes, and do chores they are assigned until finished. Martin Luther King Jr. said,

> If a man is called to be a street sweeper, he should sweep streets even as Michelangelo painted, or Beethoven composed music, or Shakespeare wrote poetry. Sweep streets so well that all the host of heaven will pause to say, "Here lived a great street sweeper who did his job well."[12]

You learn both by observation and experience that the little things often make the biggest difference. The little things make big things possible or impossible. I miscarried one row of numbers on a final math exam when I was in the sixth grade, and it cost me an *A* for the course. I missed a connecting flight in Paris by twenty seconds, and it cost me an overnight stay at an expensive hotel and a lost day on a key mission trip.

Wilhelm Reiss, a German inventor, developed a device for transmitting sound over wire. Had he moved two electrodes just one-thousandth of an inch so that they would touch each other, he and not Alexander Graham Bell would have been known as the inventor of the telephone.[13]

The second key to developing faithfulness is to always *show up whenever you are able to do so.* That means you don't call in sick when you are not. Let's face it. If all of us went in to work only when we felt like it, most of us would be on extended vacations most of the time! Don't be tempted to either let your responsibility go or let someone take your place when you should be in place.

I, along with the rest of the sports world, witnessed something in the summer of 1995 I never thought I would see. Baltimore shortstop Cal Ripken Jr. brought the entire sports world to its feet in a universal standing ovation by breaking a record that many people thought would stand forever. It wasn't a great exhibition of strength, speed, agility, dexterity, or power he was being honored for. It was just plain old-fashioned faithfulness. On September 6, 1995, Ripken walked onto the baseball field just as he had done 2130 consecutive games before. When he walked out on the field to begin game 2131, he received an uninterrupted twenty-two-minute standing ovation.

Unlike most other great moments in sports history, it was not because of a great catch, a great throw, a great run, or a great shot—a dramatic final-second victory. No championship trophy or ring was given. Cal Ripken Jr. is in the Hall of Fame, and one of the reasons is he just showed up.[14] He just faithfully did his job year after year.

A third step is *always do and give your best.* If you are faithful, you never mail it in, cut corners, or take shortcuts. The wisest king who ever ruled said, "Whatever your hand finds to do, do it with all your might" (Ecclesiastes 9:10). To do otherwise is unfaithful.

The International Olympic Creed says it best: "The most important thing in the Olympic Games is not to win, but to take part, just as the most important thing in life is not the triumph, but the struggle. The essential thing is not to have conquered, but to have fought well."[15]

John Wooden is the winningest and the greatest college basketball coach of all time. He inherited a legacy of the importance of faithfulness from his dad that he passed on to his players. At an early age his dad sat him down when he realized how competitive he was and said, "Johnny, don't try to be better than anyone else, but try to be the best you can be. You are going to be better than some and there are going to be some better than you. You've got to accept that, but you should never accept the fact that you didn't make the effort to do the best that you can do."

In his senior year of high school, Wooden's team made it to the state championship game, which in Indiana is the biggest event of the year. His team lost by one point. He was the only team member who did not cry after the loss. He later credited his reaction to his father's words to him just before he went out to play as a child: "Don't whine, don't complain, don't make excuses...just do the best you can." Coach Wooden knew he had done his best and that nothing else mattered.[16]

Finally, *be all you are wherever you are.* Treat the job you are in right now as if it is the last job you will have. If you want to go higher, to find something better, to discover a place more fulfilling, be all that you are where you are as if that is the only place you will ever be. When a young man asked Calvin Coolidge how he could go higher in life, Coolidge said, "One should never trouble about getting a better job, but one should do one's present job in such a manner as to qualify for a better job when it comes along."[17]

Os Guinness tells the story of how at the age of five he was put on a plane to go to a boarding school in Shanghai, China. He lived with his parents in Nanjing, which was the nation's capital, but few good schools existed there. He had never been away from his parents. When Os left, his father gave him two small flat stones on which he had painted his life motto. Os carried those stones in his pockets every day all the way through school. In his right-hand pocket was the stone that read, "Found faithful." In the left-hand pocket was the stone that read, "Please *Him*."

Jesus said the words we all will want to hear as we enter into eternity, "Well done, good and faithful servant!" (Matthew 25:21,23). After a life of faithfulness, those words will be music to our ears.

13

Main Character

Even those who have renounced Christianity
and attack it, in their inmost being still follow
the Christian ideal, for hitherto neither their
subtlety nor the ardour of their hearts has been
able to create a higher ideal of man and of
virtue than the ideal given by Christ of old.

FYODOR DOSTOYEVSKY[1]

As you have read this book on character, perhaps you have had the same experience as I did when I wrote it. That is, I realized I have more difficulty exhibiting some of these character traits than others, and at times I fall short of all of them. I could write a book on the times that I have been less than honest, filled with pride and ego, completely inauthentic, more selfish than generous, have given up too easily, lost self-control, harbored bitterness, and the list goes on. In short, I am not perfect, and, with all respect, neither are you!

History is the story of the world we live in, and just as every story has a main character, the protagonist, the hero, so does the story of the world's history. Jesus Christ is the main character of all characters who have ever lived. If you were grading Jesus on the character traits listed in this book, he would be the only person who would score a perfect *100*, 24/7, for his entire life.

One of the striking features of the four Gospels that tell us so much about Jesus is they provide no description of his physical appearance. From a modern journalistic standpoint, it is inconceivable that anyone writing a definitive version of a person's life would fail to tell us how they looked or any significant distinguishing feature. We live in a day and age where image is everything, and we are obsessed with the beautiful and the handsome. But to paraphrase Martin Luther King Jr., the Gospel writers seemed to be concerned not with the color of Jesus's skin but with the content of his character.[2] Suffice to say, the content of his character shines brighter than a thousand suns.

> ## The content of Jesus's character shines brighter than a thousand suns.

When you study the character of Jesus using the traits in this book, it is no wonder the Gospel writers would focus like a laser beam on his character.

Integrity

No one despised and hated Jesus more than the Pharisees. They were faultfinders par excellence and their spiritual gift was criticism. They spent the entire ministry of Jesus, three full years, investigating him full time, trying to find one flaw, one fault, one moral or ethical slipup. Yet, they had to grudgingly admit, and even said to his face, "Teacher we know that *you are a man of integrity* and that you teach the way of God in accordance with the truth. You aren't swayed by others, because you pay no attention to who they are" (Matthew 22:16, emphasis added).

Honesty

Jesus not only told the truth, but he even said that he *was* the truth (John 14:6). Jesus introduced a Hebrew word into the vocabulary of his disciples and used it to introduce so many of the things that he said: "Truly I tell you..." It is the Hebrew word *'āmēn*, which is rooted in a Semitic word that literally means "truth." Twice in the Bible, *Amen* is used as a name, once for God (Isaiah 65:16—"true God") and once for Jesus (Revelation 3:14—"the Amen"). If Jesus tweeted today he would end every one with "#truth." Jesus was never caught in a lie because he always told the truth. One of his followers, a member of his inner circle, one of the three closest to him, said after three intimate years with him, "He committed no sin, and no deceit was found in his mouth" (1 Peter 2:22).

Humility

We celebrate the humility of Jesus every year at the holiday called Christmas. This greatest act of humility ever seen was when God came down from heaven to earth in the form of a man. As if that were not low enough, he humbled himself to die as a common criminal by the most excruciating method of execution ever devised (Philippians 2:6-8).

Loyalty

In one of the most remarkable displays of loyalty anywhere in the Bible, when the greatest traitor who ever lived, Judas Iscariot, approached Jesus in the Garden of Gethsemane and, adding insult to injury, gave Jesus the "kiss of death," Jesus looked at him lovingly and called him "friend." Even in his hour of betrayal, Jesus uses a word of loyal friendship.[3] D.A. Carson calls it "an open-hearted but not intimate greeting."[4]

Respect

Jesus did more to elevate the status of women than anyone before or since. He kindly and lovingly took time to introduce himself to a Samaritan woman who would have been the scourge of Jewish society and led her to faith in himself (John 4:1-42). To a woman caught in adultery, the most shameful act in the eyes of Jewish culture, when she had been condemned and was waiting to be stoned by all of the religious authorities of that day, when she was too ashamed to look any man in the eye, Jesus looked her in the eye and said, "Neither do I condemn you. Go now and leave your life of sin" (John 8:11).[5]

Authenticity

He was, is, and always will be the real deal. The word *hypocrite* is used seventeen times in the New Testament, and every time, Jesus speaks it. He cornered the market on spotting hypocrisy and also on shunning it. He exposed it in others; it was never exposed in him. As literary records show, Jesus introduced the term *hypocrisy* into the moral record of the Western world.[6]

Generosity

Jesus made the most generous gift—that will forever remain unmatched—when he gave the gift of his birth, his life, and his death for the sins of the entire world. He gave his earthly life so that we in return could receive eternal life that we do not even deserve. A man by the name of Paul put it this way: "You know the grace of our Lord Jesus Christ, that though he was rich, yet for your sake he became poor, so that you through his poverty might become rich" (2 Corinthians 8:9).

Courage

No one has ever faced the kind of death Jesus faced with the kind of courage Jesus faced it with. Yes, other men and women have faced death with courage, but Jesus is the only person who ever faced death when he didn't have to die and never would have died had he not chosen to. And he was facing the most horrible consequence of death that anyone could ever face: complete separation from the Father. The experience was so fearful and dreadful that he sweat drops of blood in the Garden of Gethsemane prior to the crucifixion (Luke 22:44). He could have stopped it at any moment and climbed down off the cross. He could have called legions of angels to rescue him, but the courage of his character would not allow it.

Perseverance

At the end of his ministry, Jesus was able to say to the Father who sent him to complete the most difficult assignment ever given, "I have brought you glory on earth by finishing the work you gave me to do" (John 17:4). One of the last things he ever said with one of the last breaths he ever drew was, "It is finished" (John 19:30). Jesus didn't quit until the job was done and the war was won.

Self-Control

When Jesus stood before the high priest and Pontius Pilate, he could have easily pulled rank, answered every question they had, proven them wrong in what they did, but he said nothing. No matter what was done to him or said to him, he never retaliated and never responded in kind. Again, one of his best buddies, looking back at the moment when lashing out and hitting back would have been both expected and justified, wrote with amazement, "When they hurled their insults at him, he did not retaliate; when he suffered, he made no threats. Instead, he entrusted himself to him who judges justly" (1 Peter 2:23).

Forgiveness

At the exact moment Jesus was hanging on a cross, stark naked in shame and humiliation, dying an excruciating death, not even able to control his bodily functions, deserted by his closest friends, reviled and insulted by the people who hated him most, he said, "Father, forgive them, for they do not know what they are doing" (Luke 23:34).

Faithfulness

Jesus was the paragon of faithfulness. When all of his disciples deserted him, he did not desert them. When they denied him, he did not deny them. When they were faithless to him, he was faithful to them. You could always count on Jesus to show up. He showed up at the cradle. He showed up at the cross. He is indeed the ultimate Marine because he is not just always faithful, he is eternally faithful.

On and on I could go. Now consider this: Jesus asked a question that no one would dare ever ask, at least of people who know them. To his most hated detractors, to his disciples, to his family, to people he had grown up with, to the throngs that had observed him, he asked, "Can any of you prove me guilty of sin?" (John 8:46). No one has ever stepped forward with any credible proof that Jesus ever sinned. Yes, he was fully human just like us, suffered the same pains that we suffer, endured the same heartache and disappointment, faced the same temptations, bore the same injustices, and even died for the consequences of sin that we committed, but he never exhibited or experienced the conduct of sin.[7] It is a breathtaking claim to have never failed, faltered, or fallen. His enemies admitted it. His followers believed it and were ready to die for that belief, and his closest friends confirmed it.[8] Another biblical scholar said,

> If we accept the record as it stands, Jesus never had a guilty conscience, never blushed with shame, never regretted anything he said or did, never needed to apologize, never wished he could have put the clock back or turned over a new leaf, and never needed to pray for forgiveness. In the Bible's own words, he was "holy, blameless, pure, set apart from sinners" [Hebrews 7:26].[9]

Not even his most devoted followers can *be* Jesus, but all of us who claim to be followers should desire to be more *like* Jesus. The late Ruth Bell Graham, Billy Graham's wife, spoke about Pashi, a young college student from India. He told her, "We from India would like to believe in Christ, but we have never seen a Christian who was like Christ." Mrs. Graham said that when she consulted Dr. Akbar Abdul-Haqq about what might be the best response to this challenge, he answered: "That is quite simple. I would tell Pashi, I am not offering you Christians. I am offering you Christ."[10] No, we will never be perfect in our character like Jesus was, but we should strive for that perfection every day.

An estimated 108 billion human beings have lived on planet Earth.[11] Nowhere in history has it ever been recorded that one person, male or female, ever reached the status of having perfect character, except the main character—Jesus. There is nobody like Jesus—never has been and never will be.

A group of salesmen were leaving a Chicago convention and were late arriving at O'Hare International Airport for their flight home. As they hurried into the terminal, they heard the last call for their flight. They ran through that busy airport, dodging this person and that, weaving through the crowd, dragging their luggage behind them. Two of the men crashed into a table stacked with gift baskets of apples, overturning them, but they all just kept running. They reached their gate just as it was closing and managed to board the plane.

Except for one man. He stopped and told his buddies to go on—that he would catch a later flight. His conscience was bothering him, and he turned back and found the young boy who was managing that apple stand on his knees in tears, trying to pick up those scattered apples and gift baskets. The salesman got on his knees beside the boy and helped him gather the apples and baskets and set up the display again.

Some of the baskets were damaged, many apples were bruised, and a few were missing. The man then opened his wallet, gave the boy three large bills, and said, "I believe this will more than cover the cost of the damage, and I am so sorry we messed up your day. Are you okay, buddy?" The boy through his tears managed to get out a "thank you," and the salesman turned to go to the ticket counter to buy another ticket for the flight home. He hadn't gotten far before the boy called out, "Mister…" The man turned around and said, "Yes, son?" He said, "Are you Jesus?"[12]

> ## "Mister…are you Jesus?"

I will never be Jesus and neither will you, but can you think of a greater accomplishment in life than to have character of such quality that people would mistake you for Jesus? I would love that case of mistaken identity!

Our journey on the road to character has now come to its end. At times, it must have been a rough ride, calling you to deep and difficult self-reflection. Even I was convicted by what I was writing on more than one occasion. Building and maintaining character is hard and costly. There is no easy, lazy way to construct a house of character that will withstand the tests, trials, and temptations of life. But both history and destiny teach us that abandoning character is far more costly and painful, and in the end, empties life of its greatest impact. As some unknown person wisely said: "Watch your thoughts; they become words. Watch your words; they become actions. Watch your actions; they become habits. Watch your habits; they become character. Watch your character; it becomes your destiny."[13]

Golfers have a saying: "It's not how you drive, it's how you arrive that counts." May this book help us all arrive at the end of the journey of life having left a trail of good and godly impact on a world desperate for people of character.

Truly, *character still counts*. It always has, and it always will.

Notes

Introduction—Character: Don't Leave Home Without It

1. "Notes," *Reader's Digest*, October 2016, 81.

2. Adapted from Richard C. Stazesky, "George Washington, Genius in Leadership," *Washington Papers*, February 22, 2000, https://gwpapers.virginia.edu/resources/articles/george-washington -genius-in-leadership/.

3. "Most Places Named After Washington," *UPI*, February 18, 2013, www.upi.com/Most-places -named-after-Washington/50411361210145.

4. See www.quora.com/How-many-things-are-named-after-George-Washington-in-the-United -States.

5. Quoted in James Davison Hunter, *The Death of Character: Moral Education in an Age Without Good or Evil* (New York: Basic Books, 2000), 6.

6. Robert A. Wilson, *Character Above All* (New York: Simon & Schuster, 1995), 147.

7. Cited by Don Anderson, *Drawing Closer, Growing Stronger* (Sisters, OR: Multnomah Books, 1997), 1.

8. Cited by David F. Wells, *God in the Wasteland* (Grand Rapids, MI: Wm. B. Eerdmans Publishing Company, 1994), 11. Dr. Wells took these figures from an unpublished paper by Eric Nelson titled "Changes in the Public Portrayal of Death" (1991), cited with his permission. In 1786, 80 percent of the obituaries made reference to character. In 1900, that had fallen to 10 percent.

9. Ibid. In 1786, only 15 percent of the obituaries mentioned the person's occupation. By 1900, the figure had grown to 70 percent and in 1990, 80 percent.

10. David Brooks, *The Road to Character* (New York: Random House, 2015), 11.

11. David Brooks, "The Moral Bucket List," *New York Times*, April 11, 2015, www.nytimes .com/2015/04/12/opinion/sunday/david-brooks-the-moral-bucket-list.html.

12. Pelin Kesebir and Selin Kesebir, "The Cultural Salience of Moral Character and Virtue Declined in Twentieth Century America," *Journal of Positive Psychology*, July 2012. Thanks to David Brooks, *Road to Character*, 258, for gleaning this information.

13. Shelby Steele, *Shame* (Philadelphia: Basic Books, 2015), 110-11.

14. Justin McCarthy, "Majority in U.S. Still Say Moral Values Getting Worse," *Gallup*, June 2, 2015, https://news.gallup.com/poll/183467/majority-say-moral-values-getting-worse.aspx.

15. Wilson, *Character Above All*, 59.

16. Bob Barr, *The Meaning of Is* (Atlanta, GA: Stroud and Hall Publishers, 2004), 35.

17. See https://www.allgreatquotes.com/quote-396515/.

18. The Federalist, No. 57 (James Madison).

19. Everett Caroll Ladd, "To Voters Picking a President Character Does Matter," *Christian Science Monitor*, July 23, 1996.

20. Ibid.

21. Lynn Vavreck, "Why This Election Was Not About the Issues," *New York Times*, November 23, 2016.

22. Todd S. Purdum, "The 2016 Race Isn't About Issues. It's About Character," *Politico*, August 8, 2016, www.Politico.com/magazine/story/2016/08/does-anyone-care-about-issues-anymore -or-only-whether-Trump-is-crazy-214150. Interestingly, in an article in the *Weekly Standard*, Ben Shapiro said that older conservatives focused on policy and voted for Trump while young conservatives focused on character and did not (Ben Shapiro, "It Is Not a Lost Cause: How Conservatives Can Win Back Young Americans," *Weekly Standard*, May 21, 2018, 25ff.

23. Glenn Kessler, "A Year of Unprecedented Deception," *Washington Post*, December 30, 2018, www .washingtonpost.com/politics/2018/12/30/year-unprecedented-deception-trump-averaged-false-claims-day/?utm_term=.f0a28e8a75fe.

24. Danielle Kurtzleben, "POLL: White Evangelicals Have Warmed to Politicians Who Commit 'Immoral' Acts," *NPR*, October 23, 2016, www.npr.org/2016/10/23/498890836/poll-white -evangelicals-have-warmed-to-politicians-who-commit-immoral-acts.

25. Zig Ziglar, *Raising Positive Kids in a Negative World* (Nashville, TN: Oliver-Nelson Books, 1985) 49-50.

26. William J. Bennett, *The Death of Outrage* (New York: The Free Press, 1998), 5.

27. Ibid., 36.

28. Tim Elmore, *Habitudes* (Atlanta, GA: Growing Leaders, Inc, 2004), 22.

Chapter 1—Integrity: Living Under the Microscope

1. See www.azquotes.com/quote/938133.

2. Laurie Goodstein and Sharon Otterman, "Catholic Priests Abused 1,000 Children in Pennsylvania, Report Says," *New York Times*, August 14, 2018, www.nytimes.com/2018/08/14/us/catholic -church-sex-abuse-pennsylvania.html.

3. See https://johnmenadue.com/massimo-faggioli-the-catholic-churchs-biggest-crisis-since-the -reformation/.

4. The Southern Baptist Convention with almost sixteen million members.

5. Stephen Carter, *Integrity* (New York: HarperCollins, 1996), 7.

6. "Warren Buffet Looks for These 3 Traits in People When He Hires Them," *Business Insider*, January 4, 2017, https://www.businessinsider.com/what-warren-buffett-looks-for-in-candidates-2017-1.

7. Amy Rees Anderson, "Success Will Come and Go, but Integrity Is Forever," *Forbes*, November 28, 2012, https://www.forbes.com/sites/amyanderson/2012/11/28 success-will-come-and-go-but -integrity-is-forever/#382a3c5b470f.

8. See at https://daviddewolf.com/real-meaning-of-integrity/.

9. See at https://www.goodreads.com/quotes/339380-my-basic-principle-is-that-you-don-t-make -decisions-because.

10. Gary Richmond, *All God's Creatures* (Waco, TX: Word Publishing, 1991), 8.

11. Ibid., 11, 30.

12. Lee Strobel, *God's Outrageous Claims* (Grand Rapids, MI: Zondervan, 2016), 49.

13. Mark DeMoss, *The Little Red Book of Wisdom* (Nashville, TN: Nelson Business, 2006), 109-111.

Chapter 2—Honesty: Nothing but the Truth

1. Ralph Keyes, *The Post-Truth Era: Dishonest and Deception in Contemporary Life* (New York: St. Martin's, 2004), 5.

2. Karen Berman and Joe Knight, "What Did Bernard Madoff Do?," *Harvard Business Review*, June 30, 2009, https://hbr.org/2009/06/what-did-bernard-madoff-do.

3. Ibid.

4. Stephanie Yang, "5 Years Ago Bernie Madoff Was Sentenced to 150 Years in Prison—Here's How His Scheme Worked," *Business Insider*, July 1, 2014, www.businessinsider.com/how-Bernie-Madoffs-Ponzi-scheme-worked-2014-7.

5. Ibid.

6. *Today's Christian*, July/August, 2005, 12.

7. Robert S. Feldman, "UMass Researcher Finds Most People Lie in Everyday Conversation," University of Massachusetts at Amherst, June 10, 2002, www.UMass.edu/newsoffice/article/umass-amherst-researcher-finds-most-people-lie-everyday-conversation.

8. James Patterson, *The Day America Told the Truth: What People Really Believe About Everything that Really Matters* (Princeton, NJ: Prentice-Hall, 1991), 48.

9. See at https://en.wikipedia.org/wiki/Terminological_inexactitude.

10. "Cheating Is a Personal Foul," www.glass-castle.com/clients/www-nocheating-org/adcouncil/research/cheatingfactsheet.html.

11. Ibid.

12. See at http://www.glass-castle.com/clients/www-nocheating-org/adcouncil/research/cheating-backgrounder.html.

13. Ibid.

14. "Adults Cheat Too: What Started in Elementary School…," *US News & World Report*, November 22, 1999, https://www.waunakee.k12.wi.us/hs/departments/lmtc/Assignments/McConnell Scenarios/AcadHonesty_4Article.pdf.

15. Chris Matthews, "Here's How Much Tax Cheats Cost the U.S. Government a Year," *Fortune*, April 29, 2016, Fortune.com/2016/04/29/tax-evasion-cost.

16. Don Doman, "Grocery Cart Theft—Someone Has to Pay!," *Suburban Times*, March 8, 2018, https://thesubtimes.com/2018/03/08/grocery-cart-theft-someone-has-to-pay/.

17. John W. Fountain, "New York Coach Resigns After Five Days and a Few Lies," *New York Times*, December 15, 2001, https://www.nytimes.com/2001/12/15/sports/notre-dame-coach-resigns-after-5-days-and-a-few-lies.html.

18. "Adults Cheat Too: What Started in Elementary School…," *US News & World Report*, November 22, 1999, https://www.waunakee.k12.wi.us/hs/departments/lmtc/Assignments/McConnell Scenarios/AcadHonesty_4Article.pdf.

19. "Our Cheating Hearts," *US News & World Report*, May 2002, 4.

20. Kathleen Joyce, "Woman Kills Herself, Two Children After Husband Fakes His Death,"

Fox News, October 17, 2018, www.foxnews.com/world/woman-kills-herself-two-children-after-husband-fakes-his-death.

21. See at http://press.careerbuilder.com/2017-11-16-Increased-Number-of-Workers-Calling-In-Sick-When-They-Arent-Finds-CareerBuilders-Annual-Survey.

22. Lydia Dishman, "Here's the Truth About Lying at Work," *Fast Company*, July 14, 2014, www.fastcompany.com/3032863/here's-the-truth-about-lying-at-work.

23. Becky Murphy, "Is There a Crisis of Integrity and Ethics?," *Interactive Services*, June 14, 2018, https://interactiveservices.com/compliance-training/crisis-integrity-ethics/.

24. Cited by Granville N. Toogood, *The Articulate Executive* (New York: McGraw-Hill, 1996), 75-85.

25. Richard G. Capen Jr., *Finish Strong* (New York: HarperCollins, 1996), 69.

26. Charles R. Swindoll, *The Quest for Character* (Portland, OR: Multnomah Press, 1987), 67. Though many scholars doubt this meaning, one can see why the legend started, and it certainly illustrates the character quality beautifully.

27. See at https://www.psychologytoday.com/us/blog/homo-consumericus/201111/how-often-do-people-lie-in-their-daily-lives.

28. Seth Stephens-Davidowitz, *Everybody Lies: Big Data, New Data and What the Internet Can Tell Us About Who We Really Are* (New York: HarperCollins Publishers, 2017).

29. Cited in Jerry White, *Honesty, Morality, and Conscience* (Colorado Springs: NavPress, 1996), 18-19.

30. Ibid., 49.

31. Patterson and Kim, Op.Cit, 32.

32. Robert C. Williams, *The Forensic Historian: Using Science to Re-examine the Past* (Armonk, NY: M.E. Sharpe, 2013), 48.

33. "Han van Meegeren's Fake Vermeers," *Essential Vermeer 2.0*, www.essentialvermeer.com/misc/van_meegeren.html#.XKJf9KR7mUk.

Chapter 3—Humility: It's Not About Me

1. Delivering the eulogy for President George H.W. Bush.

2. "Saddam Hussein," *Wikipedia*, https://en.wikipedia.org/wiki/Saddam_Hussein#Political_and_cultural_image.

3. Andrew Alderson and Adam Lusher, "How Did He Last So Long?," *Telegraph*, December 31, 2006, www.telegraph.co.uk/news/worldnews/1538246/How-did-he-last-so-long.html.

4. George W. Bush, *Decision Points* (New York: Crown Publishers, 2010), 209.

5. David Brooks, *The Road to Character* (New York: Random House, 2015), 6.

6. Ibid.

7. Ibid.

8. Gene M. Twenge and W. Keith Campbell, *The Narcissism Epidemic: Living in the Age of Entitlement* (New York: Simon & Schuster, 2009), 13.

9. C.S. Lewis, quoted in *The International Dictionary of Thoughts* (Chicago: J.G. Gerguson, 1969), 584 (emphasis added).

10. Peggy Noonan, *When Character Was King* (New York: Penguin, 2001), 187. Incidentally, what a great title for a great leader!

11. John Cherwa, "The Kingmaker: Don Shula," *Orlando Sentinel*, August 24, 2007, http://www.orlandosentinel.com/news/os-xpm-2007-08-24-dolphinsking24-story.html.

12. Antonia Blumberg, "This Is How Many Words Are Spoken by Women in the Bible," *Huffington Post*, February 4, 2015, https://www.huffpost.com/entry/bible-women-words_n_6608282.

13. This description is taken from a message by Mark Driscoll on the Gospel of Luke.

14. I got this idea from Timothy Keller, *Encounters with Jesus* (New York: Dutton, 2013), 204.

15. "Now We Are Small Enough," Bible.org, https://Bible.org/illustration/now-we-are-small-enough.

16. Kenneth S. Davis, *Soldier of Democracy* (New York: Doubleday, 1945), 543.

17. John Ortberg, *Life-Changing Love* (Grand Rapids, MI: Zondervan, 1998), 141-42.

18. Paul E. Tan, *Encyclopedia of 7700 Illustrations: Signs of the Times* (Rockville, MD: Assurance Publishers, 1979), 1370-71, tag 6124.

19. I got that thought from Max Lucado, *Traveling Light* (Nashville, TN: Word Publishing Group, 2001), 77.

Chapter 4—Loyalty: I'll Be There

1. "Loyalty Sayings and Quotes," *Wise Old Sayings*, www.wiseoldsayings.com/loyalty-quotes/page-2/.

2. The name has been changed to protect the guilty.

3. Jonathan Merritt, *Learning to Speak God from Scratch* (New York: Convergent, 2018), 85.

4. "Loyalty Sayings and Quotes," *Wise Old Sayings*.

5. Timothy Keiningham and Lerzan Aksoy, *Why Loyalty Matters: The Groundbreaking Approach to Rediscovering Happiness, Meaning and Lasting Fulfillment in Your Life and Work* (Dallas: BenBella Books, 2010), Kindle edition, 7.

6. Ibid., 9.

7. Ibid.

8. Cited in Keiningham and Aksoy, *Why Loyalty Matters*, 6.

9. Keiningham and Aksoy, *Why Loyalty Matters*, 6.

10. Ibid., 8.

11. Ibid.

12. Cited in Amit Kothari, "Customer Loyalty–5 Surprising Facts About Its Importance," *Tallyfy*, https://tallyfy.com/customer-loyalty-importance/.

13. McKenzie Ingram, "How, and Why, You Should Calculate Customer Lifetime Value (CLV)," *Business 2 Community*, October 24, 2016, www.business2community.com/brandviews/act-on/calculate-customer-lifetime-value-clv-01687546.

14. Frederick F. Reichheld and Phil Schefter, "The Economics of E-Loyalty," Harvard Business School, July 10, 2000, https://hbswk.hbs.edu/archive/the-economics-of-e-loyalty.

15. Kothari, "Customer Loyalty."

16. Quincy Seale, "Loyalty Quotes," *KeepInspiringMe.com*, www.keepinspiring.me/loyalty-quotes/.

17. "2018 Brand Keys Customer Loyalty Engagement Index," http://brandkeys.com/wp-content/uploads/2018/01/2018-Category-Winners-tableFINAL.pdf.

18. Steve Levy, "How Many Friends Is Too Many?," *Newsweek*, May 26, 2008, 15.

19. Nancy Gibbs and Michael Duffy, *The Preacher and the President* (New York: Hachette Book Group, 2007), 321.

20. Craig Brian Larson, *1001 Illustrations That Connect* (Grand Rapids, MI: Zondervan, 2008), 331-32.

21. "Loyalty Sayings and Quotes," *Wise Old Sayings*.

22. "Top 100 Loyalty Quotes and Sayings," *Quote Ambition*, www.quoteambition.com/loyalty -quotes-sayings/.

23. Ibid.

24. "Quotes About Blind Loyalty," *Quote Master*, www.quotemaster.org/blind+loyalty.

25. I have added these questions as my own personal commentary.

26. Charles W. Colson, *Life Sentence* (Lincoln, VA: Chosen Books, 1979), 9.

27. Ibid.

28. See at https://www.nps.gov/sara/learn/photosmultimedia/saratoga-monument-virtual-tour-part -3.htm

29. J. Michael Shannon, "Illustration: Betrayal," *Preaching*, www.preaching.com/sermon-illustrations/ illustration-betrayal/.

Chapter 5—Respect: Honor Above All

1. "Ralph Waldo Emerson Sayings and Quotes," *Wise Old Sayings*, www.wiseoldsayings.com/ authors/ralph-waldo-emerson-quotes/.

2. "Americans Believe Civility Is on the Decline," *Science Daily*, April 22, 2016, www.sciencedaily .com/releases/2016/04/160422201040.htm.

3. Eugene Scott, "Poll: Majority of Americans Say Civility Has Declined Since Trump Elected," CNN Politics, July 3, 2017, www.cnn.com/2017/07/03/politics/npr-poll-trump-civility -declined/index.html.

4. Michael Burke, "Clinton: You Can't Be Civil with a Party That Wants to Destroy What You Stand For," *The Hill*, October 9, 2018, https://thehill.com/blogs/blog-briefing-room/news/ 410566-clinton-you-cant-be-civil-with-a-party-that-wants-to-destroy.

5. Hannah Hartig, "Few Americans See Nation's Political Debate as 'Respectful'," *Pew Research*, May 1, 2018, https://www.pewresearch.org/fact-tank/2018/05/01/few-americans-see-nations -political-debate-as-respectful/.

6. Andy Lewis, "CNN's Jake Tapper Talks New Novel and Why the Clintons Still Owe Monica Lewinsky an Apology," *Hollywood Reporter*, May 10, 2018, https://www.hollywoodreporter.com/ rambling-reporter/cnn-host-jake-tapper-talks-new-novel-hating-politics-why-clintons-still-owe -monica-lewinsky-an-apolo-1109806.

7. Judith Warner, "Kids Gone Wild," *New York Times*, November 27, 2005, https://www.nytimes .com/2005/11/27/weekinreview/kids-gone-wild.html.

8. Ibid.

9. Cited by David McCullough, *John Adams* (New York: Simon & Schuster, 2001), 106 (emphasis added).

10. Charles Taylor, *A Secular Age* (Cambridge, MA: Harvard University Press, 2007), 47 (emphasis added).

11. Craig Brian Larson, *1001 Illustrations That Connect* (Grand Rapids, MI: Zondervan, 2008), 267.

12. Bob Buford, *Halftime* (Grand Rapids, MI: Zondervan, 1994), 155-56.

13. "Laurence Sterne Sayings and Quotes," *Wise Old Sayings*, www.wiseoldsayings.com/authors/laurence-sterne-quotes/.

14. In this chapter, he says it in verse 6 twice, and in chapter 26, he says it in verses 9, 11, and 23.

15. "Respect Sayings and Quotes," *Wise Old Sayings*, www.wiseoldsayings.com/respect/quotes/.

16. Hussein Nishah, "Respect Sayings and Quotes."

17. "DC Woman Charged with Throwing Cup of Urine on Metrobus Driver Fails to Appear in Court," *Fox 5*, September 28, 2017, www.fox5dc.com/news/local-news/dc-woman-charged-with-throwing-cup-of-urine-on-metro-bus-driver-fails-to-appear-in-court.

18. Richard V. Reeves, "The Respect Deficit," *Brookings Institution,* August 8, 2018, https://www.brookings.edu/blog/up-front/2018/08/09/the-respect-deficit/.

19. Ibid.

20. "All Men Are Created Equal," *Wikipedia*, https://en.m.wikipedia.org/wiki/all_men_are_created_equal.

21. "400 Respect Quotes That Will Make Your Life Better (Today)," *Wisdom Quotes*, http://wisdom quotes.com/respect-quotes/.

22. Frank Luntz, W*ords That Work* (New York: Hyperion Books, 2007), 107-8.

Chapter 6—Authenticity: The Real Deal

1. Larry Hein, quoted by Brennan Manning, *Lion and Lamb* (Old Tappan, NJ: Chosen Books, Fleming H. Revell, 1986), 24.

2. Adapted from Tim Elmore, *Habitudes* (Atlanta, GA: Growing Leaders, Inc., 2004), 18.

3. "'What Is True,' the ASAP Poll," *Forbes ASAP*, October 2, 2000, 26.

4. Nancy Pearcey, *Total Truth* (Wheaton, IL: Crossway Books, 2004), 378.

5. David Kinnaman and Gabe Lyons, *UnChristian: What a New Generation Really Thinks About Christianity* (Grand Rapids, MI: Baker Books, 2017), 46-47.

6. Ibid., 42.

7. Thomas R. Ybarra, quoted in Laurence J. Peter, *Peter's Quotation Ideas for Our Time* (New York: Harper Collins/William Morrow and Company, 1977), 84.

8. "American Lifestyles Mix Compassion and Self-Oriented Behavior," *Barna*, February 5, 2007, www.barna.com/research/american-lifestyles-mix-compassion-and-self-oriented-behavior/.

9. Mark Mittelberg, *The Questions Christians Hope No One Will Ask* (Carol Stream, IL: Tyndale House, 2010), 222-23.

10. Eighty-five percent of young outsiders conclude that present-day Christianity is hypocritical. Kinnaman and Lyons, *UnChristian*, 42.

11. Cathal Dennehy, "The Simple Life of One of the World's Best Marathoners," *Runner's World*, April 19, 2016, www.runnersworld.com/news/a20793538/the-simple-life-of-one-of-the-worlds-best-marathoners/.

12. Sam Haysom, "Chris Pratt Uses MTV Awards Speech to Lay Out 9 Rules for the Next Generation," *Mashable*, June 19, 2018, https://mashable.com/article/Chris-Pratt-MTV-award-9-rules/#hyvi_Ba6Lauw.

13. Ted Koppel, cited by Richard G. Capen Jr., *Finish Strong: Living the Values That Take You the Distance* (San Francisco: HarperOne, 1996), 15.

14. Jim Edwards, "See How Lance Armstrong Humiliated Nike in These Old Ads About Doping," *Business Insider*, October 17, 2012, www.google.com/amp/s/amp.businessinsider.com/lance-armstrongs-doping-ads-for-nike-2012-10.

15. "Robert Redford," *SermonSearch*, www.sermonsearch.com/sermon-illustrations/3294/Robert-Redford/.

Chapter 7—Generosity: Give It All You've Got

1. Donna Sapolin, "22 Inspiring Quotes on Generosity," *Next Avenue*, December 3, 2013, www.nextavenue.org/22-inspiring-quotes-generosity/.

2. David Callahan, "Hold the Toasts to Generosity. In Fact, the Rich Give Away Very Little of Their Wealth," *Inside Philanthropy*, June 13, 2017, www.insidephilanthropy.com/home/2017/6/13/new-charity-data-underscores-a-depressing-truth-the-rich-part-with-very-little-of-their-wealth.

3. Christian Smith and Hillary Davidson, *The Paradox of Generosity* (Oxford: Oxford University Press, 2014), 102.

4. "Christmas Spending Statistics, Trends, and Fun Facts (US & UK)," *Much Needed*, n.d., https://muchneeded.com/Christmas-statistics/.

5. Ibid.

6. Helaine Olen, "Why Don't America's Rich Give More to Charity?," *Atlantic*, December 16, 2017, www.theatlantic.com/business/archive/2017/12/why-dont-rich-give-more-charity/548537/.

7. "Affluenza," *Merriam-Webster*, www.Merriam/Webster.com/dictionary/affluenza.

8. David Hawkins, *Breaking Everyday Addictions* (Eugene, OR: Harvest House, 2008), 152.

9. "What Would Happen If the Church Tithed," *Rethink*, May 31, 2016, https://Rethinknow.org/2016/05/31/5-things-that-could-happen-if-the-church-tithed.

10. Ibid.

11. Mike Holmes, "What Would Happen if the Church Tithed?," *Relevant*, March 8, 2016.

12. Kevin Sack, "60 Lives, 30 Kidneys, All Linked," *New York Times*, February 18, 2012, www.nytimes.com/2012/02/19/health/lives-forever-linked-through-kidney-transplant-chain-124.html.

13. "Generosity," *Wikipedia*, https://en.wikipedia.org/wiki/Generosity.

14. Jim Dwyer, "Philanthropist Wants to Be Rid of His Last $1.5 Billion," *New York Times*, August 7, 2012, https://www.nytimes.com/2012/08/08/nyregion/a-billionaire-philanthropist-struggles-to-go-broke.html?mtrref=www.google.com&gwh=94570F81FB98AB4B3C85E6417B735A3A&gwt=pay&assetType=REGIWALL.

15. "Gerda Weissmann Klein," *Wikipedia*, https://en.wikipedia.org/wiki/Gerda_Weissmann_Klein.

16. See at https://knowledgenuts.com/2013/09/09/the-weird-japanese-hole-in-one-tradition/.

17. Stephen King, "Vassar Commencement Speech," *StephenKing.com*, May 20, 2001, www.StephenKing.com/news_archive/archive/2001.html.

Chapter 8—Courage: Go Big, Go Bold

1. Quoted in James M. Strock, *Reagan on Leadership* (Rockland, CA: Forum Publishing, 1998), 216.

2. "Cost of the American Civil War," *Shotgun's Home of the American Civil War*, February 16, 2002, www.CivilWarhome.com/warcosts.html.

3. "Courage," *Twainquotes.com*, www.Twainquotes.com/Courage.html.

4. Collin Hansen, *Blind Spots* (Wheaton, IL: Crossway, 2015), 66.

5. "Maya Angelou Quotes," *Brainy Quote*, www.brainyquote.com/quotes/maya_angelou_0120859.

6. Richard Capin Jr., *Finish Strong* (San Francisco: HarperCollins, 1996), 22 (emphasis added).

7. Quoted in Franklin H. Littell, "First They Came for the Jews," *Christian Ethics Today*, vol. 3, no. 1 (February 1997), 29.

8. "Desmond Doss: The Real Story," Desmond Doss Council, https://desmonddoss.com/bio/bio -real.php.

9. Katie Lange, "Pfc. Desmond Doss: The Unlikely Hero Behind 'Hacksaw Ridge'," *U.S. Army*, February 28, 2017, www.army.mil/article/183328/pfc_desmond_doss_the_unlikely_hero_behind _hacksaw_ridge.

10. "Six Kinds of Courage," *Greenpeace*, http://moon.greenpeace.org/courage/courage.html.

11. Nicky Champ, "17 Brené Brown Quotes that Will Inspire You to Lead," *Business Chicks*, n.d., https://businesschicks.com/brene-brown-quotes/.

12. John A. Shedd, *Salt from My Attic*, https://quoteinvestigator.com/2013/12/09/safe-harbor/.

13. *Optimize*, www.optimize.me/quotes/Winston-Churchill/307042-there-comes-a-certain-moment -in-everyone's-life-a-moment/.

14. Mark Helprin, "To the New Congressional Majority," *Wall Street Journal*, January 3, 1995, 8.

15. Brenné Brown, "Courage Is a Heart Word (and a Family Affair)," *PBS Parents*, n.d., www.pbs .org/parents/experts/archive/2010/11/courage-is-a-heart-word-and-a.html.

16. Levi Lusko, *Through the Eyes of a Lion* (Nashville, TN: W Publishing Group, 2015), 157-58.

17. Abraham Lincoln, *Out of My Treasure* (Joplin, MO: College Press, 1964), 61.

18. Mark Batterson, *The Grave Robber* (Grand Rapids, MI: Baker Books, 2014), 183-84.

19. "Going to School," *Ministry 127*, n.d., www.Ministry127.com/resources/illustration/going -to-school.

Chapter 9—Perseverance: Run the Stop Sign

1. See at https://twitter.com/SportSourceA/status/701595273265618945.

2. See at https://www.cnbc.com/2017/09/12/apples-third-co-founder-ronald-wayne-sold-his-stake -for-800.html.

3. Mark Batterson, *Primal* (Colorado Springs, CO: Multnomah Books, 2009), 137-38.

4. Mike Bellah, *Baby Boom Believers* (Wheaton, IL: Tyndale House, 1988), 100 (emphasis added).

5. Lidiya K, "What Can Thomas Edison Teach Us About Success (through Failure)," *Let's Reach Success*, June 14, 2013, https://letsreachsuccess.com/2013/06/14/what-can-thomas-edison-teach -us-about-success-through-failure/.

6. John Maxwell, *The 21 Indispensable Qualities of a Leader* (Nashville, TN: Thomas Nelson, 1999), 89.

7. Lidiya K, "What Can Thomas Edison Teach Us About Success."

8. Aurelius Tjin, "These 10 Stories Will Remind You to Never Give Up on Your Dreams," *Unstoppable*

Profits, May 7, 2014, www.unstoppableprofits.com/these-10-stories-will-remind-you-to-never-give-up-on-your-dreams.

9. *Quotefancy*, https://quotefancy.com/quote/930211/Walt-Disney-Everyone-falls-down-Getting-back-up-is-how-you-learn-how-to-walk.

10. "Dr. Seuss," *Wikipedia*, https://en.wikipedia.org/wiki/Dr._Seuss.

11. "4 Things Dr. Seuss Teaches Us About Perseverance," *Mark Merrill*, n.d., www.MarkMerrill.com/4-things-Dr.-Seuss-Teaches-Us-About-Perseverance.

12. Joey Reiman, *Success Handbook* (Atlanta, GA.: Longstreet Press, 1992), 72.

13. Cited in Akash Akky, "Top 10 Most Popular Fred Smith Quotes," *Medium*, February 17, 2016, https://medium.com/@akashakky/top-10-most-popular-fred-smith-quotes-2720408d7dc.

14. Lidiya K, "What Can Thomas Edison Teach Us About Success."

15. "The Most Popular Song in America," *Reader's Digest*, July 8, 2018, 118.

16. Marvin Olasky, *The American Leadership Tradition* (New York: The Free Press, 1999), 15.

17. Quoted in Charles Swindoll, *The Tale of the Tardy Oxcart* (Nashville, TN: W Publishing, 1998), 441.

18. Ibid., 442.

19. I got this idea from Swindoll. Ibid., 23.

20. Quoted in Brett McKay and Kate McKay, *The Art of Manliness: Classic Skills and Manners for the Modern Man* (Cincinnati: HOW Books, 2011), 147.

21. Cited by Swindoll, *Tale of the Tardy Oxcart*, 42.

22. Peter Economy, "50 Encouraging Quotes to Persevere in Life and Motivate You to Succeed," *Inc.*, July 24, 2015, www.inc.com/peter-economy/50-encouraging-quotes-to-persevere-in-life-and-motivate-you-to-succeed.html?cid=search.

23. Tim Elmore, *Habitudes* (Atlanta, GA: Growing Leaders, Inc., 2004), 5.

24. "Michael Jordan Quotes," *Brainy Quote*, www.brainyquote.com/quotes/michael_jordan_127660.

25. *Houston Chronicle*, January 1, 2001, 2D.

26. John Maxwell, *Failing Forward* (Nashville, TN: Thomas Nelson, 2000), 15.

27. See at http://abolition.e2bn.org/people_24.html.

28. *Contemporary Pulpit*, October–December 1999, 7.

Chapter 10—Self-Control: Caging the Lion

1. Harry S. Truman, "Longhand Note of Judge Harry S. Truman, May, 14, 1934," Harry S. Truman Presidential Library and Museum, www.trumanlibrary.org/whistlestop/study_collections/trumanpapers/psf/longhand/index.php?documentVersion=transcript&documentid=hst-psf_naid735210-01.

2. "Prisoner of Appetite," *1001 Illustrations That Connect*, ed. Craig Brian Larson and Phyllis Ten Elshof (Grand Rapids, MI: Zondervan, 2008), 149.

3. See https://home.bt.com/news/on-this-day/september-27-1988-ben-johnson-is-stripped-of-his-olympic-gold-medal-after-failing-drugs-test-11364007354384.

4. "Pete Rose," *Wikipedia*, https://en.wikipedia.org/wiki/Pete_Rose.

5. "List of People Banned from Major League Baseball," *Wikipedia*, https://en.wikipedia.org/wiki/List_of_people_banned_from_Major_League_Baseball.

6. "The Clinton-Gore Administration: A Record of Progress," *Clinton White House*, n.d., https://clintonwhitehouse5.archives.gov/WH/Accomplishments/eightyears-01.html.

7. Daniel Akst, "Who's in Charge Here?," *Wilson Quarterly*, Summer 2006, http://archive.wilson quarterly.com/essays/whos-in-charge-here (emphasis added).

8. Daniel Goleman, *Emotional Intelligence* (New York: Bantam Books, 2005), 80-83.

9. Bradley Wright with David Carreon, "The Science of Sinning Less," *Christianity Today*, April 21, 2017, www.christianitytoday.com/ct/2017/may/science-of-sinning-less.html.

10. Matt Caron, "5 Yogic Qualities of Martin Luther King Jr. (and What We Can Learn from Them)," *Sivana East*, n.d., https://blog.sivanaspirit.com/5-yogic-qualities-Martin-Luther-King-Jr./.

11. "How Martin Luther King Jr. Succeeded with Soft Skills," *Conover*, n.d., https://Conovercompany.com/how-Martin-Luther-King-Jr.-succeeded-with-soft-skills/ and Hitendra Wadhwa, "The Wrath of a Great Leader," *Inc.*, January 21, 2013, www.inc.com/hitendra-wadhwa/great-leadership-how-Martin-Luther-King-Jr-wrestled-with-anger.html.

12. Ronald Reagan, "Inaugural Address," *Ronald Reagan Presidential Library and Museum*, January 5, 1967, www.reaganlibrary.gov/research/speeches/01051967a.

13. Quoted in Brad Whittington, *What Would Jesus Drink?* (n.p.: Wunderfool Press, 2011), 2.

14. "Christianity Without Paul," *Beliefnet*, n.d., www.beliefnet.com/faiths/Christianity/2004/04/Christianity-without-Paul.aspx#S3BursVdktl6SSvb.99.

15. Ibid.

16. I got that idea from Sam Parker and Mac Anderson, *Two Hundred and Twelve: The Extra Degree* (Naperville, IL: Simple Truths, 2016).

17. "Michael Phelps," *Wikipedia*, https://en.wikipedia.org/wiki/Michael_Phelps.

18. See at https://www.forbes.com/sites/anthonydemarco/2018/02/08/what-is-the-true-value-of-the-pyeongchang-olympics-gold-medal/#21ffb088608b.

19. Wright and Carreon, "The Science of Sinning Less," 37.

20. David Brooks, *The Road to Character* (New York: Random House, 2015), 53 (emphasis added).

21. Walter Mischel, "Points to Ponder," *Reader's Digest*, September 2014, 32.

22. Peter Drucker, *The Effective Executive* (New York: Harper and Row, 1966), viii.

23. William H. McRaven, *Make Your Bed: Little Things That Can Change Your Life and Maybe the World* (New York: Hachette, 2017), Kindle edition, loc. 780791.

Chapter 11—Forgiveness: When the Doctor Heals Himself

1. C.S. Lewis, *Mere Christianity* (New York: Macmillan, 1952), 104.

2. Cited in *Christian Century*, January 2, 2002, 15.

3. Timothy Roche/Franklin, "A Cold Dose of Vengeance," *Time*, July 4, 1999.

4. Melissa Dahl, "Why Cats Don't Forgive," *Reader's Digest*, May 2016, 31.

5. Ibid.

6. "How to Beat Burnout," *Focus on the Family*, CS315/1090, 1999.

7. "Forgiveness: Letting Go of Grudges and Bitterness," *Mayo Clinic*, November 4, 2017, www.Mayoclinic.org/healthy-lifestyle/adult-health-in-depth/art-20047692.

8. Max Lucado, *The Great House of God* (Dallas: Word Publishing, 1997), 121-22.

9. "Lou Holtz Quotes," *Brainy Quote*, www.Brainyquote.com/quotes/Lou_Holtz_384226.

10. Cited in James Dobson, *Home with a Heart* (Wheaton, IL: Tyndale House, 1996), 100.

11. David Cay Johnston, *The Making of Donald Trump* (Brooklyn, NY: Melville House, 2017), 27.

12. Cited in David Qaoud, "Joseph and Forgiveness: 5 Reflections on Forgiveness from Joseph," *Gospel Relevance*, n.d., https://GospelRelevance.com/2017/04/17/5-reflections-on-forgiveness-from-the-life-of-joseph/.

13. Don Colbert, *Deadly Emotions* (Nashville: Thomas Nelson Publishers, 2003), 163.

14. Dahl, "Why Cats Don't Forgive." The Bible talks about only one sin that is unforgiveable and that sin is the final and full refusal to accept God's forgiveness.

Chapter 12—Faithfulness: You Can Count on Me

1. "Faithful Sayings and Quotes," *Wise Old Sayings*, www.wiseoldsayings.com/faithful-quotes/.

2. "Native American Society: The American Indian Tragedy," *Wild West*, n.d., www.thewildwest.org/nativeamericans/nativeamericansociety/353-theAmericanIndiantraged.

3. See at http://www.thewildwest.org/nativeamericans/nativeamericansociety/353-theamerican indiantraged.

4. Gale Courey Toensing, "'Honor the Treaties': UN Human Rights Chief's Message," *Indian Country Today*, August 24, 2013, https://newsmaven.io/indiancountrytoday/archive/honor-the-treaties-un-human-rights-chief-s-message-7uxgczVIIEGDIUhJeBEujw/.

5. Max Farrand, ed., *The Record of the Federal Convention of 1787*, rev. ed. (Newhaven, CT: Yale University Press, 1937), 115.

6. "Jared Sparks: Journal, April 19, 1830," *Teaching American History*, n.d., https://teachingamericanhistory.org/library/document/jared-sparks-journal/.

7. Elizabeth Kwak-Hefferan, "Predicting Old Faithful Geyser Eruptions," *My Yellowstone Park*, October 19, 2015, www.yellowstonepark.com/things-to-do/predicting-old-faithful-eruptions.

8. Those titles belong to the far less predictable Steamboat geyser. "Old Faithful," *Wikipedia*, https://en.wikipedia.org/wiki/Old_Faithful.

9. Allen Barra, "Clutch Hitting Is a Big Myth," *Wall Street Journal*, September 17, 1999.

10. Ibid.

11. "United States Postal Service Creed," *Wikipedia*, https://en.wikipedia.org/wiki/United_States_Postal_Service_creed.

12. "Martin Luther King Jr. Quotes," *Good Reads*, www.goodreads.com/quotes/21045-if-a-man-is-called-to-be-a-street-sweeper.

13. Zig Ziglar, *Life Lifters* (Nashville, TN: Broadman and Holman, 2003), 137.

14. Charles R. Swindoll, *So You Want to Be Like Christ?* (Nashville, TN: Word Publishing Group, 2005), 8.

15. Richard G. Capen Jr., *Finish Strong* (San Francisco: HarperCollins, 1996), 60.

16. Andrew Hill with John Wooden, *Be Quick—But Don't Hurry* (New York: Simon & Schuster, 2001), 78.

17. Robert Sobel, *Coolidge: An American Enigma* (Washington, DC: Regnery Publishing, 1998), 80.

Chapter 13—Main Character

1. "Quotes About Jesus Christ," *Tentmaker,* www.tentmaker.org/Quotes/jesus-christ.htm.

2. Timothy Keller, *Making Sense of God* (New York: Random House, 2016), 32.

3. Frederick Dale Bruner, *Matthew: A Commentary,* vol. 2 (Grand Rapids, MI: Wm. B. Eerdmans, 1990), 69.

4. D.A. Carson, *Matthew: The Expositor's Bible Commentary* (Grand Rapids, MI: Zondervan, 1995), 47.

5. Though John 8:1-11 is not found in some of the earliest manuscripts, it has the ring of authenticity with the Jesus that is found elsewhere in the Gospels.

6. John Ortberg, *Who Is this Man?* (Grand Rapids, MI: Zondervan, 2012), 119.

7. Charles R. Swindoll, *The Greatest Life of All: Jesus* (Nashville: Thomas Nelson, 2008), 28.

8. John Blanchard, *Is God Past His Sell-By Date?* (Auburn, MA: Evangelical Press, 2002), 195.

9. Ibid.

10. Lee Strobel, *God's Outrageous Claims: Discover What They Mean for You* (Grand Rapids, MI: Zondervan, 2005), 72-75.

11. Toshiko Kaneda and Carl Haub, "How Many People Have Ever Lived on Earth?" *Population Reference Bureau,* March 9, 2018, www.prb.org/howmanypeoplehaveeverlivedonearth/.

12. Randy C. Alcorn, *Money, Possessions, and Eternity* (Wheaton, IL: Tyndale House Publishers, 1989), n.p.

13. See at https://motivationgrid.com/21-life-changing-quotes-on-building-character/.